How to Make a Million Dollars Playing the Guitar

How to Make a Million Dollars Playing the Guitar

A NO-NONSENSE GUITARIST'S GUIDE TO
MAKING A LIVING IN THE MUSIC BUSINESS

By Douglas Niedt

NIEDT PUBLISHING LLC
KANSAS CITY, MISSOURI

Published by:

Niedt Publishing LLC

Kansas City, MO

info@milliondollarguitarist.com

Editor in Chief: **Elizabeth A. Niedt**

More Editors: **Alex Niedt, Mom** and **Dad**

Cover and Interior Design and Production: **Richard Leeds | bigwigdesign.com**

Back Cover Photo: **Robin Gentile,** New York, NY

Proofreader: **Tom Hassett**, San Francisco

HOW TO MAKE A MILLION DOLLARS PLAYING THE GUITAR

Library of Congress Control Number: 2009908999

ISBN-13: 978-0-9824178-0-5

Printed in the U.S.A.

This book is dedicated
to Elizabeth and Alex,
and to all whose passion in life
is for music and the guitar.

contents

Prelude: Sorry, But I Have to Tell You How to Read This Book 1

PART ONE: It's All About You

1. One Million Dollars: No Bull, No Spin 7
2. The Mission and the Million 15
3. The Downbeat: The Nine Questions
   Do You Really Want To Do This?
   Do You Have What It Takes? 23
4. You Have to Know What You Want 65
5. Setting Goals 73
6. Positive Attitude 77
7. Luck 87
8. The Pursuit of Opportunity 91
9. Education 103
10. Talent Is *Not* the Answer 117
11. When Am I Ready? How Much Am I Worth? 125
12. Don't Let Perfection Get in the Way 131
13. Reliability and Honesty Count 135
14. Quitting? 139
15. You're a Failure—Congratulations! 143
16. Keeping Your Financial Head On Straight 151
17. How to Get Along With People 161
18. Age Has Nothing to Do With It 171

PART TWO: This Is How You Do It

19. Go For Great 175
20. The Right People 179

contents

21. The Brutal Facts of Reality.................................. **185**

22. Foxes, Hedgehogs, and Success **193**

23. The "D" Word: Discipline **213**

24. Technology May *Not* Be the Answer **219**

25. It's a Road, Not a Racetrack **225**

26. What Exactly Am I Going to Do to Earn a Living?.......... **231**

PART THREE: Recording and Selling Your Own CDs

27. Do-It-Yourself vs. Commercial Studios **243**

28. Buying Equipment... **249**

29. Why You Don't Want to Sign With a Major Label **255**

PART FOUR: Good Business Procedures for All Musicians

30. Nutz 'n' Boltz Business Basics **265**

31. Your Website **273**

32. Selling Stuff on the Internet **281**

33. How Much Is It Worth?....................................... **291**

34. Shipping... **295**

35. Customer Service **305**

36. Taxes.. **309**

37. Of Course You Have a Database…Right?.................... **315**

38. Time to Be Religious—About Backing Up Your Data.......... **323**

PART FIVE: You Are Running a Business

39. Your Pyramid **329**

40. You Will Need Help... **343**

41. This Is the Part You Will Want to Skip Over................. **347**

PART SIX: Once More, With Feeling

42. Things I *Must* Do 357

43. Coda and Fade.. 359

Sources 363

SORRY, BUT I HAVE TO TELL YOU HOW TO READ THIS BOOK

In this instant information age, many are losing touch with reading books for comprehension. You cannot read this book the way you read a computer screen. Don't scan it looking only for what is of immediate interest to you.

Read carefully, page by page, digest, and have a conversation with yourself about how each idea and concept might relate to your life as a guitarist.

TO GET THE MOST OUT OF THIS BOOK:

1. Read a chapter to get a broad overview of the information. If you are passionate about making a living playing the guitar, your mind will begin racing. You will have a cascade of thoughts, reactions, and ideas. You will be tempted to rush on to the next chapter—don't. Go back to the beginning of the chapter, slow down, and reread the chapter thoroughly.

2. ■ Stop frequently and think about how the information applies to you and your own career, hopes, and dreams. Ask yourself, "Can I do this? Do I want to? How will it change my life? How will it improve my career? Should I at least try it?"

3. ■ Be sure to have a pencil, pen, or highlighter in hand. Mark up this book like crazy! Write in your reactions and ideas. Highlight, circle, and underline ideas you think you can use. This will make it much easier to find and review the information later. You won't have to read through pages and pages to find the ideas that jumped off the page at you when you first read them. Those are the ones that could be crucial to your career success. When you are done, I hope every page is yellow.

4. ■ The rate at which we forget important information and concepts is astonishing. Don't think that reading through this book once or even studying it carefully one time will work. If you want to receive real, lasting benefits from the book, and reach your goal of earning a million dollars playing the guitar, reread the book or skim through your notes and the highlighted passages every few months. It will help keep your fires burning and ward off negativity. Maintaining a good mindset and using the principles in this book are only possible by a constant and vigorous campaign of review and application. If you don't stay on top of things, your career may founder. Also, a set of ideas or information may not be of use to you at certain times in your career. But those same ideas and information will be pivotal at another time in your development. If you don't review, you won't remember them when they will be most useful to you.

5. English author George Bernard Shaw once remarked, "If you teach a man anything, he will never learn." Shaw is completely correct. Learning is an interactive process. We learn by doing. Apply the information in this book to your own life and career at every opportunity. Otherwise, you will forget most of the principles, ideas, and thought processes. Only knowledge you *use* will stick with you.

6. From time to time (maybe every three months), step back and look at your career. Ask yourself, "What mistakes have I made? What opportunities did I miss? What did I do right? What have I learned? What do I need to do next?" This will improve your ability to make decisions and help keep you on track. Reread sections of the book that are applicable to your life at that moment, or that will soon be applicable, and formulate new goals or adjust old ones. Stay on your path to success.

PART ONE:
It's All About You

ONE MILLION DOLLARS: NO BULL, NO SPIN

Starving musician, starving artist—you know the cliché. I'm here to put a stop to that—at least for you, the reader. Leave that starving musician nonsense to others. You will *not* be part of that scene.

This book is not a get-rich-quick, anybody-can-do-it scam. I will *not* tell you how to make a million dollars overnight or even in the next five years. This book is about how to earn a million dollars playing the guitar *over the course of your career*. I will explain what to do, and especially *how to think* in order to achieve success *over the long haul*—note I strongly emphasize *over the long haul*.

Also, I use the phrase "playing the guitar" loosely. You may not make your million dollars actually *playing* the guitar. More likely, you will make it in a musical niche related to the guitar.

This is not about making easy money. This will be very hard—so hard that, to be honest, even though I will tell you what to do to succeed, many of you will be unable to do it. Once you understand what it will require, many of you will not *want* to do it.

Although our subject is earning a million dollars over the long haul, I will also help you earn a good living *as soon as possible* doing what you love to do—play the guitar. Those who are unsure how to get started on the pursuit of your dream will find this book to be a valuable guide. Those who have already begun, but find your journey temporarily thwarted, will find the book helpful to get you back on track.

This book is written for the entrepreneurial guitarist or musician. In other words, its content is targeted to those who want to be *self-employed*—to go it alone. However, those who want to work as employees for someone else—a record label, music publisher, recording studio, university, school, or other business—will also find it useful, especially as a supplement to other resources.

Today's market is teeming with a multitude of books on how to achieve success. The authors bloviate on how to find happiness, create wealth, and achieve goals to create a life that matters. But they vary widely in quality, and many are not always easily applicable to musicians.

These success gurus imply that they never failed at anything. Or, they say they *failed at everything* until they discovered the "secrets" of success—which they are breathlessly about to share with lucky you. Either way, they now have everything all figured out. A rule of thumb: *Don't believe anyone who has everything all figured out.*

I'm a classical guitarist and have done extremely well in the music business. I've had much success. But I've also had many spirit-crushing failures throughout my career. As a matter of fact, the failures (and successes) continue to this day, even as I write this book.

I'm not a success guru. I'm still figuring things out, testing, and experimenting. I'm still failing. I'm still succeeding. The things I will recommend have usually worked for me, but not always. Some of them will not work for you at all. I don't have everything figured out.

One of the really annoying things about many success books is that the writers have never succeeded at anything other than *telling* other people how to succeed. They are charlatans, like the people who write how-to-play-the-guitar books but can't really play. They're full of baloney. I want to read books by people who are really good at what they're writing about. I *have* made a million dollars playing the guitar. I don't claim to be as successful as guitarists like Eric Clapton, John Williams, Leo Kottke, or Tommy Emmanuel. But I think most guitarists trying to build their careers would be pretty happy trading places with me. Even those who are well on their way to success and have prospered more than I have will benefit from the information in my book.

I'm writing this book to make money. Absolutely. But I'm not writing it because I couldn't hack it in the guitar world and decided to write how-to-succeed books instead. I'm doing quite well, thank you. Playing the guitar is and will remain my major occupation in life. In a lifetime of playing the guitar I've learned things that no one else has written about and things that are seldom mentioned—things I think are vitally important to achieving success and satisfaction in a music career.

My name is not a household word. I'm not even well known in the guitar world. What I hope will be an enlightening and freeing thought for my readers is this:

> *You don't have to be well known or famous to make a million dollars playing the guitar.*

When I was young, I thought what most people think: I need to be well known and become famous in the guitar world to make serious money playing the guitar. It has amazed me through the years to learn that is absolutely not the case. Notice that the title of this book is not *How to Be a Superstar Guitarist* or *How to Be a Famous Guitarist*. The title is *How to Make a Million Dollars Playing the Guitar*.

People search for different kinds of success in the music industry. Some people are looking for overnight success. Others want to be superstars, but realize it may take some time and effort to become one. A third group is comprised of those who aren't concerned about superstardom. They would be happy being able to earn a living in music any way they can. They realize they must pay their dues and build their careers slowly over time.

The first group is chasing a dream of stardom. They may have good intentions. Or they may be incredibly egotistical. Either way they are probably unrealistic and do a lot of wishful thinking. They want the glamour of success but have no idea how much hard work and study is required. They don't realize overnight success is a rarity. When they don't succeed, they usually blame it on "I just don't know the right people" or "I just haven't gotten my big break" or "I'm just too good and those idiots don't know it."

As for the second group, the truth is that only a very few guitarists make it to the "top," overnight or not. But music is not about stardom. It's about pursuing a mission in life. If your goal is to become filthy rich, to be a household name, to be on network television and have your picture in magazines, this book is probably not for you. However, the advice and information here can still be useful. I just want to warn those who are looking for mega-success, quick or not: unless you are one of the chosen few (a Michael Jackson, Garth Brooks, Paul McCartney, etc.), you are probably headed for a life of grave disappointment, and possibly poverty, desperation, and despair.

This book is directed toward the third group—those willing to pay their dues and patiently work and study, those for whom music is their passion. You will be the architect of your success. You will learn how the music business works and how to make and prepare for opportunities. You will learn how to be in the right place at the right time. You will meet the right people who you can help and who will in turn help you. Stardom? Fame? Maybe. Maybe not. You can make your million dollars with or without them. You will be flexible and realistic. And perhaps above all, you will have the right mindset. *The development of that mindset is a major topic of this book.*

In addition to the countless books on the market about general success, many books have been written about "making it" in the music business. Most of the books are written by professional authors, journalists, a few musicians, some educators, and entertainment lawyers. And that's fine. On my website, MillionDollarGuitarist.com, is a Recommended Reading List that includes many books of that type. Most of these books offer solid hardcore advice and information on the basics of the music industry, including invaluable facts about contracts and copyright law. Some give specific instructions on how to approach key people at record labels and publishing companies or how to get gigs. All of that is information you should know. But again, my book is more about mindset and how to think. While I have included specific information about many nutz-and-boltz aspects of building a successful career as a guitarist, *the most important information in my book is that concerning your thinking and your attitude.*

This information will not go out of date. Although technology and public taste will change, the information in this book concerning your mindset and how to think will remain totally accurate and relevant.

I have filled the book with my personal stockpile of clichés—I like clichés. Sometimes we forget the basic, obvious things that are actually of great importance, and need a tired cliché to remind us of them. "Trite but right," as my dad would say. Skeptics may think that much of my discussion of mindset is corny and simplistic, especially the motivational stuff. And yes, if you only do the motivational stuff, success will not just automatically come to you. But a positive mindset is an essential ingredient to achieving success in every aspect of the music business. Don't discount it.

You may not like some of the things I say. That's fine, but don't just reject them immediately. Reconsider and give the ideas a close look. You have little to lose by trying them. And remember, if you keep doing the same things you've always done, you will probably keep getting the same results. If you want new results, if you want to move forward, you have to try new approaches and attitudes.

As a guitarist, you know how important mindset is when you perform. Your audience knows very well whether you are "into it" or not. *Your attitude is contagious to your listeners.* Your confidence and belief in what you are doing is reflected even in your fingers. If you aren't sure of yourself, if you aren't positive and confident, you just don't play as well physically. You can practice twelve hours a day, but your performance comes 95% from your head and only about 5% from your fingers. All the practice and preparation you do before the performance doesn't really matter much if your head is not in the right place.

This is also true of your career. Achieving success in music is determined 95% by what is in your head and only 5% by your knowledge, talent, contacts, and whatever else. You must have a positive, I-can-do-this, I-can-surmount-all-obstacles attitude in order to succeed in music. Doubts and negative thoughts in your head about your career or your music can have *serious negative consequences* for your future in music.

> **Positive mental attitude is crucial to success in both your performances and your career.**

If you learn to think about yourself and your career in the way I describe in this book, you will immediately advance to the front ranks of the millions of people trying to break into the music business. From what I've observed, easily 90% of those millions vying for a career in music aren't thinking straight and therefore won't succeed, regardless of how well they play the guitar or how talented they are.

Because every person is unique in personality and gifts, every person's journey to success will be different. In fact, if you ask two mega-successful people what is essential for success, sometimes you will receive opposite answers. But the answers *are* there. The secret is to learn from everyone and figure out what is relevant and necessary for your own personal journey.

IT'S A LIFE ADVENTURE

This book is about making money—a million dollars playing the guitar, to be precise. But as an entrepreneurial guitarist, you will be concerned with far more than just making money. Building a music career is about pursuing your passion in life. This exciting, spirit-building, and satisfying quest for success literally becomes a life adventure.

You will have ups and downs. You will take detours and sometimes end up at dead ends. Sometimes it will be a real roller coaster ride.

You may have an incredible ride upward followed by a bad low or a crash. But those wonderful "ups" give you a glimpse of the world you are seeking. That world is waiting for you if you do things right and don't give up. The "ups" are telling you that you are on the right track—keep going. Think of those good times as shots of courage and motivation. They will keep you going through the low points and you will keep learning.

Remember, when you fail a test *and give up*, you're through. It's all over. But wait. Defeat is only a temporary condition. Giving up is what makes it permanent.

The journey is important. In an interview, singer, songwriter, and guitarist Kenny Rogers was once asked, "What was the most exciting time in your life? Was it when you looked at your bank account and realized you had a million dollars sitting there? Was it when you bought your first mansion?"

Without hesitation, Kenny answered that the part of his life that he treasured most and was most rewarding was when he was a street musician in San Francisco, struggling to earn enough money to pay his hotel bill. As he counted every penny and every dollar dropped into his guitar case, he knew his talent would carry him through.

To Kenny, each step he took in those humble beginnings, though small in the eyes of others, were steps to the destination he saw so clearly in his mind. At the time of the interview, Kenny Rogers was the highest-paid performer in the world. But the period in his life he remembered most fondly was when he struggled every day to buy his dinner.

THE MISSION AND THE MILLION

Most of us have a goal that goes beyond making a bundle of money playing the guitar. Let's call this goal our mission. The mission relates to filling a need or solving a problem, combined with a desire to serve as many people as possible. For us guitarists, the mission may be as basic as using our music to make the world a better place, or to bring happiness to as many people as we can. Ask yourself, "Why do so many mega-successful rich musicians continue to concertize, release CDs, make television appearances, etc. when they already have all the money they could possibly need?" Cynics might say they do it so they can afford their mansions, fancy cars, and lifestyle. That could be true of some, but I think most have a mission or have a calling in their lives that goes beyond amassing a huge fortune to support a materialistic lifestyle.

For successful people, some life choices are not a question of "or." The decision is not whether to serve and help others OR make a bundle of money pursuing their passion. The choice becomes "and." One can make money AND make a contribution to society. They can serve themselves AND a cause. They choose both. It isn't even a 50/50 proposition. It is 100%/100%. As they pursue their passion, the joy it provides for their fellow human beings is as exciting as what it does for them.

Successful people realize that service to others is in their own self-interest. Let me emphasize that serving others is *not* the same as pleasing others. Serving others isn't a type of validation, or done to win approval or applause.

And let's not get carried away by the mission thing. Don't put it on a pedestal or couch your goals in highfalutin philosophical "save the human race" terms. Successful people have a very intense focus on the thing they want to do—that one thing that really matters to them and drives their passion. They choose to do it because they love it. They pursue it *despite* the opinions of others.

You may find that having a mission attracts more people to help and support you than if you only had goals of financial gain. Some people (whose influence and assistance will be of considerable aid to you financially) will only be attracted to partner with you on your spiritual mission. If the mission is only financial, they may not get on the bus with you.

However, don't go the route of the tortured "artiste" and denounce money as the enemy of art. Someone once commented to Paul McCartney about how the Beatles were so altruistic and anti-materialistic. McCartney replied, "That's a huge myth. John and I literally used to sit down and say, 'Now, let's write a swimming pool.'" Derek Sivers, founder of CD Baby, admonishes:

> *Never underestimate the importance of making money making music. You've got to let go of any weird taboos you have about it. Money is nothing more than neutral proof that you're adding value to people's lives. Making sure*

*you're making money is just a way of making sure you're
doing something of value to others.... So, be one of the few
who is clever enough to make money making music instead of pretending it doesn't matter.*

It may sound trite, but especially for a performing artist, the more
people you serve, the richer you become. This is true both spiritually
and financially. To give an obvious example, if you serve more people
you will have a larger audience. And guess what? You will sell more
CDs, or have more students, or have larger audiences (buying more
tickets) at your gigs. Not exactly rocket science, is it?

FEROCIOUS RESOLVE

Many people in the entertainment world seem to be uninhibited
and gregarious. At least that's the way it appears when we see them in
public life and onstage. In their private lives, a sizable number of them
are actually shy, introverted people. They are very different human beings onstage and offstage. If you are a wallflower, a private person, or
a shy person, do not think you don't have what it takes to succeed as a
guitarist. Very successful people in general are often very shy. *But what
they do have is ferocious resolve.*

Artists have a fierce resolve to do whatever it takes to make their
music the best it can be. Most work at achieving musical excellence,
though not for egotistical reasons. Rather, their focus is on the music itself or the enjoyment of their audience. Admittedly, some good
performers are in it for selfish reasons and ego. But the greats usually
go beyond that. Yes, they may have an oversized ego and strong self-
interest. They are incredibly ambitious. But they use that ambition first

for the mission or the destination, not for themselves.

How often have you found yourself working hours and hours to make a song the best it can be? Do you do that because you're thinking you will get something out of it? No, you do it because it never occurred to you to do it any other way.

Great artists are usually fanatically driven, infected with an incurable need (their close friends or spouses would call it an incurable disease) to produce great music for the sake of the music. They are diligent and committed to doing whatever it takes to make their work great. It doesn't matter how long it will take, how hard they have to work, or what else they have to sacrifice to achieve their goals. The focus is on the work, not their *personal* sacrifices, considerations, rewards, or discomforts.

Concerning recognition, Beethoven wrote, "I care nothing for it, because I have a higher goal."

Let's look at the great composer Franz Schubert, profiled by Patrick Kavanaugh in his book, *Spiritual Moments with the Great Composers*:

> *Schubert spent most of his short thirty-one years in poverty. He composed hundreds of masterpieces—songs, symphonies, sonatas, chamber music, and choral works. But at the time, he was ignored and neglected by almost everyone. Many of his greatest works were not even performed during his lifetime. But the poverty and neglect had no effect on his incredible work and creativity. He once stated, "When one piece is finished, I begin another." He even wore his glasses to bed so that he could begin composing immediately as soon as he woke up. Schu-*

bert created his masterworks because he strove for excellence, not success. He didn't care if anyone responded to his work or not. He just had to do it. He had a mission. Unfortunately, even when he did write a "hit" such as his extraordinary song the "Erl King," his lack of business savvy resulted in his selling the rights to the song for a pittance. Poor Franz was too busy creating masterworks to consult a business adviser!

Some of the greatest artistic works throughout history were created by people who refused to let rewards and recognition distract them from their purpose. Here we are, trying to make a million dollars playing the guitar. But to do that, ironically, we can't allow approval and rewards to distract us from our purpose. The mission, our passion, is number one. If the execution is done correctly, the million dollars will follow.

When you have the extra dimension of a spiritual mission, guiding philosophy, or core ideology (which consists of core values and a purpose), you can go far beyond just making money. The mission serves as an inspiring standard. The pursuit of money will not be the focal point of your life, your career, or the reason you play the guitar. As Quincy Jones remarked, "When you chase music for money, God walks out of the room." You may say, "But Doug, the title of your book is focused on money." Yes, that is correct. But if you follow the advice I give, in truth, your focus on money will be secondary. Your primary focus will be on your core ideology that drives you to play the guitar and enjoy music. But bottom line: your choice is the mission *and* the million.

PASSION AND FULFILLMENT

I want you to earn piles of money. But I also want you to achieve the much higher goal of living a happy, fulfilling life doing what you love to do—playing the guitar and making music. I want you to have a life filled with passion for what you love.

Your strategies and activities will endlessly adapt to the ever changing music business at large. You will want to stimulate change, improvement, innovation, renewal, and creativity in everything you do. But your core values and purpose in life will be steadfast.

Most people ignore what matters to them and do things for approval (to fit in), popularity, safety/security, or recognition. But the people who find success pursue and accomplish goals because those goals matter to them, *not* for approval, popularity, adulation, safety/security, or recognition. They take chances and risks in spite of social and outside pressures, not because of them. They are committed to doing what they love rather than being loved by others.

In fact, in the entertainment business, pursuing a career because of a need for attention, affection, or approval is risky. That career path can lead to a very slippery slope. You can never predict what people will think of your work. Their opinions will change from day to day. If you crave adulation and have a deep need for public approval or recognition, you could be headed for trouble if that external approval eventually withers away. To keep yourself psychologically healthy, keep your focus on the mission. If you do, you don't have to wait for a standing ovation to validate what matters to you.

Although the traditional definitions of success—wealth, fame, and power—are nice, they pale in comparison to the power of having a mission in life, the satisfaction of giving to others, and the joy of simply doing what you love to do and being paid for it.

The mega-successful eventually find that making a difference, making a lasting impact, and finding personal fulfillment become more important in their lives than wealth, fame, and power. Their ambition is very powerful, but never blind. They have clear reasons why they work as hard as they do. Berry Gordy of Motown fame remarked, "Money had never been the main thing for me. The legacy is what is important."

Ask yourself, "What is the fuel behind my ambition? Why do I want this so much?" Knowing the answer will galvanize your efforts and dramatically increase your determination and will to succeed.

I want you to earn your million dollars playing the guitar. But don't forget that the real reward is not about becoming filthy rich and famous. Yes, your million dollars will come gradually over the years. But pursue the mission—your passion. Pursue it with ferocious resolve. Make your journey a life adventure. Enjoy your years of struggle *and* success. The journey may be the most memorable and treasured part of your reward. Let's begin.

chapter 3

THE DOWNBEAT: THE NINE QUESTIONS

DO YOU REALLY WANT TO DO THIS?
DO YOU HAVE WHAT IT TAKES?

Before you dream one more dream, before you announce to your spouse that you're quitting your job to become a famous guitarist, or before you tell your parents you don't *need* to go to college because you're going to be a rock star, you must answer the following nine questions. For now, browse through them. We will look at each of them in detail shortly.

1. **Does the phrase "I can't imagine myself doing anything else" ring a bell?**
   - Is playing the guitar and earning a living as a guitarist a burning desire within me? Is it my life's mission?
   - Can the guitar be absolutely #1 in my life?
2. **Do I want to be an entrepreneurial guitarist instead of an employee?**
   - Do I have the entrepreneurial spirit?

- Can I go it alone without the security and safety net of a "real job"?

3. **Am I clear on what level I will compete?**

4. **Am I willing to work harder than I've ever worked before, and then some, to play the game?**

   - Am I willing to pay a staggering price for this?

5. **Am I willing and humble enough to pursue every opportunity possible to further my career? (Many of these opportunities will not pay a dime or have any obvious immediate benefit.)**

   - Or, am I just going to make excuses?
   - Am I willing to pay my dues?

6. **Do I have an insatiable thirst for knowledge?**

   - Do I want to read, read, read, research, research, research *all* aspects of my field? For hours every day? (Mind you, this is in addition to your hours of guitar practice or other musical activities every day.)

7. **Am I willing to fail?**

   - Can I learn from and be positive about failure and mistakes?
   - Or, am I afraid to fail?

8. **Can I take heavy-duty soul-crushing criticism?**

9. **Do I have the persistence and determination to put countless hours of time into my career with no immediate rewards?**

   - Am I willing to persist through endless criticism, doubt, fear, and failure?
   - Do I have the mental strength to never give up?

Now, we will look at each question in detail. The profundity, relevance, and ramifications of each question must be clearly understood before attempting to answer it.

1. DOES THE PHRASE "I CAN'T IMAGINE MYSELF DOING ANYTHING ELSE" RING A BELL?

- *Is playing the guitar and earning a living as a guitarist a burning desire within me? Is it my life's mission?*
- *Can the guitar be absolutely #1 in my life?*

I Can't Imagine Myself Doing Anything Else

When I was sixteen or seventeen, I started gathering my thoughts about going to college. I was a very good student in school. I usually got A's and B's, worked fairly hard, and really enjoyed school because I enjoyed learning. I had a strong interest in meteorology and the sciences from age seven to twelve. I could have majored in just about anything and done very well.

But I started playing the guitar at age seven and it grabbed hold of me like nothing else ever had before or since. Its grip on me never lessened. By the time I was in junior high school, during the summers I practiced ten to twelve hours a day. I got my first teaching job (teaching guitar classes at the YWCA in St. Louis) when I was thirteen. I began playing gigs and concerts by age fifteen.

I was a pretty popular guy in junior high. I was student council VP, quarterback on the football team, and lettered in basketball and track. But when I got to high school, I gave all that up. There wasn't time for everything if I wanted to be a good guitar player. Subconsciously following the advice of King Solomon, "Do not love sleep or you will grow poor," I cut my sleep down to 3–5 hours a night (not something I recommend for others, but it worked for me). That way I had time to go to school, study, and still get six hours of guitar practice in every day. My life was centered totally on music and the guitar.

When the time came to think about college, I had no thoughts about doing anything else. Doing anything else never even *occurred* to me. I was fully planning to major in music.

My dad, however, when we discussed my going to college, frequently interjected the thought, "Why don't you take your music courses but minor in business?" I remember him suggesting that over and over again. It didn't bother me at all—after all, he has always provided me with stellar advice throughout my life. It just kind of rolled off my back. I heard the words, but they never engaged my brain. The only thing I could imagine doing was music. There just wasn't anything else. So, despite my dad's efforts, my college and life focus was to be 100% guitar.

As the great conductor, composer, and pianist Leonard Bernstein (one of my personal heroes) said,

> *The only reason to go into music is if you can't imagine doing anything else.*

Music industry exec Clive Davis said essentially the same thing:

> *You've got to love music, because it's all-consuming. You can't do it unless you're committed to it as a passion. … You can only consider music if you just can't get enough of it.*

Although I'm sure my dad feared for my future as a musician (he is a successful businessman), I had no qualms about it whatsoever. It never crossed my mind that I would have any financial difficulty. Young and naïve, you might say. But honestly, money was not and has never been high up on my list of needs, wants, and desires in my life. My love of the guitar and the joy I experience with music was and continues to be my focus. Playing the guitar is fun. Music is tremendously gratifying and feeds my soul in a way nothing else does or ever has.

If you're like me, and can't imagine earning a living doing anything else but music, you are passing through Question #1 with flying colors. If you love music, but think you could be satisfied being a doctor, police officer, teacher, psychologist, whatever: forget music and pursue the other job. The decision is that simple.

Is Playing The Guitar and Earning a Living as a Guitarist a Burning Desire Within Me? Is It My Life's Mission?

You will succeed in music if the guitar (or music) is the thing that drives and energizes your life and gives it meaning. You can call it your mission in life, purpose in life, or higher calling. Strong missions produce strong results. You will be driven by values far more important to you than the pursuit of money. Your passion for the guitar and music and love for your art must matter more than money. Remember, people who find success pursue their mission because it matters, not for popularity, recognition, or fortune.

Is your passion for music directly connected to how much money and fame you expect to gain? Would you pursue your passion for music and the guitar regardless of the financial rewards? You had better answer "No" to the first question and "Yes" to the second.

Many artists see their music as something that *must* be done. It disturbs them to think that something so magical, valuable, and wonderful would not be done. Some see their musical ability as being a gift from God. Some see it as a serious responsibility to develop their gift into something that will benefit others. Serving other people is the primary driving force behind their music.

However you see it, music must be your life's mission. If that is not the case, get a real job.

Can the Guitar Be Absolutely #1 In My Life?

This last element in Question #1 can be troubling for some. Its importance and relevance first came to my attention when I was 15 or 16 years old. My mom used to listen every day to a live radio show on St. Louis' KSD-AM 55 starring Russ David. He was a very well-liked, prominent, and influential musician. He was a pianist, radio personality, big band leader, and booking agent. One day he related a story about how, early in his marriage (or maybe before), his wife Jean asked him, "What's more important—me or the piano?" He said he remembered immediately breaking into a sweat, realizing the consequences of giving the "wrong" answer. But he told his radio audience he quickly realized that if he was going to have any chance at all with this wonderful woman, he owed it to both of them to give the real answer: "The piano is most important to me, Jean." They had a long, happy marriage, till death did them part. In any relationship, both partners must have a clear understanding of this calling as did Russ David and his wife.

There is no easy way around this. If you are thinking, "Yes, I really want to pursue music as my life's mission," then the guitar *is* your life. Without the guitar, you would be a different person. You are defined by your music. The guitar or music must occupy the top spot in your life.

I always feel a little uneasy saying this, but music and the guitar must come before spouse, before children, before lover, before family. If you must hedge a bit, let's say they are at least equal. If that isn't the case, if you can't bring yourself to do that, if it feels too selfish, that's okay. Make the guitar a hobby or a source of supplemental income, not your potential profession. Put spouse, lover, etc. back at the top, keep or get a real job, and carry on. Your real job can still be in music, but working as an employee. Teach at a music store, or a university. Work at a music store or for a music publisher. All kinds of jobs can be found working for others. But don't go the route of working for yourself as an entrepreneurial guitarist. It will probably be disastrous. You can sell this book on eBay.

I know this viewpoint is very controversial. Many will say that one can balance both dedication to music and a personal life. Yes, I agree. You will have to put your dream, desires, and responsibilities to others in perspective and maintain a balance. If you do it right, you won't have to give up one for the other.

Don't lose the dream. Burying your dream is bad. You will become angry and bitter over the years, possibly becoming unbearable to everyone around you. Nothing is worse than dying with unrealized potential or never having tried to find your dream. But the welfare of your family or loved ones is important—you can't abandon that. You will have to adjust your career plan to encompass and feed both. Compromising the financial and spiritual well-being of your loved ones in the wake of achieving your goals would only lead to guilt and hard feelings. Success would be bittersweet indeed.

You will have to maintain a precarious balance so that your dreams are not buried or brought crashing to the ground and your personal responsibilities are not neglected. It doesn't have to be an either-or situation. If you do it right, everyone will win.

Timing is everything. Maybe you can't take the full plunge right now. If you have a family, you may have to suspend your dream for a while. At the very least, keep your career moving at a perceptible steady forward speed. Persistence will be the word by which you live. Remember the story of the tortoise and the hare. We're in this for the long haul.

But when it comes down to the nitty-gritty and hard choices, I believe that if you are going to be successful (and true to yourself and others around you), music must come first. Music is the driving force in your life, an all-consuming passion transcending everything else. The amount of focus required to succeed as a guitarist is incredible and can't be diluted or thrown off course by others. I believe this is one reason that performing arts types have such poor track records in marriage and domestic life. That's not to say it can't be done. Many great artists form many deep friendships and have great marriages. But again, those around them understand that music comes first.

2. DO I WANT TO BE AN ENTREPRENEURIAL GUITARIST INSTEAD OF AN EMPLOYEE?

- *Do I have the entrepreneurial spirit?*
- *Can I go it alone without the security and safety net of a "real job"?*

Earning a living as a guitarist is very much like being an entrepreneur. An entrepreneur is a person who organizes, manages, and assumes the risks of a business or enterprise. You are an entrepreneur running an enterprise called "(Your Name Here), Guitarist." Your enterprise or company will probably involve multiple streams of income. Some may be as an employee of someone else. But most will be the result of activities you pursue as a self-employed individual with no guaranteed weekly paycheck. You are responsible for managing all the streams of income, even those as a paid employee. Being an entrepreneur and for the most part self-employed can be a frightening experience for many people. You go it alone with no steady paychecks, no health insurance or retirement plan, no paid vacations, no security. If you get sick, you don't get paid.

Few people who are used to being employees, or have friends or family who work for others, have the courage to become entrepreneurs. They fear not having a regular, steady income to pay the bills. If you become self-employed, you are now responsible for setting up a home office; purchasing a computer system, software, copier, scanner, paper, pens, postage, brochures; paying for health insurance, liability coverage—the list can go on and on.

A clash of philosophies exists between those who seek to find a rewarding job as an employee and those who seek to become entrepreneurs. The employee seeks security, the entrepreneur seeks freedom.

For the entrepreneurial guitarist with a dream, one of the downsides of choosing a life of security is that you will always be living two lives. While earning a dependable paycheck from an unfulfilling job, from afar you will still be dreaming about the life you have always wanted. It can be a very tough choice, especially if you have a family that depends on you. Having a family may require you to have that secure job.

Some people burn all the bridges behind them before they proceed on their journey to mega-success. Once they decide to pursue their passion, they quit their real jobs and stake their entire future on their life purpose, leaving no possible retreat. They make the decision to win or perish.

Personally, I'm a bit of a coward and a realist, so I have always kept a few bridges behind me. Had I burned them all, I would have taken different roads and perhaps become even more successful than I am. But I have no regrets. Which bridges you burn is your choice. Have you heard the expression "feed the soul"? Well, listen to your soul, but be certain it has been fed with adequate knowledge and common sense before making huge decisions such as this.

One of the driving forces behind the entrepreneurial guitarist is courage. The word courage comes from the Latin word *cor*: the heart. You will proceed with your life guided by your heart and soul, tempered with a strong dose of intellect, knowledge, and reality checks.

Your passion for the guitar and your music matters. In fact, you would pursue your passion for music even if there were no money. As a value-driven self-employed entrepreneurial guitarist, you will experience one of the greatest joys in life: being able to do what you love to do and get paid for it.

Most employees, on the other hand, are passionate about their work only as long as they receive a paycheck. A good employee will try to do a good job, but in the end it's still just a job. They would rather be at home doing something they really want to do.

You won't have a "real job." But, you may have to get involved in projects you're not wild about. Occasionally, you will have to do something you don't like. But doing so will benefit your work on the things you do enjoy. That will make the task less onerous. It may turn out to actually be fulfilling.

For example, maybe you've said to yourself, "I *never* want to teach guitar lessons." Well, at some point in your career you may need money to finance an important project. In that case, teaching the guitar might not be so bad. You can earn good, easy money. You sit with your guitar in hand in comfortable surroundings. If you're any good at teaching, you will get to listen to some pretty nice music for a few hours each day. Then, when you go home, you won't be wiped out and can focus on other projects that are more important to you. No? Okay, work all day at the Quik Trip. Or, how about a physically draining job doing manual labor? Does teaching the guitar sound a little better now? If it makes you feel any better, in Mozart's and Beethoven's day, teaching was often the primary source of income for composers.

Even if you have to work retail, if you choose a good music store, at least you will be around what you love as well as other people who might share your enthusiasm for the guitar. You could learn a lot about the music retail business that might be useful to you later in your career. And you never know who you might meet. It would sure beat working at The Gap.

For me, one of the most rewarding parts of being an entrepreneurial guitarist is the personal freedom I have day to day. In fact, a major component of my personal definition of success is: the successful person can pretty much do whatever he wants whenever he wants to do it. I set my schedule. I don't have to please a boss or meet any deadlines except those I set for myself. I don't have to go to meetings or write reports.

REALITY CHECK: It takes tremendous personal discipline to live like that. You *do* have to set deadlines for yourself. You *do* have to set up appointments. You *do* have to practice, read, study, listen to music, study videos, make phone calls, send and reply to emails. You have to work *much* harder than an employee. And, you have a very demanding and relentless boss—YOU.

The big difference, though, is that when you are self-employed, *you* are in control and for the most part you are doing things *you want to do*. Once again, freedom for the entrepreneur versus security for the employee.

Therefore, the big questions you have to ask yourself are, "Do I want to go the entrepreneurial route? Am I willing to take chances and go out on a limb without a safety net? Do I want to work my fingers to the bone 24/7 with no steady paychecks, no health insurance, no retirement plan, no paid vacations, no security? Can I put up with little income or take on other music jobs I'm not real interested in for a few years until my career begins to click and pull in more money? Or, am I better off working a real job with an employer and just playing the guitar and pursuing music on the side?"

3. AM I CLEAR ON WHAT LEVEL I WILL COMPETE?

Half of all new businesses fail within the first five years. Music careers fail even faster. Or, they never even get off the ground. Sometimes, especially in the pop world, careers succeed too much and too fast, resulting in the guitarist making stupid decisions. Some musicians lose focus on what's important (their music) and become self-indulgent fools, sinking into a world of mindless partying, spending, or alcohol and drugs.

To avoid either extreme, the guitarist must plan and stay focused on his goals. If you thought that being in the music biz meant you could avoid things like plans, goals, and schedules, you are very wrong. Plans, goals, and schedules will provide much-needed direction for your career. Merely staying home and practicing for hours and hours will not make a career. Remember, you are running a business. You cannot just be a guitarist. You will have a career plan with goals you want to accomplish. You will know, or have a good idea, how you will reach those goals and when.

You don't have to be a great guitarist or a performer to make your million dollars. You may end up focusing on some other area of music and become great at that. But if you want to be a performer, face reality. Look with brutal honesty at yourself and your talents. Don't compare yourself to other guys who play the guitar at your school or in your city.

Look at yourself and ask:

1. How do I compare with the best in the world?
2. Can I get to that level?
3. Do I have the heart, desire, and gift to be at that level?
4. Can I do a workaround? Persist? How will I do it?
5. What combination of traits and strengths do I have that will put me at the top on my terms?
6. What advantages do I have over my competition and what do I have in me musically or personally that will distinguish me from my competition in the minds and ears of the public?
7. Do I have the courage to constantly put myself in situations where I am at the limit of my skills, always testing myself so I continually get better?

Those are really hard questions that must be answered early on. A performance or recording career is already a tough business. If you don't have the answers to those questions, it will be even tougher. If you lack needed skills or knowledge, you will have to find a teacher, an adviser, or information to help you acquire those missing links.

Regardless of what area of the music business you pursue, ask yourself, "At what level do I want to play the game? Do I want to compete in the major leagues or the minors? Or even something more local?" You can make your million dollars in any of those leagues.

You may be a local band enjoying a lot of success. The temptation or next logical step is to build on that and go to the next level and the next. As you move up the ranks and perhaps go for the major label deal, just remember, you are a successful local band until you get the record contract. As Sam Llanas of the Bodeans discovered, once you sign the contract and crank out the CD, then, all of a sudden, Bruce Springsteen is your competition.

Know where you will realistically best succeed. You needn't worry about or direct all your energies to a major-label recording deal if you are more interested in local success. Ask yourself the old question, "Do I want to be a little fish in a big bowl, or a big fish in a little bowl?" Or, do you want to go for broke and be the big fish in the big bowl? Those decisions and choices determine how you will map out your road to success.

4. AM I WILLING TO WORK HARDER THAN I'VE EVER WORKED BEFORE, AND THEN SOME, TO PLAY THE GAME?

- *Am I willing to pay a staggering price for this?*

Your friends, your family, your teachers all say you have an incredible talent. You're wonderfully gifted. Or, they say you're a loser, you're a no-talent bum—go out and get a real job. I say it doesn't matter a heck of a lot either way. Talent, especially others' perception of it, is way down on the list of attributes needed to succeed in the music world. Look around you. Listen to the radio. Watch television. You hear and see people of limited or questionable talent all the time who achieve tremendous success.

As I mentioned earlier, you don't have to be a great guitarist to earn a million dollars from your music career. But whether you have talent or not, the abilities you do have must be developed. The better you are (at anything), the more you improve yourself, the easier your journey to success will be. The development of your maximum potential, whether in guitar playing or another area of music, is essential.

Even people who are seemingly blessed with natural talent often have below-average or nonexistent careers. Why? Because developing one's abilities and giving the gift of music to others is extremely hard work. Most people do not want to work that hard.

If you plan to make your million dollars in music, you will have little time for play. Forget about "work hard, play hard." If you have time to play, then you aren't working hard enough. Pursuing an entrepreneurial career in music means giving up many things that others take for granted:

> After a pianist gave a fabulous concert, a woman ran up to him gushing about how wonderful it was and declared, "I would give anything to play like that." The pianist looked her straight in the eye and replied, "Oh no you wouldn't." The woman, somewhat taken aback, asserted, "Yes I would." The pianist explained, "I doubt you would prac-

tice six hours every day, every day of your life, sacrificing time with friends, family, and your children. I doubt you would spend the rest of your waking hours studying music and listening to it to learn everything you could about it. I doubt you would maintain a rigorous touring schedule of constant travel and endless hours in motel rooms. I doubt you would enjoy the sometimes crushing criticism of your work when you have an off night." And he went on quite a while longer while the poor woman came to terms with reality.

All people, even so-called child prodigies, have to develop their gift with endless hard work. Not too many people are up to the task. I explain this in detail in Chapter 10, "Talent Is *Not* the Answer."

Depending on the focus of your career (especially if you aren't a performer), you may not spend thousands of hours actually practicing the guitar. Instead, you will find a niche in the music field—something you can do better than anyone else in the world that will bring you success. But you will still have to put in endless hours and punishing sacrifice pursuing that niche activity.

Derek Sivers spoke about the importance of focus to an entering class of freshmen students at the Berklee College of Music:

You are surrounded by distractions. You're surrounded by cool tempting people hanging out casually, telling you to relax. Unfortunately, the casual ones end up having very casual talent and casual lives.

Looking back on my Berklee classmates who really got

successful, were the ones who were fiercely focused, deter-
mined, and undistractible.

You are being tested and your enemy is distraction. So
stay offline, stay off the computer, and stay in the shed.
Daily events, even political events will be only so much
noise that really doesn't matter, that years later you will be
happy you avoided.

If you master focus, you are going to be in control of your
world. If you don't learn to focus, your world will always
control you.

My personal focus is playing the guitar. I have forgone sleep since my early teen years to have more time for music. After about five hours of sleep, I still enthusiastically wake up at 4:00 am every day to get four to six hours of practice or recording in before anything else comes along that might distract me from it. I spend two to six hours teaching. The rest of my time is spent studying music, reading about it, writing about it, or taking care of business. The activity is absolutely non-stop.

Non-music types might think, "Boy, Doug, you have it easy. You get to play the guitar all day and listen to music. Wish I could do that." I have heard that all my life. Guess what? Those people couldn't do what I do if their lives depended on it. Just like the woman who heard the pianist and asserted she would give anything to play like him.

A performing artist focuses 100% on their four to six hours of daily practice. Most people don't have the ability to focus on one activity for that long. They don't have the stamina to do it every day, holidays included. They don't have the will to forgo going out with friends or spouse to stay home and practice instead. They couldn't stick to the disciplined schedule of a performing artist. They don't have the patience to practice and improve little bit by infinitesimal little bit over weeks and weeks. They don't have the focus to immerse themselves totally in one subject their entire lives. They don't have the will to learn every day, to aggressively seek out new information. They don't have the will or discipline or psychological strength to continually evaluate their work, constantly finding weak spots that must be fixed in order to improve without becoming discouraged.

Remember, this mindset applies not just to playing the guitar. It applies to any striver—a person who is totally committed to the relentless pursuit of their life mission or passion. It takes a degree of focus, mental and physical stamina, discipline, patience, will, and psychological toughness that most people don't possess. The difference between a successful person and others isn't a lack of talent or knowledge, but rather a lack of will.

I must admit that although I put in a tremendous amount of hours and effort into what I do, it never feels like work to me. I have never had a real job. In my mind, I've never worked a day in my life. I love what I do. For the most part I only engage in the activities I like to do. I would do what I do (or try to) even if I weren't paid to do it. That is the huge difference between performing artists (or strivers on a mission) and others. That joy and contentment is what others see when they think what we do is easy.

Sacrifice is another large part of the life of a performing artist and striver. For many, health is even sacrificed. Ballet dancers know going in that to perfect their art probably means causing problems for their bodies down the road. Artists sometimes literally work themselves into the grave—not something I'm recommending, but it happens.

Little stuff will be sacrificed, like spending time with friends. Much bigger stuff will be sacrificed, such as spending time with your children or on relationships with lovers or spouses. Sometimes those sacrifices can be avoided, but many times they cannot. The performing artist's ability to maintain relationships is pretty abysmal by most accounts.

Many performers and strivers live in periods of penury early in their careers while perfecting their art or pursuing their mission. Many artists' entire lives are spent in poverty, all because their art is something they simply must do, regardless of the consequences. Some of this may sound like romanticized baloney, but the true artist's sacrifice is real.

One way or another, you will pay heavy dues to achieve your success, to earn your million dollars. Not everyone can do it. Not too many people even *want* to do it once they realize what is truly involved.

We also need to distinguish between an amateur guitarist and a professional guitarist. If your career is dependent on your guitar playing, understand the difference and ask yourself, "Which am I?" In this case, I am not talking about whether you are making a living as a guitarist and are therefore a pro or that you are not making money and therefore an amateur. Nor am I alluding to the professions such as doctors or lawyers.

I am distinguishing between the two in terms of commitment. The amateur plays the guitar for fun. The pro plays for keeps. For the amateur, playing the guitar is fun and rewarding. For the pro, playing the guitar is certainly fun and rewarding, but is also his life. Music is so elemental, like oxygen or water, that he can't live without it. The amateur plays at it part-time like a weekend warrior. The pro is at the guitar full-time seven days a week including Thanksgiving and Christmas. The pro eats, lives, and breathes the guitar. Many people think of amateurs as pursuing their interest out of love whereas the pro does it for the money. That is absolutely not the case in music. The amateur guitarist loves the guitar but on a comparatively shallow uncommitted level. The pro loves it so much that he dedicates his very being to it. He is totally committed. If you think famous musicians "sell out" and are in it for the money, how many musicians can you think of who quit playing music *after* they were great successes and made millions of dollars? The answer is: hardly any. They aren't in it for the money. Their mission drives them.

The work is endless. Perfection is the Holy Grail performing artists and strivers seek. We know it doesn't exist, but that doesn't ever stop us from trying to reach it. Creating artistic works and achieving a mission is about effort, more effort, and then some. We keep going the extra mile and the extra nanometer for improvement. It's okay, it's good, it's very good, but we always want it better. We want it to be great. If you don't have that mindset, please find another career.

5. AM I WILLING AND HUMBLE ENOUGH TO PURSUE EVERY OPPORTUNITY POSSIBLE TO FURTHER MY CAREER? (Many of these opportunities will not pay a dime or have any obvious immediate benefit.)

- *Or, am I just going to make excuses?*
- *Am I willing to pay my dues?*

Being an entrepreneurial guitarist doesn't mean just practicing real hard and keeping busy. An employee is paid for keeping busy. The entrepreneurial guitarist is paid for results. Your checking account will not grow if you stay home all day and practice, hoping for something to come up. It doesn't matter that you play better than everyone else or write songs better than anything you're hearing on the radio. No matter how good you are, concert promoters will not call you, begging you to give concerts. People will not automatically buy your CDs. You aren't making any money unless you're *selling* your CDs, playing concerts, collecting royalties, etc.

You have to take steps—pursue opportunities every day. You can't play the guitar all day, thinking, "Well, I'll work on pursuing contacts, gigs, opportunities later, tomorrow, next week, or next month." Steps need to be taken *every day* so you are walking steadily down a path where opportunity breeds opportunity. That path leads to breaks, big and small. Pursue every opportunity regardless of how insignificant or unglamorous it seems at the time. It doesn't matter if you're just starting out or already have a career in motion. Begin taking those steps now. Even when opportunity knocks, you still have to get up off the couch and open the door!

Excuses

Don't let excuses discourage you from pursuing opportunity. Excuses will derail your dreams and career before it begins or even while in progress. Here are some real gems:

1. "I don't have the money."
2. "I have a family to support."
3. "I don't have any contacts."
4. "I don't play well enough. I don't read music. My songs aren't any good. I get stage fright. My technique isn't good enough..."

5. "I'm not smart enough."
6. "I don't have enough time."
7. "I can't find anyone to help me."
8. "This is going to take too long and take too much time and effort."
9. "I'm afraid of poverty." (Or any other noun that applies to your situation.)
10. "I'm shy. I don't like dealing with people, especially business types."
11. "I'm too old." Or, "I started too late."
12. "I'm not good at asking people for things."

The infamous "ifs and whens" list will be familiar to many:
1. "If I wait until tomorrow, circumstances will be better."
2. "I'll do it when the perfect opportunity appears."
3. "I'll do it when the time is right."
4. "I'll do it when I have more time."
5. "I'll do it when I find the right partner."
6. "I'll do it when the kids are out of school."
7. "I'll wait to see if I get another promotion. If I don't, then I'll do it."
8. "If I take some classes first for a few years, I'll be better prepared."
9. "What happens if I fail?"
10. "If I fail, I'll be embarrassed."

You can probably add a few more lame excuses of your own if you give it some thought. One of the big ones endlessly discussed on talk shows and in self-help books is lack of self-esteem. Don't have much self-confidence? Well, get off your butt, do the work, and accomplish something—anything, no matter how small or seemingly unimportant. And voilà, you will experience confidence in your next endeavor. It works every time. Forget self-esteem. Criminals and sociopaths often rate highly on confidence tests. The quality of your effort is what produces results. Don't allow the power of your excuses to be more powerful than your dreams.

I'm Gettin' the Blues Payin' My Dues

You have to recognize that if you're starting out, you will probably start at the bottom. Accept it. You don't want to carry the equipment? You don't want to play for free? You don't want to play that type of music? You don't want to play that kind of gig? Tough. Man up. Use every experience to your advantage. Try to get something good to come out of it. Learn. Recognize and take advantage of opportunities. Don't sit back and wait for things to happen. They won't. If a door won't open or closes on you, go around to the back door. Try. Go after it.

Working for free is part of your learning experience, especially when you're starting out. I know many guitarists who get insulted when asked to do a freebie gig or concert, donate their time to a cause, or take a drastically reduced fee. I see this with students and even seasoned artists who should know better. When you refuse to do these, all you do is shut the door on opportunity and goodwill. This is true at any level of your career. Yes, you have to earn a living and can't do that by playing for free all the time. But you have to realize that great opportunities may lie in wait down the road when you do the freebies. Sometimes playing for free at a fundraiser, a wedding, a funeral, or to get someone out of a jam, can pay off big-time in goodwill and enhance your personal reputation in your community.

If you expect to get paid for everything you do, you will have problems. You can't be greedy. Musicians tend to get more than their share of the bad times in life. You will have to do jobs you think are beneath you or a waste of time. But survival is survival. Seize every opportunity to learn and broaden your background and experience. It doesn't matter how seemingly menial the task is or whether you think there will be a payoff. Go for it.

Most guitarists and other performing artists have to pay their dues their entire lives, not just at the beginning of their careers. In fact, most begin paying before they even get started on their career. They pay with endless hours of practice when they are very young. Classical guitarists must practice for hours every day to keep their skills top-notch. Unlike most athletes who cease grueling physical activity by middle age, guitarists must maintain their physical skills into their sixties, seventies, and beyond. Since we usually aren't paid to practice the guitar, those are thousands upon thousands of unpaid hours! It may sound like a large amount of money to hear that a guitarist gets $5,000 for a single concert. But by the time you figure in the number of hours of practice the guitarist has put in to get to that level, he's probably being paid pennies per hour.

Your task is to willingly pursue every opportunity possible to advance your career. You are choosing a career that involves endless preparation, endless work and research, unrelenting harsh criticism of everything you do, repeated failure, and no guarantees. You will be paid pennies per hour. Do you have a problem with that?

6. DO I HAVE AN INSATIABLE THIRST FOR KNOWLEDGE?

• *Do I want to read, read, read, research, research, research all aspects of my field? For hours every day? (Mind you, this is in addition to your hours of guitar practice or other musical activities every day.)*

I don't know about you, but people who think they know all the answers to everything really annoy me. When I was twenty-one, yes, I knew everything. As I grow older, I am finding I know less and less about more and more. In the music business, thinking you know everything is very limiting and dangerous to your career. On the other hand, even though you realize you will never be able to know everything, give it your best shot.

A type of wealth and power exists that, with effort, anyone can attain. It is called knowledge. Be very greedy in acquiring as much intellectual "capital" as possible to achieve your goals. Opportunity comes from expertise, not just luck, talent, or even passion. If you say something matters to you, but immersing yourself in learning about it is just too tedious or too much trouble, you are only dreaming about your dreams. You aren't really engaged enough to pursue them. If you are unwilling to get dirt under your fingernails from digging to discover new things, you will never uncover the treasure.

Digging isn't easy and takes a tremendous amount of time, energy, persistence, and thoroughness. If you don't persist your entire life in learning as much as you can about your area of interest, you will fail when the inevitable obstacles are thrown at you. Being the best at what you do is essential. You must have the willingness to learn as much as you can about what you do for its own sake. To be blunt, *if you aren't doing your homework and research, you probably have little chance of succeeding as an entrepreneurial guitarist.* If you are unwilling to dig deep, don't bother digging at all. Do something else, because you are wasting your time. This isn't my opinion. Nor is it a revelation. You will hear these words from every person who has achieved lasting success.

The music industry is very cutthroat. Thousands and thousands of other guitarists are out there, wanting to achieve many of the goals you are pursuing. It's called competition. Many of them are smarter than you, cleverer than you, and more talented than you. You usually don't have to confront them head on. You don't have to engage them in battle. You just have to figure out how to get around them. A sizable number of them are aggressively pursuing their homework, their research. To give yourself the edge, equip yourself with as many tools, advantages, and information as possible.

One of the biggest mistakes young people make is underestimating how competitive the world is. They underestimate their competition and overestimate their abilities and chances for success. They think there is a way to find success without having to do the heavy lifting. Many young people waste their time in bars and clubs or surfing the net, flirting on Facebook, and playing videogames. They expect to find a shortcut, but time is passing. Meanwhile, the competition is at home, working their butts off. Derek Sivers quotes a martial arts maxim: "When you're not practicing, someone else is. When you meet him, he will win."

Think of your career development as a long journey. You need a map to help keep you on track so you don't waste time and money going in the wrong direction or going around in circles or missing important turnoffs or on-ramps. The way to develop your career map is through research. Become a sponge. Be hungry for every morsel of information you can find. This is critically important.

Basing your decisions on good, not faulty information is crucial. If you limit yourself to interacting and learning from only your immediate circle of friends and acquaintances, you're in trouble. Arm yourself with the best and most current information so you are prepared. Check with successful people you know and trust, to be certain you are in possession of the right information.

Even with thorough preparation and good research, your career path may not proceed exactly as planned. That's okay and expected. With the knowledge you gain through your study, you will be able to alter your route to get around an obstacle and proceed forward. You won't end up in a rut or rolled over at the side of the road.

Seek out information aggressively every day of your life. You have much to learn and must learn it fast. When you aren't actually playing the guitar you should be reading, listening, and studying and then applying what you learn to the improvement of your guitar playing and advancement of your career. Set up a schedule to do this. Maybe every Saturday and Sunday afternoon from 2:00 to 5:00 you will go to Borders or Barnes & Noble and just sit there and read.

Go to a library and read books, articles, music trade publications (the back issues too), and listen to CDs that are applicable to your interests. You don't have to buy anything! Read for free and take notes. Make copies of important articles. Make a notebook to collect ideas and information. Put your photocopied articles or clips in the notebook organized by topic.

Or, just stay home! While libraries are still great places in which to spend time, the Internet is the largest library in the world. You have 24-

hour access to an absolute goldmine of information. Mine the Internet for important information, ideas, and contacts. Go deep. Bing and Google are important research tools for success. Read, search, and read some more. Many trade periodicals have online editions. Don't have a computer? Use the computers at the library or, if you are a student, at your school. It's FREE.

If you are a poor or slow reader, I would strongly recommend you take courses to improve your reading skills. Completing a speed-reading course will give you the skills needed to effectively wade through the mountain of information you must absorb.

As an entrepreneurial guitarist, be thirsty for knowledge about everything relevant to your art and career. Learn everything possible about the guitar and the type of music you're playing. Depending on your focus, it may be necessary to know all the ins and outs of subjects such as:

1. CD production
2. Recording
3. Music publishing
4. Television
5. Radio
6. Films
7. Music performance rights
8. Songwriting and composing
9. Copyright law
10. Agents, managers, and lawyers
11. Video production
12. Record producers
13. Mechanical royalties

14. The Internet
15. Building websites
16. Contracts
17. Computers and software
18. Music retailing
19. Music education

Those are just a few broad topics. Obviously, you cannot know everything about all these topics. But having a good understanding of most of them is important. Look at the Recommended Reading List on my website, MillionDollarGuitarist.com. If you don't read at least 90% of these or something similar, you should probably reconsider pursuing a career in the music business.

My son told me that's a ridiculous statement. He said plenty of musicians have achieved success who haven't read any of those books. That's true. But, they probably haven't made a million dollars. Or, they won't have lasting success. Some of the mega-successful artists also may not have read these or similar books. But, if your name isn't Madonna or Justin Timberlake, start reading.

Other important subjects not directly related to guitar playing that you should know about include:

1. Public relations (PR)
2. Sales and marketing
3. Accounting
4. Insurance (personal, liability, equipment)
5. Sales and marketing
6. Finance (taxes, raising capital, personal finance)

7. Sales and marketing
8. Investing
9. Public speaking
10. Sales and marketing

Hmmmm…do you get the feeling that I believe sales and marketing is important?

Everyone has their strengths and weaknesses. If you are weak in a certain aspect of your guitar playing, fix it. Read about it and seek help from someone who *is* good at it. You may not be a natural salesman. Therefore, read up on it to find out how to improve yourself in that area. After all, if you are not applying basic principles of sales, marketing, and PR to your career, you are going nowhere.

Finally, if you think preparation, study, practice, research, and learning are only done while you are in college or in the early stages of your career, you are sadly mistaken. Once you commit yourself to being a pro, the work not only continues, but intensifies. As you move ahead, the competition increases. After your first modest or even big success, if you get lazy you will lose your edge. Adopt and retain a mindset of discovery throughout your life. Keep yourself in top shape in every area: intellectually, physically, guitar chops, knowledge, and commitment. More preparation and more study are always ahead of you. The more you know, the more you will have to draw on.

Perpetuating a mindset of discovery and gathering information will not only make you a better guitarist, but will help you survive through the rough times. It will be one of the most important habits to maintain in order to achieve success and earn your million dollars.

7. AM I WILLING TO FAIL?
• *Can I learn from and be positive about failure and mistakes?*
• *Or, am I afraid to fail?*

Failure? Expect it! We *learn* from failure and mistakes. A toddler doesn't one day just stand up and walk. Learning is a gradual process of trial and error. The toddler falls down, gets up, and tries again. He does it over and over. Remember when you learned to ride a bicycle? At first you just couldn't get the hang of it. You fell down. You tried again. Eventually you figured it out and you wondered later, why was *that* so difficult? It feels totally natural now. Look at how you learn to play the guitar. Mistakes, mistakes, mistakes! But you fix them. You *learn* how to fix them. In fixing the mistakes and especially in learning *how* to fix the mistakes, you become a better guitar player. Mistakes are a natural and essential part of learning.

All successful people have significant failures and losses. They suffer bitter disappointments. In fact, if you didn't know better, you might think they were losers. They get knocked down. But they get up again. They take two steps backward and three steps forward. They learn their lessons along the way. They learn what works. They avoid things that don't work. They are not superhuman. When they fail, they suffer like the rest of us. They get angry. They hurt. They may go into shock for a while. But they don't try to "fix" their feelings. The fix is to learn from the experience and keep moving onward. The temporary defeat matters far less than their ultimate goal. They bounce back from adversity.

As I espouse many times in this book, positive thinking is crucial for success. But achievers don't "waste" mistakes by glossing over, dismissing, or trying to cover up failure with superficial positive thinking, or by pretending to be happy or unaffected. They don't want to miss the opportunity to learn from mistakes. They don't want to miss receiving the benefits of the insights they gain from failure.

Successful people don't obsess for one moment about defeats and setbacks and certainly don't blame others for their failures. They harvest information from their failures (and successes) so they can improve, regardless of whether the setback was their own fault or just bad luck. They focus on their goals and on things they can control. They keep taking action. They make things happen instead of letting things happen to them. *They never surrender.* As Winston Churchill (one of my personal heroes) wrote:

> *This is the lesson: never give in, never give in, never, never, never, never—in nothing, great or small, large or petty— never give in except to convictions of honour and good sense. Never yield to force; never yield to the apparently overwhelming might of the enemy.*

Life is all about making mistakes, learning from them, and moving on. Some mistakes can be very serious and life altering or even life threatening. As nineteenth-century philosopher Friedrich Nietzsche said in his famous quote, "That, which does not kill us, makes us stronger." Something to remember on a rough day.

Things will go wrong, and events will turn against you. It will be your job to figure out what happened and where you went wrong. If you are the type that pretends you don't make any mistakes or, worse yet, blames others for mistakes and bad turns of events, you are not honest with yourself. You don't face the facts. You will not learn the lesson. If you are unwilling to learn from your mistakes, and face up to what *you* did wrong, your career will falter if not fail completely.

8. CAN I TAKE HEAVY-DUTY SOUL-CRUSHING CRITICISM?

To be successful as a guitarist or achieve any worthwhile goal, you will probably have to do things differently from anyone else. Playing the way everyone else does, or writing the same type of songs as everyone else, will not get you very far. If you play just like (insert name of guitarist here) or write songs that sound just like (insert name of artist here), guess what? People will buy the CDs and go to the concerts of the originals, not you!

When you do something different and out of the ordinary, I guarantee you will be criticized for it—sometimes severely. If you get strong reactions, you are probably doing something right. You somehow have struck a chord.

Throughout your career, people will tell you that you have no talent, no personality, you're not a very good guitarist, your voice is bad, your songs are stupid, and you should have kept your old job. If your focus is on a mission not directly related to actually playing the guitar, they will tell you that you aren't smart enough to achieve it, or you're too lazy, or your idea is stupid, and on and on. Some of the people who say these things will be people you respect in the music industry. Some will be close family members. Others will be total idiots.

REALITY CHECK: Ironically, even when you're doing your best, you will be bombarded with cruel criticism. You will receive harsh reviews of your music, your product, your intent, your plans, anything and everything. For a significant portion of your career journey, your hard work at innovation and creativity will be rewarded by stinging criticism. Lucky you! Successful people suffer through this just like anyone else. They feel the hurt and the pain of being beaten up by unfair or brutal criticism. But the difference is that they tolerate it, learn from it, and continue doing what matters to them.

You will have to take it and keep moving forward. If you believe in what you are doing with your heart and intellect, you can't let others bring you down. You can even use negative words and reactions to motivate you—the old "I will prove them wrong." If you believe in what you're doing, ignore what "they" say, especially when you are met with temporary defeat. "They" probably don't know that every failure has within it the seed of an equivalent success. You will put up with all the grief you get from pursuing your dream, because for better or worse, you know *you must pursue it.*

Always guard against criticism that results from jealousy, as opposed to criticism that may be valid. Never confuse the two. Jealous criticism is commonplace. Don't let it become personal and get under your skin. But valid criticism is another matter. Listen to and examine the naysayers' words. Is there some truth in what they say? Can you learn from it? What can you improve? Also, take it as a positive that the person making the critical comment took the time and effort to do so and therefore cares about what you are doing. Feedback and criticism can be a valuable way for you to find your bearings—to evaluate where you are and where you should go next.

As you become more successful, the criticism will intensify. Once you are up on a pedestal, it seems you are fair game for every nutcase out there to take shots at you. Even seemingly normal and rational people will chime in. Not only will you become the object of controversy somewhere along the line, but you may very well do something stupid, then watch it become magnified way out of proportion, just because you *are* successful.

You will face heavy criticism. Deal with it. But if you are thin-skinned and just can't handle it, forget about the idea of being an entrepreneurial guitarist. Get a job where you fit in. Do things the way everyone else does so you will find acceptance. Nothing is wrong with that and for many people it will be the better road to take. The danger is that some months or years later, you may find yourself beating yourself up for having given up so easily. When the going gets tough, persistence and determination will come to your aid.

9. DO I HAVE THE PERSISTENCE AND DETERMINATION TO PUT COUNTLESS HOURS OF TIME INTO MY CAREER WITH NO IMMEDIATE REWARDS?

- *Am I willing to persist through endless criticism, doubt, fear, and failure?*
- *Do I have the mental strength to never give up?*

Once you honestly face the brutal reality of where you are (more about that later), you will move forward. You will pursue your dreams and goals. But you will be discouraged by many things. Criticism is one. Failure is another. In fact, sometimes it will seem like a demon has been specially assigned to you to throw as many discouraging experiences in your way as possible. It will be the old "everything that can go wrong, will go wrong." You will find yourself frequently asking, "Why me?" The only way to get through difficult times is with persistence and determination. My favorite quote, and one I live by to a great extent, is by Calvin Coolidge:

> *Nothing in the world can take the place of persistence.*
> *Talent will not; nothing is more common than unsuc-*
> *cessful men with talent.*
> *Genius will not; unrewarded genius is almost a proverb.*
> *Education will not; the world is full of educated derelicts.*
> *Persistence and determination alone are omnipotent.*

The world is littered with talented people who did not persist, who didn't put in the time, who thought they could ride in on talent alone. The ones that succeeded showed up and stuck with it the longest. Persistence trumps talent. Persistence trumps education. Persistence trumps genius. Doggedness delivers massive returns.

Perseverance means never giving up. It means continuing on a journey to achieve a purpose, or continuing to pursue a course of action in spite of opposition. Difficult goals and incredible dreams take time. Impossible ones take a little longer.

Optimism plays a huge role in perseverance and determination. When you believe in yourself and believe that things will work out for you, a huge tipping of the tables occurs in your favor. "But Doug, I'm kind of a dark person by nature," you say. My answer: it doesn't matter. You can choose the light instead of the dark. You can choose and will yourself to be optimistic, to have a positive attitude. It benefits you directly and also attracts people to want to work with you. *Attitude is a choice.*

This doesn't mean you only see the world through rose-colored glasses. The ability to be brutally and analytically critical and to see the bad side of things can be an asset—when combined with optimism.

You can be an optimist even in the bad times if you have a contingency plan for the worst-case scenarios. Optimism brings you a positive sense of the world and of the people around you. It energizes you. Doom and gloom are paralyzing.

Your determination to succeed will define what is possible and what is impossible. Let's take a moment and have a look at Ludwig van Beethoven. In his book, *Spiritual Moments with the Great Composers,* Patrick Kavanaugh tells us:

> *Beethoven possessed a tremendous resolve to persevere in the face of a musician's worst affliction: deafness. Beethoven's music as well as his own written thoughts reveals the powerful convictions he maintained in the midst of trial and tragedy. He considered his talents a sacred trust from the Creator and strove to use them in the face of affliction compounded by humiliation and disgrace. He did not surrender to the difficulties and dejection created by his deafness. Over the years as his deafness worsened, his new compositions actually grew increasingly profound.*
>
> *In Beethoven's day, deafness was a visible disability. If Beethoven wanted to hear anything clearly, he had to hold up a large, awkward ear-trumpet. This is a far cry from today's hearing aids, as unobtrusive as eyeglasses. And, in contrast to today's public, which is relatively accepting of physical handicaps, Beethoven's world was ignobly unsympathetic. Street urchins taunted and jeered as he shuffled through the streets of Vienna.*

The tenacity that caused him to be seen as rude and discourteous enabled him to persevere and write pieces late in his career that were of unrivaled splendor and complexity. They were heard only in his mind, never by his natural ear. Genius yes, but fueled by absolute perseverance.

To be successful as an entrepreneurial guitarist, you must be willing to fly in the face of conventional wisdom. Doing things like everyone else usually doesn't work in the music business. You will be working on things that all the people around you say can't be done. Your mindset is that you will persist and figure out how you can do it. You might even figure out how you can do something that has *never* been done.

During the bad times, in the midst of doubt and fear, you may feel like you are trudging through deep mud with a heavy weight on your shoulders. Ninety percent of the perseverance battle is knowing that what you are doing is right and worth the fight. Remember your mission? See the vision in your mind. Know where you are going and where you want to be. Don't give up. As Thomas Edison once wrote, "Many of life's failures are people who did not realize how close they were to success when they gave up." You will face adversity many times throughout your career. Tough times don't last. Tough people do.

YOUR ANSWERS TO THE NINE QUESTIONS

Okay, you've made it through the Nine Questions. You have asked yourself specifically:

1. Does the phrase, "I can't imagine myself doing anything else" ring a bell? Is playing the guitar and earning a living as a guitarist a burning desire within me? Is it my life's

mission? Can the guitar be absolutely #1 in my life?

2. Do I want to be an entrepreneurial guitarist instead of an employee? Do I have the entrepreneurial spirit? Can I go it alone without the security and safety net of a "real job"?

3. Am I clear on what level I will compete?

4. Am I willing to work harder than I've ever worked before, and then some, to play the game? Am I willing to pay a staggering price for this?

5. Am I willing and humble enough to pursue every opportunity possible to further my career? (Many of these opportunities will not pay a dime or have any obvious immediate benefit.) Or, am I just going to make excuses? Am I willing to pay my dues?

6. Do I have an insatiable thirst for knowledge? Do I want to read, read, read, research, research, research *all* aspects of my field? For hours every day? (Mind you, this is in addition to your hours of guitar practice or other musical activities every day.)

7. Am I willing to fail? Can I learn from and be positive about failure and mistakes? Or, am I afraid to fail?

8. Can I take heavy-duty soul-crushing criticism?

9. Do I have the persistence and determination to put countless hours of time into my career with no immediate rewards? Am I willing to persist through endless criticism, doubt, fear, and failure? Do I have the mental strength to never give up?

If some of your "yes" answers are weak or come with qualifications, you will run into some problems in your career. If you have even one "no"—*a "no" that has no chance of being turned into a "yes" with work and change of attitude*—I would seriously reconsider pursuing a career in music, at least on the scale on which this book is focused. In fact, I am tempted to tell you to close the book right now. Keep the job you have or go to college or a trade school. Get yourself a "real job." You will save yourself and everyone around you heartache, pain, and frustration.

I realize my stance is uncompromising and merciless. But I know that by choice, or because of a lower energy level, some people simply don't have the total commitment necessary to earn a million dollars playing the guitar. That's fine. You could set a smaller goal and still succeed at that goal. Other goals can be honorable and satisfying, especially in music. Those of you who can be content with less grandiose types of success will have rich lives in other ways. You can actually have the time to develop and maintain a good marriage, have time to go to movies and go on dates, hike with the kids, indulge in the joys of personal friendships, and just hang out with people you care about. This book can still be useful to you too.

Or, you may decide to pursue music and play the guitar for fun rather than as a full-time occupation. That is absolutely wonderful. Keep enjoying your music. You might even be able to earn some good income on the side to supplement your regular job income. I'm all for it. I'm with you. But if you had a "no" answer to any of my questions, don't kid yourself and think that you will be able to make a million dollars playing the guitar or have a financially solid, sustained living in music. I would love to have you prove me wrong—write me in twenty years and let me know how you did it—but I sincerely believe it won't happen.

If, however, you are one of those gunning for a full-time career, and all your answers to the Nine Questions are a strong "yes," you are in great shape mentally to pursue your million dollars playing the guitar. You are in for an exciting ride. You have the boundless energy, enthusiasm, and obsessive burning desire to achieve almost any goal you choose. You will forgo many simple pleasures others take for granted. But your commitment is not sacrifice. You do it willingly. You will have a satisfying, fulfilling, challenging life that few others have the privilege to experience. It will be hard and you will get very discouraged. But at the same time, you will be having more fun than a human being should be allowed to have. You will have a mission, a purpose in life which will benefit many, not just yourself.

When you operate at this level of total commitment, the rest of the world will tell you that you have misplaced values. You will be accused of being self-centered. Wrong. "Balance," as understood by pop culture and television psychologists, is incorrectly defined. You are striving to make a dream come true. That is healthy. Balance is finding a place for everything important to you. You will spend most of your time doing exactly what you want to do by choice and will love doing it. That isn't being a workaholic. That isn't imbalance. That is fulfillment.

Actress Katharine Hepburn once said the secret to her success was elimination. "I simply got rid of anyone and anything that really didn't matter one bit to me. You know, dead weight, excess baggage, that sort of thing."

Researchers have found that successful people in general are healthier than those who are not. People who strive for success undergo tremendous stress. But rather than being debilitating, stress is often a positive factor for the achiever. The person who relentlessly pursues their passion in life actually enjoys the stress of coping with and overcoming difficulties. They get a buzz out of controlled risk. It energizes them and makes them come alive.

Yes, you are different from others. You are pursuing what you love most in life. You reach higher than the people around you. And you will gladly pay a staggering price for the joy you give to others and receive for yourself.

What? Are you still waffling about your ultimate answer? Just don't know? Should I or shouldn't I? You very likely already know the answer in your heart. When you think you don't know, *you know.*

chapter 4

YOU HAVE TO KNOW WHAT YOU WANT

Not many people really know what they want in life. Ask twenty acquaintances. Few if any will be able to tell you. Those who can will use very general terms. Some will say security. Some will certainly mention happiness, good health, or money. Mothers will say they want their children to prosper. But seldom will you get a well-defined specific answer. In the rare instance that someone has a definite answer, seldom do they have a definite plan to make their desire become reality.

If you want your life to be filled with riches, you have to know what you want. I'm using the word riches in the broad sense: financial, spiritual, material, relational, intellectual. Figure out what *you* want, not what you think you should want or what someone else says you should want. What do you want to do with your life?

To answer that question, say in one sentence:

1. The main thing you want out of life

2. Your definite major purpose in life

3. Your mission

4. Your passion

5. Your goal

6. Your dream

7. Your burning desire

These phrases and words all mean the *same thing.* Whatever you want to call it, identify that one thing you want more than anything else.

That one focused goal will now become the driving force in your life. Fuzzy, general desires don't survive disappointment, soul-crushing discouragement and criticism, failure and temporary defeats, or constantly hearing the words "waste of time." Find a definable purpose that will become an all-consuming passion for you, transcending everything else. It doesn't have to be earthshaking or grand. Since you are a guitarist, I would imagine your dream will somehow involve the guitar or music. But it may not involve actually *playing* the guitar. That's okay.

Once again, although the subject of this book is how to make a million dollars playing the guitar, that may not be your own personal goal. The "all I need to be happy is money" thing is a myth. Not many people think about it, but our real primary goals are programmed into us genetically. They are called prepotent needs. Until these needs are met, we have difficulty moving ahead in life to higher goals. Here, in order of necessity, are the prepotent needs that have priority over everything else: air, mothering, water, food, and sex. Now stay with me on this, because knowing this stuff is essential to figuring out what you want in life.

If these prepotent needs are not met, the consequences are devastating.

In our modern society, money is required to purchase basic needs such as food, clothing, and shelter. But money itself is not a basic need. Money is the *means* by which we gratify those basic needs. Once our primal and basic needs are met, we are free to move on to the things we wish to achieve as individuals. *Money is a means to an end, not an end in itself.*

YOUR REAL DESIRES

Money can mask your real desires. For example, on a materialistic level, you may say you want a bundle of money. But what you really want is a fancy car and a mansion. Why? If you're a guy, you think those things will attract beautiful women. Why beautiful women? Because you want connection, love, fulfillment, sex. I know some of you guys might cut that list down to one thing. Again, money is a commodity— something you use to get what you really want. Money itself is not your desire. That realization will help you clarify your thoughts to figure out what you really want.

Our prepotent needs are clear. But our wants or desires are very complex. Some examples of wants are love, power, fame, excitement, success, status, a good marriage, a fulfilling sex life, well-adjusted children, friends, fun, beauty, good health, spiritual contentment, respect, and self-sufficiency. Most people want combinations of any or all of them.

For example, a woman may have a career goal to be chairperson of the board of the Acme Corporation. But that isn't her real want or desire. What she actually wants or desires is power or status. A young guitarist's career goal is to be a rock star. What he really wants is fame, status, attention, sex, etc. In other words, basic wants loom behind the outer career goal.

Identifying your true desires will help ensure that your career choices are helping you attain those desires. In the big picture, life isn't so much about the career. Living a fulfilling and rewarding life is about attaining your innermost desires.

FOCUSED THOUGHT

The power of the human mind is nearly limitless. Your focused thought is one of your most powerful tools to get what you want. Choose a goal (or goals) that will help you obtain your innermost desires. Pursue it obsessively with focused thought, faith, unrelenting persistence that does not recognize defeat, knowledge, the right people around you, and, most of all, a white-hot burning desire. If you do that, most likely you will achieve your dream. You have the power to force life to pay you whatever is asked.

Here again are the tools:

I will pursue my goal obsessively with:
1. Focused thought
2. Faith
3. Unrelenting persistence that does not recognize defeat
4. Knowledge
5. The right people around me
6. White-hot burning desire

Does this sound overwhelming? It might if you are unaccustomed to thinking big or have never been obsessed by an idea. But research and thousands of in-depth interviews with the mega-successful overwhelmingly confirm that these are the tools they used to achieve a mission. Wishing and hoping won't cut it.

THE SILENT SCREAM

You may be frightened by words like passion, power, obsession, desire, unrelenting, and force. You may think, "Oh my. I don't think that's for me. I don't want my life to be taken over by something I probably won't get anyway. I just want to be happy." Be careful. Another side to this exists that is more frightening.

In *Success Built to Last*, Jerry Porras writes about "The Silent Scream." Have you ever been aware of a little voice in your head that occasionally whispers to you from the background, telling you very clearly what you *should* be doing? The voice is very quiet. People often try to ignore it or decide to go against it, much to their detriment.

That voice is telling you what truly matters to you. It strains to be heard not by being loud, but by being unceasingly persistent. It keeps on nagging. You try to drown it out with logic, or reject it by convincing yourself that even though you know it's right, the circumstances are just not right at this time.

That whisper can be drowned out by the loud voices of your own fear and self-doubt. It can be drowned out by well-meaning loved ones, friends, or business partners whose "concern" for you is vested in seeing that you don't change. Others (and you!) are frightened by your changing. Maybe it would be best if you lock your secret dream away in an unused dusty drawer. Then you'll be safe and the others will be happy.

Tragically, as you attempt to drown out that little whisper, it becomes the silent scream. Remember, it knows the truth. It knows what really matters. Even with your dream bound, gagged, and locked away, you will still hear and feel that desperate, ever-persistent cry deep within. It will eat away, and eat away, and eat away.

Steve Jobs, head honcho of Apple Computer, once mentioned a quote that had made a big impression on him. It read, "If you live each day as if it was your last, someday you'll most certainly be right." In a commencement address at Stanford University in June 2005, he related this story:

> *The quote made an impression on me, and since then, for the past 33 years, I have looked in the mirror every morning and asked myself, 'If today were the last day of my life, would I want to do what I am about to do today?' And whenever the answer has been 'no' for too many days in a row, I know I need to change something.*
>
> *Remembering that I'll be dead soon is the most important thing I've ever encountered to help me make the big choices in life, because almost everything—all external expectations, all pride, all fear of embarrassment or failure—these things just fall away in the face of death, leaving only what is truly important. Remembering that you are going to die is the best way I know to avoid the trap of thinking you have something to lose. You are already naked. There is no reason not to follow your heart. No one wants to die; even people who want to go to Heaven don't want to die to get there.*

But Jobs says we can't escape it, so face it head on.

> *Your time is limited, so don't waste it living someone else's life. Don't be trapped by dogma, which is living with the results of other people's thinking. Don't let the noise of others' opinions drown out your own inner voice,*

heart and intuition. They somehow already know what you truly want to become. Everything else is secondary.

Those who succeed in life ignore their own fears and self-doubt. They ignore friends, spouses, and family members who want to control them, who want to keep them "safe" where they are. They ignore outside forces like the media telling them things are bad, now is not the time, what they want to do has been tried and not attained. The list goes on and on. Don't give in to it. Decide what you want and pursue it with ferocious resolve and unrelenting persistence.

chapter 5

SETTING GOALS

For many of you, goal setting may already be well understood, even rudimentary. But for others, we need to talk. Because musicians are so immersed in the creative side of things, many lack focus and fail to make clear plans or set goals.

Goal setting is a proven key ingredient to success. Nearly every person in any successful endeavor has used some form of planning or goal setting. Successful people know where they are, what they want, and where they are going. Through study and research, they know or have a pretty good idea of the steps they need to take to get there. As a result, they reach their destinations faster and more easily than people who don't plan. The dynamic of goal setting is very simple and very basic.

Goals give direction and keep things on track. Goals repel indecision. Indecision leads to standing still or walking in circles. Indecision leads to doubt, then fear. Indecision is an enemy. You are playing the game of life. *Your ultimate opponent is time.* If you hesitate too often or move too slowly, your opponent will overtake you. You are playing against an opponent that makes huge advances on the game board when you are indecisive.

Making plans is necessary in order to achieve goals. Plans provide a step-by-step approach to maximize your time and focus your efforts.

This greatly increases your chances for success.

With a clear plan you will be more likely to stay disciplined to attain your goal. A step-by-step plan is also a great way to measure your progress. As you look back at your plan, you can see which steps you have successfully completed and which ones still need work.

To achieve a goal, do this:

1. Set a main goal—the one thing you want to accomplish. Make it definite. Make it precise.
2. Figure out the secondary goals necessary to achieve the main goal. You may have no idea what it will take to accomplish your main goal. This is where your research enters the picture.
3. Figure out the tasks you have to do to reach the secondary goals. These are your working goals that require day-to-day work and continual effort to accomplish. You don't get anything for nothing. Give to receive. Take heart—most things are not particularly hard to do if you divide them into small jobs. Your research and study will help you figure it out.
4. Have a timeline. Decide *specific dates* to accomplish your secondary goals and main goal. Not number of years, months, or weeks—*dates.*

All of this will fall into a reasonable and logical order. Every goal and every task can be broken down into additional goals and tasks to make each step even easier so the journey doesn't seem so formidable.

BEGIN AT THE END

Making goals, measuring your progress toward achieving them, and finally reaching them keeps you moving on a path. However, you have to understand that achieving goal after goal doesn't tell you if you're headed in the right direction. If you're going the wrong way you will receive little benefit. In other words, you can successfully be climbing the foothills to a mountain without any assurance that particular mountain is the one you should be climbing. This is why beginning with the end in mind is important. Ask yourself, "What is my life-driving mission?" In Chapter 22, I will tell you how to develop a "Hedgehog Concept." Your Hedgehog Concept will help you define your mission and guide you toward achieving it.

THE BIGGER PICTURE

Some say that detailed, clearly articulated career plans don't result in long-term success. They say that having a plan where you will do x which will lead to y which will put you at z will not work. The world is too tumultuous, too unpredictable. Such carefully crafted plans fall apart.

Yes, of course. If you make an inflexible plan that doesn't evolve as circumstances change, it has no hope for success. That is why, *as circumstances continually change, you must constantly adjust and change your plan.*

Goal setting is very logical and produces clear results on day-to-day tasks. But yes, how they benefit you and where you end up in the big picture usually doesn't turn out as expected. The path you end up taking will probably bear little resemblance to the road map with which you started. The goals and the map give you a vision and direction in which to proceed. But the journey is like shooting for the moon, and instead hitting Venus! Not very close to what you were aiming for, but possibly an even better outcome than you could have believed possible. Realize that if you hadn't made the plan, set the smaller goals, and mapped it out, you would still be sitting on the couch in front of the HDTV.

Having direction is crucial. But the road map will continually change. When you go deep for knowledge, plan, and relentlessly pursue opportunity, unexpected things happen that lead you down unexpected paths and ultimately lead to unforeseen treasures. You will live with the ambiguity of not knowing what will happen next.

In my own life, I have always had very specific goals and plans. Because I kept my eyes and ears open to change and opportunity, things turned out far better than I could ever have imagined, with wonderful, unexpected results. So, you may be tempted to say, "Why bother making a plan if something very different is going to happen anyway?" Because plans produce results. Having no plans leads to nothing.

chapter 6

POSITIVE ATTITUDE

So, you are the most talented musician that has ever walked the earth. Guess what? That doesn't mean you will have a successful career in music. You still have a tremendous amount of work to do. To develop a career you have to focus on strategy—what you do and when. I don't care how talented you are. If you can't implement a strategy to achieve your goals, you will fail. Set your goals and map out your path—make a plan.

However, in order for your plan to work, you must *decide* the plan is going to work. This is essential. If you don't believe in your plan, it will be worthless.

Success begins with a state of mind. Once you have made the decision that your plan will succeed, push negative thoughts out of your mind. Concentrate on thoughts of success. Positive mental attitude is a vital key to making your plan work.

POSITIVE VERSUS NEGATIVE

I talk about being positive and optimistic throughout this book. Many people will try to cut you down, even people close to you. The odds for real success in any endeavor are usually against you. If you decide to go for it anyway, the last thing you want is a negative outlook. You don't have to lie to yourself or ignore the bad stuff. Just make up your mind to think about the good things that have happened, are happening, and can happen. It will become a positive cycle. If you focus on the good, you will believe the good. Then, more good things will happen. It's trite, but right. Remember, attitude is a choice.

Negative energy is prevalent in the music business. Negativism, pessimism, and darkness are actually part of the makeup of certain segments of pop music. Heavy metal, Goth, and rap immediately come to mind. If you are creating music that contains that attitude, fine. Just don't let it creep into your "I want to succeed" mindset. The last thing you want is to become another angry musician drinking or abusing drugs and sitting around complaining about the system not recognizing your genius.

Yes, people will tell you your music stinks. It's not this, it's not that. It's too this, it's too that. Condition your mind against all such negativity. Don't let the doubters and the criticizers shake you. Don't let them weaken your resolve and your belief in yourself. You know these names: Elvis Presley, Bruce Springsteen, The Beatles, Barbra Streisand, Michael Jackson, Bob Dylan, Madonna, Tina Turner. You wouldn't know them, however, if they had listened to the high-level music industry "experts" who told them they would never make it. All were told in one way or another that they sucked. They didn't listen—neither should you.

Rush Limbaugh, who has faced countless naysayers his entire life, offers this sage advice:

> *Whether looking for a job or career advice, don't listen to*
> *whiners and complainers. If you want to succeed at some-*

thing find someone who has succeeded and listen to and learn from them. Don't listen to someone who has failed and let them tell you how rotten and unfair the business is that you want to get into.

Find someone who has succeeded and loves it and learn from them. It takes effort and work to remain positive. So don't hang around people who moan and whine and complain all the time because eventually it will get to you. And then you'll get depressed and stop trying.

The lesson is to hang around positive people. Negative people don't give energy, they take energy.

Though you can't avoid them, learn not to let negative friends or family bring you down. Unfortunately, some have a vested interest in keeping you where you are. Though they want to be supportive, your desire to achieve lofty new goals threatens them. They're afraid they might lose the old "you." They are far more comfortable with the "you" they know. Learn to handle rejection and discouragement on the friend and family level to successfully overcome rejection and discouragement as you enter the professional world of dealmakers, managers, agents, critics, colleagues, and the public. Don't listen to naysayers. Follow your resolve. Believe in you.

OVERCOMING REJECTION

One of the main ingredients of success is the ability to overcome rejection. You will hear this again and again in this book and in the stories of successful people. People who succeed are people who keep on trying. They never give up.

Lack of persistence is a common weakness and one of the major causes of failure. Just remember, your ability to persist in achieving your life purpose is directly tied to the intensity of your desire to achieve it. You have to want it. You have to be hungry for it. It must be an obsession. Maintain a positive mental attitude to make it happen.

No matter what you are pursuing, from securing an audition with an important person to getting a concert at an important venue, don't even think of being discouraged until you've been rejected at least 30 times. Thirty rejections for anything is pretty much par for the course. Learn from each rejection. Figure out if something needs to be changed. Don't let it slow you down. Use it to make you work harder and smarter. Then forget about the rejection and move on. Let it go. You have things to do, things to accomplish. Sometimes, someone who rejected you a year ago will suddenly do a 180 (usually without realizing it) and become your strongest advocate. Only when your rejection tally tops 50 should you perhaps begin thinking about a significant change of strategy. I'm not saying that facetiously. That is reality.

KEEP THE FAITH, BABY

If you doubt the benefits of positive thinking, think back to a situation in which you *didn't* believe you could accomplish a task. What happened? Either you didn't try at all or you gave it a half-hearted attempt that failed. Success couldn't happen. You were doomed to fail with your negative thoughts.

"I can't do it" becomes a self-fulfilling prophecy. Negative thinking is disastrous. If you remember situations in your past when negative thinking led to failure, then it follows that positive thinking can lead to success.

This duality of positive and negative thinking is captured very well in the poem "The Victor," attributed to C. W. Longenecker:

> *If you* think *you are beaten, you are,*
> *If you* think *you dare not, you don't.*
> *If you like to win, but you* think *you can't,*
> *It is almost certain you won't.*
> *If you* think *you'll lose, you're lost,*
> *For out in the world we find,*
> *Success begins with a fellow's will—*
> It's all in the state of mind.
> *If you* think *you are outclassed, you are,*
> *You've got to* think high *to rise,*
> *You've got to be* sure of yourself *before*
> *You can ever win a prize.*
> *Life's battles don't always go*
> *To the stronger or faster man,*
> *But soon or late the man who wins*
> *Is the man WHO THINKS HE CAN!*

Your unconscious mind is always working, whether you try to influence it or not. If you leave it to its own devices, it will absorb positive *and* negative thoughts. Through your constant effort and steady habit, you can close the gate to the negative but allow the positive to pass into your mind. Take control and use this powerful tool for your benefit.

Positive thinking is closely allied with faith. Faith can be induced, created, or nurtured by repeated affirmations to the conscious and subconscious mind. Faith gives life, power, and action to our thought. *Faith removes limitations.*

Try to imagine a world without faith. I can't. Faith is in our being, a primary part of our humanity. Nurturing and strengthening faith in every aspect of our lives is vital for our well-being.

Success begins with faith. The most powerful tool we have in pursuing our passion and achieving our definite purpose in life is faith. Have I lost you? Okay, let me bring you back down to earth and put it in materialistic words. You've gotta have faith you will make your million dollars playing the guitar. If you don't, it ain't gonna happen.

VISUALIZATION AND AUTOSUGGESTION: POWERFUL TOOLS OF THE HUMAN MIND

Visualization is imagining a detailed mental picture of an activity or process to improve one's performance of that activity or bring that process to fruition. It works for mundane tasks, such as improving your golf swing and of course, your guitar playing. Some advocates recommend its use for preserving health or fighting illness. Many success gurus believe that by using visualization techniques every day, you can achieve almost any goal. They say if you imagine yourself already in possession of your goal, you will eventually reach it. Of course, it involves much more than that, but you get the idea.

Autosuggestion uses the subconscious in a similar way. By affirmation or repeated instructions, either spoken aloud or written down, we place a plan, idea, or purpose in our mind through repetition of thought. Any plan, goal, or purpose persistently held in the mind with repetition eventually seeks expression or becomes real in a practical manner.

Have you heard of the phrase "the power of the spoken word"? Many success gurus say that one way to succeed is by *saying out loud* positive affirmations and goals every day. They claim that what you repeatedly say out loud tends to actually happen.

Napoleon Hill in his classic book *Think and Grow Rich* recommends reading aloud twice daily (after waking in the morning and before sleep at night) a written statement of your desire for success (Hill speaks more in terms of making a certain amount of money). Then, see yourself in possession of that success. Hill maintains that this will implant in your subconscious mind absolute faith in the belief that you will achieve your desire. Repeating your words creates habits of thinking that continually keep your thoughts focused toward reaching your stated desires. The mind begins to filter out information that isn't useful to your stated goal and instead seeks out and focuses consciously and unconsciously on information that *will* be of help to you.

In my personal experience, I have found that having a burning desire for an outcome combined with visualization and written-out affirmations works amazingly well *without* daily verbal affirmation. I have experienced it my entire life. Does saying your statement *out loud* produce a stronger result? Personally, I can't say it matters, but for what it's worth, many of the success gurus say it does make a difference.

Writing out goals and desires, however, produces impressive results. A Ford Foundation study of what makes people successful determined that only 3% of their research sample reached their target goals. What was the determining factor for these 3% that enabled them to reach their goals? *They had written them down.* Once you write down your goals, desires, and plans on paper, you give them concrete form. You can see them in front of you, staring back at you. The mind tends to follow what it sees. Writing down your goals greatly increases your power to turn your desires into reality.

In 1966, when I was fourteen years old, I wrote out a list of career goals that included performing a solo recital in Carnegie Recital Hall. I even specified April 1973. I hit it on the nose. I didn't use verbal affirmation and I didn't look at the list very often—maybe three to six times a year. Other goals for which I specified completion dates I missed by a year or two, but still reached almost all of them. A few goals I missed altogether—never got a booking on television's "The Tonight Show" with Johnny Carson. I came close, but it didn't happen. Nevertheless, I think the fact that I achieved most of my written goals, many of them by the date I had specified years before, is pretty amazing and not at all coincidental.

Napoleon Hill maintains that the subconscious mind will act on any orders given to it if given with absolute faith. He emphasizes that the orders must be repeated over and over again before the subconscious will engage. And then, continue to repeat the orders to keep the subconscious working for you until your desire becomes reality.

Hill is adamant that simply reading a statement of your desire will be worthless unless your words are filled with emotion and feeling. Your subconscious mind acts only upon words and thoughts that are charged with intent or emotion. Plain, unemotional words will not engage or influence the subconscious mind. The successful use of autosuggestion is dependent on the intensity of your desire. Your desire must be genuine.

Skeptical? Hill saw it coming. He reminds us that skepticism of new ideas is characteristic of all human beings. He asserts that if you follow his instructions your skepticism will be replaced by belief, which will soon become absolute faith.

SUCCESS LIES BEYOND THE PLATITUDE

Don't misinterpret the use of autosuggestion as "if I can think it, I can do it." As you've just read, it involves much more effort than that. Autosuggestion and positive mental attitude will only work when used in combination with other well-known principles, such as endless hard work. And, all by itself, even endless hard work will not bring success. *Neither hard work nor a positive attitude will work alone.* Your outcome is contingent on the *joint application* of hard work, planning, positive mental attitude, willingness to fail, the endless pursuit of opportunity, and going deep for knowledge. Even then, the sparks begin to fly only when your desire for the outcome becomes a burning obsession.

chapter 7

LUCK

The greats often credit good luck with their success. Being self-effacing, they give credit to things outside of themselves when things go well. If they can't think of a person, event, or circumstance that deserves the credit, they credit good luck. At the same time, when things go wrong, they take personal responsibility—they don't blame bad luck.

But the self-effacement of the mega-successful can be misleading. In reality, their good luck is usually earned at great cost. They focus on doing work that means everything to them. They are passionate about their goals (which are clearly in focus at all times) and completely engaged on all levels in their pursuit. As a result, they are better prepared to turn seemingly inconsequential or unrelated things into opportunities. The successful may appear to be brilliant, heroic, and endowed with supernatural talent. The truth is that their success is a result of passion, skills developed by 10,000-plus hours of work, and the endless acquisition of knowledge from "going deep." Their passion inspires them to acquire the skills and knowledge to make their "luck" happen. Focusing on developing skills and acquiring knowledge allows them to see things others don't, and use them to their advantage.

Roman philosopher Seneca the Younger said, "Luck is where preparation meets opportunity." Television personality Matt Lauer once commented, "Luck is knowing how to take advantage of breaks; knowing how to take advantage of the kindness of strangers. Being fortunate enough to meet the right people at the right time, and then capitalizing on those opportunities."

To capitalize on opportunity, always do the absolute best you can at any job you do. You will derive satisfaction from doing things well, and you will develop a mindset of *always producing excellence*, regardless of the payoff. That mindset needs to be ingrained. Make it a habit. Then, when the big gig comes, when the cards are on the table and it really counts, you will come through:

> Unknown trumpet player Chris Botti was playing a wedding gig where talk-show host Oprah Winfrey was in attendance. Oprah loved his playing, got a copy of his CD and invited him to play on her show. The result? Botti's CD was number one in sales on Amazon.com twenty-four hours later.

Luck requires preparation. It also requires being present. You literally have to be there. You have to be in the room for luck to find you. Show up. Be seen. Be involved. Experience things, see things, and meet people with no immediate payback in mind. Make it happen.

Here's a mundane example from my own career of how showing up and doing what you do can lead to a significant opportunity.

> I attended and graduated from the Conservatory of Music and Dance, University of Missouri—Kansas City. I was a good student. My teachers liked and respected me. I had a good relationship with the Dean and Assistant Dean (who

later become Associate Dean and then Dean).

A year after I graduated I got a call from the Dean's office. I thought I was in trouble—that maybe they discovered I hadn't passed some class or didn't have enough credits and shouldn't have graduated.

But no, they were looking for a new guitar instructor. It was a tenure-track position (which meant nothing much to me then) for a pretty lousy salary even back then in 1976 of $10,000. I had also just signed with Columbia Artists Management, one of the biggest agencies at the time, for concert bookings in North America. Since I signed with Columbia Artists, I thought I had it made. I took the teaching job at the University almost as an afterthought. The University hired me because I had made a good impression as a student, they knew my character, and they knew that I played well.

I was in the right place at the right time and I was available and cheap. I had gone to classes and did what I was supposed to do. I showed up. I also did my absolute best.

As it turned out, that job led to hundreds of other opportunities (and still does). It also helped to fuel the rest of my career financially. I used that income to produce promotional photos and brochures, do mailings, make demo records, etc.

I happened to stumble into a stream of income that not only contributes substantially to my overall cash flow, but also carries with it security and benefits such as health and life insurance and an excellent retirement plan (although what idiot wants to retire from music?).

In the end, luck is something you attract. *You create luck by creating opportunity.* The only "big break" you can depend on is one that is self-made. Luck begins with having goals and a mission, and is created with the application of persistence.

Thomas Jefferson (one of my personal heroes) wrote, "I am a great believer in luck, and I find the harder I work, the more I have of it."

chapter 8

THE PURSUIT
OF OPPORTUNITY

Harvard professor Howard H. Stevenson defined entrepreneurship as "the pursuit of opportunity without regard to resources currently controlled." Wow. That's a great description of the situation of most guitarists just starting out on their career. You don't have much money and you don't know any important people. You just don't know much of anything. But you love playing the guitar or you love music and want to make it your life's work. You're beginning to pursue or are in the process of pursuing opportunity as an entrepreneurial guitarist.

As a guitarist, you must be driven by the *perception* of opportunity. Don't be discouraged just because at present you don't control many resources. Those will come. Do not allow yourself to think, "I can't afford it." Or, "I can't do that." Instead, if you are planning to be a successful guitarist, ask, "How can I afford that?" Or, "How can I do that?" Look at and pursue every opportunity that has the potential, however slight, of helping your career. Or, to put it another way, look for things that will drive your career.

I have also found that rather than knocking, opportunity has a sly trick of tiptoeing in through the back door, unannounced. Sometimes it even comes disguised in the form of bad luck or a setback. For that reason, many people fail to recognize opportunity. Thomas Edison quipped, "Opportunity is missed by most people because it is dressed in overalls and looks like work."

Opportunity leads to opportunity. Or if it doesn't (which is actually very rare), you learn from that. Often the seemingly normal or even insignificant things you do turn out to be important later in your career.

For example, when I was teaching guitar in my early twenties, I had a student named Bill Piburn and another named Mitch Gallagher. They were great students and I enjoyed teaching them. Thirty years later I found out that Bill was the editor of *Fingerstyle Guitar* magazine and Mitch was editor of *EQ* magazine. I ended up on the cover of *Fingerstyle Guitar* with a nice feature article inside, and a nice page and photo about my home recording studio in *EQ*. Needless to say, that coverage led to other coverage and additional attention, which led to increased sales of my CDs, DVDs, and published music. That type of thing has happened to me throughout my career and will happen for you too if you keep the right mindset.

Let's see how some famous musicians got their first "breaks" that led to major careers. Look at the humble beginnings of country music legend Porter Wagoner, related by Patrick and Barbara Kavanaugh in their book, *Devotions from the World of Music*:

> *At the age of ten, poverty forced him to leave school and work on his father's farm. He loved singing and playing his guitar, but he was so bashful he would never play for anyone. In fact, he was so shy that no one who knew him (not even himself) could ever imagine him having a public career in music.*
>
> *As a teenager, Porter worked in a butcher shop in West*

Plains, Missouri. He used to sing to himself in the back room. One night his boss accidentally overheard Porter singing. The butcher (unlike the execs at most modern-day record labels) recognized talent when he heard it and offered Porter a raise if he would sing some commercials for his butcher shop on the local radio station. A much larger radio station in Springfield, Missouri heard one of Porter's commercials. The bewildered young boy was offered a job at the big station for seventy dollars a week. Next, he swerved into an opportunity to appear on a new television show, The Ozark Jubilee. From there he was noticed by RCA and signed to a recording contract. Soon after moving to Nashville and releasing his first hit, Porter moved on to become a mega star in country music.

Imagine the terror the shy, young Porter Wagoner must have felt at his first radio and television appearances. At each step in his career, he could have slipped back into his wallflower persona and ended up back at the butcher shop. But instead, little by little, he overcame his fears and seized each new opportunity. In fact, as his career matured, Wagoner became known for his relaxed stage presence on television and his live performances.

Here's another story from Patrick and Barbara Kavanaugh:

Two of Nashville's top songwriters, DeWayne Blackwell and Earl "Bud" Lee, decided one day to purchase some new boots. The salesman who waited on them had no idea who they were. But they were very impressed with his expert customer service. He was cheerful and polite and knew everything about each pair of boots he brought out to show them. Bud Lee later commented how much he liked the guy because he was so polite and did everything he could to give them a good deal.

During their conversation the salesman found out his customers were songwriters. His face beamed as he shared his dreams to become a singer. He had come to Nashville to get into the music biz. After finding out that their salesman had a solid background in music and singing and was already working hard, pursuing his dream, they made an appointment to hear him. The boot salesman's name was Garth Brooks.

The songwriters hired Brooks to sing on their demo tapes. Within a few months, he got a contract with Capitol Records and was on his way to stardom. His seminal break came about simply because he was polite, enthusiastic, and offered great customer service to two strangers in a shoe department.

Again, you never know when or where opportunity will knock. Never dismiss an opportunity as too small. At the time it appears, you can never know its potential significance and consequences later down the road. But it can change your life.

MEETING PEOPLE

Some say that meeting the right people is pure luck. That isn't true.

Luck does enter into everything you do, but at the same time *you* have to help make things happen. You are the one who must reach out to make connections with other people. You must make yourself visible and available, so the right people notice you and can find you. Luck that leads to results doesn't usually happen on its own. To a large extent, you make your luck.

You will deal with many people throughout your life and career. You never know where those people will end up. You may not know that the somewhat annoying guy talking to you after a long gig and asking endless questions is the best friend or cousin of an important person at a major record label, newspaper, or magazine. Many successful people in the music industry "jump tracks" many times. A guy in a band you met ten years ago at some obscure club may now be in the A&R department of a significant record label. The lowly assistant at the studio where you made your demo years ago may now be a top-notch producer or mastering engineer. Your old student who could barely hack his way through "Stairway to Heaven" may now be a hotshot entertainment lawyer or record label honcho.

Anyone and everyone can help you in your career, not just music people. You never know who knows who. When you meet a person, you don't know what special talent they may have. No one contact will "do it all" for you. It takes many people to open doors for you that lead to opportunities. In fact, some of the very best people you will meet are the ones who help you out but have nothing to gain personally from doing so.

Like other creative types, you may be inhibited and shy. But you have to communicate with others. Introduce yourself. Circulate. Go to some parties. Hang out with people. Bother people. Ask for favors. Ask for what you want. This may be difficult for you. It is for me. But you have to force yourself to get out there. Do it for your career.

You can join professional organizations and attend workshops, meetings, and seminars. Every showcase, every audition, and every music-related job gives you an opportunity to meet people who can give you advice. They might be helpful to you somewhere down the road. After you meet someone, follow up. Don't just forget about them. Develop and maintain that initial encounter. Build a good reputation and relationship with *everyone*. Don't make everything me, me, me. Nurture a group of people *you can help*. They in turn, will want to help you. The street runs both ways.

Stay in contact with people who have done favors for you in the past. Contact one person every week that you haven't seen or spoken with in a while. There's nothing wrong with telling someone you were thinking about them or were wondering how they were doing. The more you maintain contact, the more you will be on their minds. You want to maintain a presence in their minds. When you contact them, don't begin by saying, "You probably don't remember me but…" Instead, remind them of the contact you had previously and what you've been doing recently.

Don't be offended if people don't return your calls or respond to your emails and letters. It doesn't necessarily mean they don't want to talk to you. Try again later. Some people (myself included) sometimes take weeks to get back to someone if the matter is not urgent. Don't be discouraged. Don't take it personally. If they say no to a request, fine. But that doesn't mean they will reject your next request. To paraphrase author Jack Canfield, it doesn't matter if you're asking for a record deal or asking for a date, your life is the same if the answer is no. Rejection is really of no consequence. If the answer is no, try again or ask someone else.

Don't be afraid to ask for help or favors. If you don't ask, you don't get. In fact, if you don't ask, the answer is always no. Things won't happen just because you are talented or worthy. You have to decide what you want and ask for it. Ask yourself or someone, "How can I get what I want?" Otherwise, opportunities perfect for you will go to someone else. Just be certain your demands or wants are commensurate with your abilities. If your abilities don't measure up, work on them until they do.

And *please*, do your homework before trying to get a job, asking for help, or selling something. Find out the name of the person you must talk with. *Know how to pronounce their name correctly and how to spell it.* Look into the person's background and find out about their company. The more you know going in, the better your results will be coming out. When you call someone for information, go in for an interview, or try to sell to someone, make it clear you have taken the time and made the effort to do your homework. You will impress the person and set yourself apart from the hundreds of others who don't.

LOOKS CAN BE DECEIVING

Often, important and powerful people don't look important or powerful. They don't drive flashy cars or dress in expensive clothes. They look like regular folks. I know your mother has told you this many times, but I'm telling you again: don't judge people by how they look.

I remember when I was a little boy taking weekly guitar lessons at the Mel Bay guitar studios in St. Louis back in the early 1960s. My dad often talked to Mel during or after my lesson. At this time the store was just a little shop in

Kirkwood, a suburb of St. Louis. I knew that the parent company, Mel Bay Publications, published a multitude of books and music, but I didn't think much about it. I only visited the small retail shop.

One evening I came out of my lesson and Mel and my dad were winding up their conversation. Mel just looked like an old guy in a rumpled suit and tie. There was nothing special about his appearance at all. As we walked to the car my dad said to me, "You know, Mel Bay is a multi-millionaire." My eyes lit up and my mind did somersaults. I had seen "millionaires" on television and the movies. But Mel didn't look anything like those "millionaires." Here I was standing in front of the real thing and didn't even know it. I didn't have a clue.

I've thought about that evening many times over the years. You just never know who you're talking to. The eyes you're looking into could be those of an angel, a murderer, or, worse yet, an entertainment lawyer (just kidding). Again, you will come into contact with a multitude of people. They may be in positions of power and be able to help you. Or, if they aren't at the time, you never know where those people may end up someday down the road. Don't make enemies, don't give people the brush-off, and don't burn bridges. Be courteous and gracious to everyone, even if they can't help you today.

DON'T OVERDO IT

Some people say all you need are the right contacts to climb the career ladder to success. But that isn't true. You meet people who seem to know everyone, but still don't achieve success. Some people go head over heels into networking before they should. Ask yourself why you are networking. Examine the benefits and how you will be perceived. Don't expose yourself to too many people before you are ready. You want others to notice your achievement, not your networking skills. If you meet someone too early in your career, they may perceive you as just another kid or novice trying to break into the music industry. Be sure you have some accomplishments under your belt. That way, when you meet someone, they have reason to be interested in you. You have something to say. You have a story. That's when you have a real reason to network.

Others say networking is very overrated. Radio host Rush Limbaugh says he didn't get anywhere in his early radio career:

> *I made no effort to find out whom the insiders were. I just focused on my own achievement. Eventually, after 20 years, my own achievement finally overshadowed not knowing the insiders. That's why when I arrived on the scene in 1988 nobody outside of the people who had worked with me had ever heard of me, 'cause I was not a networker. I didn't go to the conventions. I didn't glad-hand. I didn't try to get where I was going with contacts, because largely in this business, you don't know who to trust anyway. Which is the case in any business.*

That is not to say you can exist in a cocoon. You do need to meet people. But don't depend on networking to produce opportunities. Focus on your work and achievement instead.

THE ESTABLISHMENT

Occasionally, you will meet an obviously influential and powerful person. You might think, "Oh wow. This person is my ticket to success." Unfortunately, they will often be of little or no help to you at all! Sometimes they may not connect or click with you personally. Or, in their judgment, you may not be at the right stage of your career for them to work with you. Or they may think you just aren't any good. Of course that won't bother you, because you believe in yourself and are aware of your potential. The numerous times "knowledgeable" and influential music biz types have been wrong in their judgment about talent are legend. Once again, in *Devotions from the World of Music*, Patrick and Barbara Kavanaugh have an apropos story:

> On January 2, 1962 four London lads were feeling very discouraged after auditioning for Decca Records, one of the most powerful record labels at the time. They gave it all they had, but Decca turned them down and signed Brian Poole and the Tremeloes (sic) instead.
>
> The future of John, Paul, George, and Peter (later Ringo) looked pretty bleak at the moment. They had no idea if another break might come, so they did the one thing they could still do. They kept working on their music.
>
> When the next opportunity finally rolled in, they were ready. The Beatles were soon on their way to world domination. They had hung in there despite the rejection by a major music industry company that supposedly knew talent when it heard it.
>
> Although probably apocryphal, legend has it that the

Decca execs pulled the Beatles' audition tapes out of the vault every Christmas and figuratively wept at having rejected signing the greatest rock band in history.

So much for industry "experts."

For a mainstream "I want to be a star" career, the establishment record labels and music industry groups are still very important. But for the entrepreneurial guitarist, they probably won't be helpful or catalytic to your career. Because you aren't seeking overnight or mega-success, you aren't dependent on industry heavyweights to advance your career. You will find a way around them. Yours is a niche-oriented long-haul approach. Perhaps you will form your own "parallel music universe" where you find your success. The catalyst to your career, the breaks that come to you will probably come from individuals or organizations outside the establishment.

In the same way, the importance of living in the major music centers (New York, Los Angeles, and Nashville) has decreased. Dealing with the industry establishment headquartered there is not crucial for us. Of course, being in the heat of the action and meeting people in the flesh rather than by phone or email has many advantages. Nothing beats face-to-face human contact. But this is a new world of email, instant messaging, cell phones, and texting. One can do quite well from about anywhere in the world as long as you have access to such technology.

Regardless of how you meet or interact with them, you have chosen a people-centric business. People are your audience. Without an audience, you cannot succeed. Ultimately, other people will be the providers of your opportunity and will play a part in constructing your road to success. They will be one of your most valuable assets. Appreciate and treat them well.

RELENTLESS PURSUIT

The pursuit of opportunity is the lifeblood of the entrepreneurial guitarist. The guitarist who waits for opportunities will have a non-career that never gets off the ground. The successful entrepreneurial guitarist makes and pursues opportunity relentlessly. Sometimes the greatest opportunities are brilliantly disguised as impossible situations.

Don't focus on or get distracted by problems. Managing and solving problems will certainly make you good. But building opportunities will make you great.

chapter 9

EDUCATION

You do not need a music degree from a university to earn a million dollars playing the guitar. It might help, it might not. A degree guarantees nothing. And this is coming from me, a university professor for thirty years. Thousands of students graduate with university music degrees every year. Many of them have no clue what they will do with that education. If they have some goals they want to pursue, most have no idea how to go about achieving them.

KNOWLEDGE

Two kinds of knowledge are available for our use. One is general knowledge and the other is specialized knowledge. No matter where you get it (even from a great school or prestigious university); no matter how much of it you have; no matter how many degrees or diplomas you have, certifying that you possess it—neither general nor specialized knowledge is of much use for making money. A typical university professor has a tremendous amount of general and specialized knowledge, but most professors don't have much money. They are gifted at imparting knowledge, but they don't organize or use it (or teach their students how to organize and use it) to accumulate money.

General knowledge is not power. General knowledge is only potential power and will not attract money or mega-success. Specialized knowledge is equally ineffectual unless organized, focused, and intelligently targeted according to a practical plan of action. Only then does knowledge become power. The plan of action must be born from a burning desire, an obsession for the achievement of a mission (a definite major purpose).

To achieve success playing the guitar, you will need *specialized* knowledge, and plenty of it. As I spelled out in Question #6 of The Nine Questions, you must have an insatiable thirst for knowledge. You don't have to know everything, but the key point is this:

> An educated person is one who knows where to get accurate information when he needs it, and how to target that knowledge into specific plans of action.

Knowing how and where to find information means knowing how to use a computer, the Internet, and a library, how to discriminate between accurate and false or biased information, and how to read thoroughly and analytically for deep understanding.

It also means surrounding yourself with or knowing the right people, or knowing how to find the right people who have the knowledge you need. This is especially true if you need specialized knowledge that you don't have the ability or time to acquire on your own. It also holds true for knowledge you don't understand or don't know how to use in your plan. Although you personally don't have to know everything, you do have to be an expert in gathering specialized knowledge.

A music professor teaching a class on the music business will have the knowledge to teach the course. He will even have specialized knowledge of the technical and legal aspects. But what he probably won't have is any clue regarding how to use that knowledge to make a successful career in music. If he did, he probably wouldn't be in the classroom teaching the course. You might want to ask him how his career is going—he may be a good professor, but how is he using his knowledge and experience in his *own* career in the *real* world of music? Does he even *have* a career? But be nice. However, if he is teaching the course and really does have a very successful career outside the university in the real world, you, my friend, have hit pay dirt. You want to be this professor's very best friend and stay in touch with him a long time. His expertise and experience will be invaluable.

How one gathers and uses knowledge will vary from person to person. Some people may benefit from a formal university education, whether in music or general studies. But everyone is different, everyone has different goals, everyone has different strengths and weaknesses. Those differences determine what type of education is needed by an individual. And realize that no one will really teach you anything. You have to teach yourself. Don't expect teachers to teach you. They will give you information, but it's up to you to figure out how to use it and make the most of it. Learn how to help yourself instead of expecting others to do it for you.

UNIVERSITY MUSIC SCHOOLS

If you want to work on being a better guitarist, you certainly need good teachers. But most university guitar programs are oriented toward the classical guitar. I have had several students audition for me who said, "Well, I really am interested in rock. But I thought if I can play classical, I can play anything." Or, "If I can play classical, I'll be a better rock guitarist." Or, "My parents really want me to have a degree in something." What did I tell them? I told them not to come to our music school. If rock is what you're interested in, put all your efforts and energy into that. If your parents want you to have a degree, do it in something that will directly contribute to your goals of becoming a rock guitarist—a degree in music production or technology, composition, computer science, or even a business degree to learn accounting, marketing, promotion, etc. Or, a rock guitarist could pursue a guitar degree at a university with a jazz program—at least that's a little closer to what he needs than classical.

And look. Music school is still school. Some people thrive in a structured school environment. Others have a very rough time. Yes, studying music theory, counterpoint, and conducting sounds much better than biology and geometry. But music school is still a school environment with assignments, reading, tests, and papers to write. Even a music major has to take some non-music courses. These will not kill you, but at the same time, you have to ask yourself what you want to be doing with your time.

If you want one of your streams of income to come from a university teaching job, these days you will need at least a bachelor's degree, probably a master's, possibly a doctorate. Or, maybe two master of music degrees, one in guitar, the other in another area such as theory to increase your employability. I say "these days" because when I started out in the early 1970s, some of our best music faculty members did not have any degrees. They had studied with famous people or had achieved some significant career success. But now, so many people are seeking these jobs, you need the degrees, the documented career success, and the advanced study with renowned artists.

Even though I had formal university music school training, I learned more by hanging out in the library than I ever did in classes. Reading books in which I was interested, and listening to as many recordings as possible, opened my mind to knowledge and opportunities directly related to pursuing my career as a guitarist. If I only sat in the library and never went to music school, I would be just as good a guitarist as I am now. The degree itself really didn't make any difference. My guitar lessons at the music school with Joseph Cozad certainly made a difference. But I could have done the lessons with Professor Cozad outside of the university and saved tens of thousands of dollars.

Having said that, my year at The Juilliard School in New York was invaluable. But not because of anything I learned in classes at Juilliard. Music classes are pretty much the same anywhere. The value is being able to have on my resume that I studied at Juilliard. The name denotes prestige to others in the classical music world and the university world. Having studied at Juilliard is a stamp of approval, a mark of credibility.

In my case, being a graduate of the Conservatory of Music and Dance at the University of Missouri—Kansas City led to my being offered the job of chairman of the guitar program the year after I graduated. So obviously, I'm glad I went to music school!

But again, getting a music degree is not for everyone and guarantees nothing. This holds true for other fields as well. But the market value of a law or business degree (in terms of getting a real job) is greater than a music degree. Those with degrees in guitar enter the job market with about the same job prospects as someone graduating with a degree in philosophy. (About two years after I graduated, I remember running into my American Philosophy professor. He had become a stockbroker.)

RESULTS, RISK, HUNCHES, AND CONSTRUCTIVE WORRYING

Your own personal development matters most. School smarts are not absolutely necessary (Bill Gates didn't finish college), but they do help tie everything together and give everything perspective. As a parent and educator, I often hear teenagers (mostly males) point out that many famous entrepreneurs didn't finish college (some didn't even graduate from high school). Thomas Edison, Henry Ford, Bill Gates, Michael Dell, Steve Jobs, and Ted Turner all fall in that category. But let's face facts: these were and are extraordinary individuals. What they lacked in academic credentials, they made up for in tenacity, brains, guts, and strong business sense. For the rest of us mortals, formal education is not necessarily a negative thing.

Street smarts, on the other hand, are of incomparable worth in the music business. Knowledge gained by experience in the school of hard knocks is invaluable. Just remember that in real life, results and actions are what count. It doesn't matter what your education was, how many degrees you have, or even if you finished high school. Being a good student or an achiever in school does not mean you do or do not have the qualities necessary to be an entrepreneur. Education is the ability to meet life's challenges. A good education should spur one into action.

Education is also essential for evaluating risk. We are in a risky occupation. We don't just roll the dice and plunge into every scheme that comes our way. We monitor the risk with smarts. We calculate. We take one step at a time, giving thought to each one and evaluating its effectiveness. That's the way you build a solid foundation. Each step builds on the previous one. Each step may indeed be somewhat risky, but because you give thought and consideration to each, the foundation on which you are building remains fairly stable and will usually hold.

You've probably made a decision, now and then, because "it feels right." The reason it feels right is because previously known, accurate information was applied (sometimes unconsciously) to the situation. The entrepreneurial guitarist doesn't make decisions on a whim. He doesn't chase fantasies. He doesn't jump off a cliff and expect good things to happen. Successful people make seemingly impulsive decisions with thought and preparation. They have a large amount of information swimming around in their conscious and subconscious minds to intelligently guide their decisions. They trust their hunches. Hunches are usually based on accurate information filed away in the mind just below the conscious level.

The educated entrepreneurial guitarist is also able to worry constructively. Although he survives on positive thinking, he knows if anything can go wrong, it will. So he looks ahead at every turn in the road to see what might go wrong and figures out what he will do if it does. When a problem rears its ugly head, the educated entrepreneur has already anticipated a solution for it or figured out a way to turn it to his advantage. Now *that's* smart.

SEEK INFORMATION AGGRESSIVELY, BUT ORGANIZE IT

Whether you attend school or not, one thing you must do *all your life* (real education begins when you *leave* school, not while you're there!) is aggressively seek out information. If you are not reading books, cruising the Internet, seeking out mentors, listening to music, reading newspapers and magazines, you are in trouble. Learn, learn, and learn. Read, read, and read. Listen, listen, and listen. You will soon realize you cannot find enough hours in the day to learn and listen.

When I was in high school, I used to try to get to school early every day so I could spend forty-five minutes in the library reading. What did I read about? Anything and everything I could find that related to playing the guitar. I remember I was working on some music by Debussy and Ravel. So I read every art book about Impressionist painting that the school library had on its shelves.

As a student at the University of Missouri, I used to spend my weekends in the Conservatory music library (this was before the Internet). I would randomly walk through the stacks until I found something that looked fascinating (it usually took under two minutes). It was usually related in some way to what I was doing with the guitar at the time. It might have been a book about careers in music, or about a composer, music history, or composing. I would also grab recordings at random and listen for hours. Sometimes I would go to the university's general library and study books on marketing and advertising. I would read the Sunday *New York Times* arts section to keep up on the latest news in the classical music field in New York.

Usually, every book I looked at and every recording I listened to sent me down a trail of discovery that was perpetually fascinating. One book or recording led to another. The trails were endless. Just like pursuing opportunities in music.

I have learned more at the library and on the Internet than I ever learned in college or from the best classical guitarists in the world. How you think, and *how you educate yourself when you are away from school* (rather than your formal education), is what matters. To paraphrase a quote often attributed to Mark Twain, "Don't let school get in the way of your education."

Steve Jobs of Apple Computer fame is an excellent example of someone who knows the value of seeking out what is of interest without any expectations of immediate rewards, but knowing the payoff will come in some form, somewhere down the road.

He dropped out of college after six months. He says it was one of the best decisions he ever made because it enabled him to stop taking the boring required classes. Instead, he could drop in on the classes in which he was interested. He said, "Much of what I stumbled into by following my curiosity and intuition turned out to be priceless later on." He goes on to tell his story:

> *Reed College at that time offered perhaps the best calligraphy instruction in the country. Throughout the campus every poster, every label on every drawer was beautifully hand-calligraphed. Because I had dropped out and didn't have to take the normal classes, I decided to take a calligraphy class to learn how to do this. I learned about serif and sans-serif typefaces, about varying the amount of space between different letter combinations, about what makes great typography great. It was beautiful, historical, artistically subtle in a way that science can't capture, and I found it fascinating.*
>
> *None of this had even a hope of any practical applica-*

tion in my life. But ten years later when we were designing the first Macintosh computer, it all came back to me, and we designed it all into the Mac. It was the first computer with beautiful typography. If I had never dropped in on that single course in college, the Mac would have never had multiple typefaces or proportionally spaced fonts, and since Windows just copied the Mac, it's likely that no personal computer would have them. If I had never dropped out, I would have never dropped in on that calligraphy class and personal computers might not have the wonderful typography that they do.

Of course it was impossible to connect the dots looking forward when I was in college, but it was very, very clear looking backwards 10 years later. Again, you can't connect the dots looking forward. You can only connect them looking backwards, so you have to trust that the dots will somehow connect in your future. You have to trust in something —your gut, destiny, life, karma, whatever—because believing that the dots will connect down the road will give you the confidence to follow your heart, even when it leads you off the well-worn path, and that will make all the difference.

This kind of education opens opportunities that lead to more opportunities. Without opportunities, you will not make a million dollars playing the guitar.

Although I'm all for knowledge, I do want to caution you that, especially on the Internet, drowning in information is very possible. Your head will begin swimming with too much information and you can lose your focus and analytical discrimination. In-depth study becomes surface skimming, the words flying by without engaging the brain.

One way to prevent that and to get the most out of your research is to organize the information as you find it. A great tool I use is the Microsoft Office OneNote software program. Remember 3-ring binders with the subject dividers? OneNote is a 3-ring binder on steroids that resides in your computer instead of on your desk. OneNote lets you organize different kinds of information—text, videos, audio, images—in one notebook, or separate notebooks by subject. You can save Web content directly into OneNote, link to Web pages or other notes, scan anything into it, and even use drawing tools to capture an idea. It has auto save and backup to protect your notes. The Instant Search feature allows you to find almost any information, whether in text, image, or even audio or video format. You can search for text within pictures and for spoken words in audio and video recordings. This amazing, powerful, and user-friendly program will help keep your research organized and useful.

CAUTION

Be careful. Don't ever fool yourself into thinking, for example, that since you know all about music contracts and the recording industry, you can sign a contract with a record label and save yourself the cost of an entertainment lawyer. Overestimating your abilities and knowledge is foolish and oftentimes downright dangerous. The arrogance of thinking that you know everything is pure stupidity. Sometimes the smartest thing to do is to seek outside help. Take time to develop the skill of finding who to ask for help. Then, when you don't know something, admit it and ask someone who does.

While you must not overestimate your abilities, in promoting your career you can do many things yourself. In fact, you may be able to do them as well as and cheaper than a professional. This is especially true of sales and marketing in the early stages of your career. You know your product better than anyone. You know your strengths and weaknesses. You believe in yourself 100%. Who better to promote you than you?

MENTORS

Mentors are important. You are familiar with mentors in learning to play the guitar. Usually a teacher becomes an inspiration for you, and teaches you not only about the guitar, but other things as well. Or, perhaps you have a guitar hero. You listen to everything he plays, and read everything he says and writes.

Choose your mentors carefully. Unfortunately, most people's mentors are their best friends. That can be a problem. According to one study, you can determine an individual's income by averaging the income of his or her ten best friends. Do you want to double your income? Find new, richer friends!

Look at your guitar playing. If your guitar mentors are friends who play the guitar, your sights are probably set pretty low. You will not become a very good guitarist. But if your mentor is a top-notch player, or if you are emulating the very best guitarists, you will be aiming for a higher level from the get-go and ultimately become a much better player. Mentors relating to the business aspect of your career are equally important. They will guide you with their experience and wise counsel.

Hang out with people and listen to people who are really good at what they do. They will set an example for you every moment you are with them. Watch them. Listen carefully to every word they speak. Be certain the words you listen to or read come from people who really know what they're talking about. Don't listen to someone tell you how to play an *Emaj7b9* chord if they can't play it themselves. Likewise, don't listen to someone tell you how to make a million dollars playing the guitar if they haven't done it themselves.

chapter 10

TALENT IS *NOT* THE ANSWER

"Talent Is *Not* the Answer" is true on several levels. First, get it into your head that the only guarantee of success is to have an audience. Your audience might be thousands of people who come to your concert to hear you play. It might be thousands listening to you on the Internet. It might be a handful of computer execs examining your newest software. It might be two performers perusing the songs you have written. Whether a couple of people or hundreds of thousands, you must have an audience to buy your product.

IF YOU HAVE AN AUDIENCE, WHO NEEDS TALENT?

As a performer, if you have an audience, whether or not you have talent matters very little. That explains why the music world abounds with wretched music and untalented performers on radio, television, and on CDs. If your audience loves you, it doesn't matter that you can't sing in tune or can only play the guitar or piano with a couple fingers. If you have an audience, they will buy your stuff and you will make money. Because you are making money, other people will be interested in you. You will have power. But be careful being a bottom feeder in the talent pool. Your audience may love you today, but will they tomorrow once the novelty wears off? Long careers aren't usually built on shallow novelty.

REAL TALENT

On another level, what about real talent? Are you born with it? How do you nurture it? How do you develop it?

New research shows that being an exceptional performer has little to do with any innate talent or skill. Exceptional people are not gifted. They are not born geniuses. Exceptional performers are a product of:

1. Deliberate practice
2. Enthusiastic family support or support by a mentor throughout their developing years
3. Study with devoted teachers or coaches

The amount and quality of practice are key factors that determine the level of mastery a person achieves. Consistently and overwhelmingly, the evidence shows that exceptional performers are always made, not born.

Rigorous research studies, using scientific methods that are verifiable and reproducible, have examined exceptional performance. Most of the research studies are compiled in a 900-page handbook called *The Cambridge Handbook of Expertise and Expert Performance*, edited by K. Anders Ericsson. It includes studies by more than 100 leading scientists who studied exceptional performance in many fields including surgery, acting, chess, writing, computer programming, ballet, music, and many others.

Ericsson states:

The journey to truly superior performance is neither for the faint of heart nor for the impatient. The development of genuine expertise requires struggle, sacrifice, and honest, often painful self-assessment. There are no shortcuts. It will take you at least a decade to achieve expertise, and you will need to invest that time wisely, by engaging in "deliberate" practice—practice that focuses on tasks that are beyond your current level of competence and comfort. You will need a well-informed coach not only to guide you through deliberate practice but also to help you learn how to coach yourself.

But, putting in tons of practice doesn't mean you will master the guitar or any field. The practice must be what Ericsson calls *deliberate practice*. Deliberate practice is a huge, sustained effort to do things you are unable to do well, or even not at all.

Most people tend to practice what they already know. Golf champ Sam Snead once said, "It is only human nature to want to practice what you can already do well, since it's a hell of a lot less work and a hell of a lot more fun."

Only by long-term work trying to do what you *can't* do will you become a master guitarist or expert in your field. You will work continually—hours every day for all your life—to eliminate specific weaknesses. It must be focused, deliberate practice.

The word "deliberate" cannot be emphasized enough. Practicing mindlessly on autopilot will not produce mastery. For you, the musician, mastery is not so much the result of how many hours you practice and exercise the fingers. What matters is how many hours you practice with your head. Research shows that very few experts, including musicians, writers, and athletes, can engage in highly focused deliberate practice for more than four to five hours at a time.

As Sam Snead pointed out, deliberate practice is very easy to neglect. Even master performers who reach high levels of performance may begin to rely on intuition and respond by habit to specific situations. This can cause problems when they encounter new challenges because they can lose their ability to analyze the problem and fix it with the required new solutions. But research has shown that musicians over 60 years old who continue deliberate practice for about ten hours a week can match the speed and technical skills of expert musicians in their twenties when tested on their ability to play an unfamiliar piece of music.

Ericsson's research shows that even the most gifted performers need a minimum of ten years or 10,000 hours of *intense training* to achieve mastery in their field. He says (and I absolutely concur) that in music and some other fields, the "apprenticeship" is longer. "It now takes most elite musicians 15 to 25 years of steady practice, on average, before they succeed at the international level." That translates to 15,000 to 25,000 hours of practice.

Ericsson and his colleagues found no exceptions to the 10,000-hour rule. There weren't any "naturals" who practiced less than their peers and still became top performers. In music, the people who reached the top didn't practice somewhat harder than the others. They practiced *thousands* of hours longer than the others.

This finding, that a critical minimum number of hours of deliberate practice must be met to achieve mastery in complex tasks, surfaces again and again in studies of expertise. Neurologist Daniel

Levitin states, "The emerging picture from such studies is that ten thousand hours of practice is required to achieve the level of mastery associated with being a world-class expert—in anything.... Of course, this doesn't address why some people get more out of their practice sessions than others do. But no one has yet found a case in which true world-class expertise was accomplished in less time. It seems that it takes the brain this long to assimilate all that it needs to know to achieve true mastery."

Some child prodigies (or a chess master like Bobby Fischer) are able to beat the ten-year rule by practicing more hours per year. And times are changing. Before the early 20th century, people could reach world-class levels more quickly. The music world did not have nearly as many performers. And from what we can tell from written accounts, technical execution was not on the level of today. With the advent of advanced recording technology, we now have the expectation of perfect technical execution on CDs, which has translated into expecting technical perfection in concert performances as well. The bar has risen significantly since pre-recording days. The ten-year 10,000-hour rule is now almost impossible to beat. It seems to be the magic number of greatness.

Most people are naïve about the effort and time it takes to become an expert. Leo Tolstoy once said people often told him they didn't know if they could write a novel because they hadn't tried yet. After all, everyone writes. Many people have a natural ability to write. They learn to do it in school. What's the big deal? It irritated him to no end that they thought if they just got started, they too could produce a brilliant novel.

Equally irritating to me is that this type of person, if they do get around to creating their book or musical composition, or if they work on their skill at playing an instrument, will think their work is equal to that of a true master. They are clueless.

Self-help authors tend to promulgate this same type of thinking. They tell their readers they are essentially ready for success and just need to take a few easy steps to turn their lives around.

Leaving out the flash-in-the-pan, here today/gone tomorrow celeb types, researchers unfailingly have found that so-called born geniuses, natural talents, and "overnight successes" spent an incredible amount of time in practice and preparation. They didn't find any exceptions. Remember, the researchers are not talking about people who achieve popular success because of their lifestyle, sexual adventures, and out-rageous behavior. They are talking about people who are masters of their skill—true experts.

Let's look at Wolfgang Amadeus Mozart, one of the most famous examples of a child prodigy who is commonly cited as a born genius. No one questions that Mozart's achievements were head and shoulders above others of his time. What is forgotten is that his *training* was also head and shoulders above others of his time. Mozart's father, a violin-ist, was a superb and insightful musician. He wrote an important violin instruction book. He was also a skilled composer. Mozart's dad began teaching Wolfgang when the child was only four years old. Dad provid-ed an environment where the young boy could hardly do anything but put in his 10,000+ hours of deliberate practice. Wolfgang had an expert teacher encouraging him and feeding him knowledge 24/7, from the age of four. *That* is what started Wolfgang on his path to genius. Not even Mozart was born an expert—he became one.

Not only must you put in your 10,000+ hours. In many fields, start-ing when you are young is crucial. Motor skills for playing a musical instrument are most easily learned at an early age. Also, one's available time to engage in endless hours of deliberate practice decreases as the demands of a job or caring for a family come into play.

Being in an environment where you are encouraged to practice your skill or at least where few restrictions are placed on you is an extremely important part of achieving mastery. The support and encouragement can come from family or from an outsider. Either can provide that environment or opportunity for 10,000 hours of deliberate practice.

But that is still not the whole picture. You know you have to put in your 10,000 hours. You are in a supportive environment where you are free to do it. But now, you need a teacher, coach, or mentor.

Ivan Galamian is acknowledged as one of the best violin teachers of all time. He once made the point that even the best students don't necessarily engage in deliberate practice all by themselves. Galamian said, "If we analyze the development of well-known artists, we see that in almost every case, the success of their entire career was dependent on the quality of their practicing. In practically every case, the practicing was constantly supervised either by the teacher or an assistant to the teacher."

Scientific research on world-class performers confirms Galamian's observation. Interestingly, it also shows that the future performer needs different kinds of teachers at different stages of their learning.

The research shows that in the beginning, most students have loving and caring local teachers who are able to give them plenty of praise and time. Eventually, the student studies with a teacher who is an expert himself, who has achieved international levels of achievement. This caliber of teacher gives not only expert instruction, but also intensive and sometimes painful feedback. At this level, however, motivated students actually seek out this type of take-no-prisoners feedback. At the same time, the student is skilled at recognizing what advice from the teacher works for him and what doesn't. The budding elite performer is fully aware of what he is doing right and concentrates on fixing, with deliberate practice, what he is doing wrong. Performers who want to be the best deliberately choose unsentimental teachers who will challenge and drive them to higher levels of performance.

The best teachers also identify things that will need to be improved when the student reaches the next level of performance skill. While the teacher must be tough and demanding, he must also be sensitive to pushing too hard and too fast, which might produce frustration or burnout, even in advanced students.

The ultimate goal of the master teacher is to become obsolete—to teach the student to teach himself. As the student's experience and ability increases, he becomes more independent, able to develop his own plan for his future development. The student leaves the nest to fly on his own.

If your passion in life involves being a master performer or expert in your field, take these facts to heart. This is reality. Now you know what you must do to become an expert. Now you know how to *make* your talent. No more discouragement that you were not born a genius. Geniuses are made, not born.

Having written all this about what is required to master the guitar or any other instrument, let me remind you: *You don't have to be a great guitarist or performer to earn a million dollars playing the guitar.* Instead, focus on your Hedgehog Concept (coming up soon in Part Two). Put those 10,000 hours into that.

chapter 11

WHEN AM I READY? HOW MUCH AM I WORTH?

PREPARE

What does "ready" mean? If you want to be a performer, as you read in the previous chapter, it certainly means putting in 10,000-plus hours of practice on the guitar, your singing, or compositional skills. It means putting in thousands of hours reading, listening, and studying about everything to do with the guitar and music. While others around you entertain themselves, relax, or waste time on mindless diversions, you will be constantly preparing yourself for a lifetime of brilliance. Some people have hope that they will succeed, but they aren't willing to knuckle down and discipline themselves to work hard to prepare for the future. Being prepared, being ready, is an important part of diligence.

Always ask yourself, "What am I doing today that will help prepare me for tomorrow?" After all, as American author Jack London once quipped, "You can't wait for inspiration. You have to go after it with a club."

Preparation is necessary, but is also an ongoing process. Don't wait forever to begin your march to success. Whether you are in school or preparing on your own, getting out in the real world to learn and hone your skills in the school of hard knocks is invaluable. If you get out there and play some gigs, meet people, record some demos, write some software—whatever your focus is—you will learn much more quickly than working in isolation. You might even pick up a few fans. You will certainly meet people who can give you feedback. They might even be in a position to help you in some way. You will find out what you don't know and what needs improvement. You will learn many types of skills—musical, life, and people skills.

When you are in a learning phase, it's not a good idea to throw piles of money into any projects or make any significant appearances. Many guitarists are chomping to jump as soon as possible on some great opportunity or big break that comes their way. But if you are not ready, that big break will make you look utterly foolish. Prepare.

Take the example of a young jazz pianist named Al Haig:

> Like thousands of other pianists in the 1930s and 1940s Haig had dreamt of performing in the big time. But he knew most of the preparation needed to succeed came in the hours of practicing alone, not on stage. He practiced incessantly, getting himself ready in case his big break ever came. One of his first professional gigs was with the Tiny Grimes Quartet in a small club in New York City. The young man was playing his heart out when he looked up and to his astonishment, saw Dizzy Gillespie and Charlie Parker enter the club. Gillespie and Parker jumped up

on stage with their instruments. Dizzy barked out "I Got Rhythm" and started to play. The hours of preparation Haig had put in were immediately apparent to Gillespie and Parker. After the "audition," they asked him to join their band.

Haig had prepared for a significant number of years and he was ready at the right time.

HOW MUCH AM I WORTH?

Be sure to ask for what you are really worth. If you ask $1,000 for a gig, you better give a really good professional performance. If you ask $50 an hour for guitar lessons, you had better be one heck of a good teacher. Just think about how you feel when you purchase something that's expensive or even medium-priced and it turns out to be poor quality or doesn't work very well. It leaves a bad taste in your mouth, you steer clear of anything like it in the future, and you tell your acquaintances about it so they won't be duped. You don't want that to happen with your career. Word travels fast and for a long time.

You may be saying, "But Doug, how will I earn a million dollars if I'm playing gigs for fifty bucks?" The answer: you won't be playing fifty-buck gigs for long. As you become a better guitarist and get more and more experience, you will ask for more money. Look at the market, be brutally honest about who you are and how good you are, and go from there. Your fees will steadily increase and you will develop a good reputation if you work from a solid foundation. Don't get greedy and ask for too much before you're really ready. If you proceed too fast, without a solid foundation of experience and without steady development of the quality of your artistic skill, your career will falter.

Nothing is worse than getting a great opportunity or big break and then blowing it because you were inexperienced. I have had students who had almost no performing experience and expected to get paid for every gig they did, or asked for too much money relative to their ability and experience. They didn't get far.

THE BOX-OFFICE FACTOR

Another important factor to consider is the name or box-office factor. I book guitarists to play formal concerts on the Kansas City Guitar Society's Guest Artist Concert Series. "Name" guitarists such as Christopher Parkening, Tommy Emmanuel, Pepe Romero, etc. command and deserve pretty hefty fees. Not only are they top players, *they draw audiences*. An artist who can draw an audience helps us make money too. But we receive calls from younger, inexperienced guitarists wanting to perform on our series wanting high fees of $2,000 or more. Yes, they may be fabulous players, maybe even as good as the "name" guitarists. What they don't understand is that nobody knows them. Even if they have CDs out, even if they have won major competitions, even if they have performed on important concert series in Europe, the general public doesn't know them. In Kansas City, maybe 150 people will come out to hear such a guitarist. The Guitar Society would lose money on the concert after paying the artist, promotional costs, and production costs. These young players may be really fine guitarists, but they have to pay their dues just like everyone else. Playing well is not enough. They have to gain experience and make a name for themselves. Then they can gradually increase their fees as they are able to attract larger audience numbers.

The same realities apply when the entrepreneurial guitarist approaches a record label or artist management. If you aren't well known, they won't invest their money in you. Why? You simply won't sell enough CDs or get enough performance bookings to justify the investment—they will lose money on you. The situation is a classic catch-22. The record label won't sign you because you're unknown, but how do you become known without being on a record label? Or, you can't get concert bookings because you're unknown, but how do you become known without playing concerts? Fortunately, plenty of ways can be found around this problem. And take note that, especially early in your career, much of the rejection you encounter will be because of the box-office factor, not because you don't play well.

Unfortunately, it works the other way too. We see financially successful artists who can barely hold their guitars, let alone play them, or performers who can't sing, act, or dance. But they sell hundreds of thousands of CDs or get tons of performance bookings. How do they do it? They pull off some outrageous PR stunt, become romantically involved with a celebrity or notorious character, adopt an outlandish persona, and on and on. I'm sure you and your friends have found yourselves sitting around saying, "How come *he's* so famous? He can hardly play." Usually these statements are made punctuated with a fair number of expletives! Well, that's show biz. Oftentimes that's just how it works. I used to say that most of these people are just flash-in-the-pan entertainers. But more and more, I see them able to sustain their careers through ongoing PR stunts and extreme behavior that keeps them in the limelight. I guess that's a type of talent in itself.

DON'T LET PERFECTION GET IN THE WAY

Most artists, whether musicians, dancers, singers, painters, or film-makers, are perfectionists. We love what we do and we want our work to be the best it can possibly be. As artists, we strive for perfection. Creating artistic works is about effort, more effort, *and then some*. We keep going the extra mile for improvement. Our work is good, but we want it better. We want it perfect. We want it great.

AND THEN SOME

The great Russian composer and pianist Sergei Rachmaninov was known to go the extra mile even as a student at the Saint Petersburg Conservatory. If three problems were assigned, he would complete five. If he had to learn a composition within one week, he would learn it in a day so that he could polish it all week.

Bob Dylan began writing his well-known song "Like a Rolling Stone" by starting on the chorus. But then came the laborious work of writing all the different verses. Frustration set in. But he wrote and wrote until he had a song about twenty pages long. He whittled it down, adding and deleting material. Most of the twenty pages ended up on the floor, but each sketch and rejected idea was important to the work's creation. The song would not have come to fruition without the extra effort, *and then some.*

In his address at the Berklee College of Music, Sivers told the students:

> *You don't get extreme results without extreme actions. If you want to be above average, you must push yourself to do more than is required.... If you're a songwriter, you should not only write a song every week, but spend twice as long improving it as you do writing it. Inspiration is a really good start, but it's the diligence to make every note and every word perfect, that really sets you apart.*

Saying "that's good enough" is easy. But you have to look ahead a little further, and realize that a little more effort could make all the difference. If you give it all you've got...*and then some*, you will have begun to reach your potential.

DON'T GET BOGGED DOWN

However, some guitarists get bogged down by their perfectionism. They wait for all the stars to line up before embarking on their career or pursuing an opportunity. If they are working on a CD, they endlessly tweak this and that, wasting months and months on things that no one else will notice, and things even *they* will not notice in a year. I'm guilty of that myself. In fact, perfectionism has plagued man throughout time. In the thirteenth century Tai T'sung issued his *History of Chinese Writing* with the words, "Were I to await perfection, my book would never be finished."

As a musician, you probably work with computer software. And you've noticed that software is issued in versions such as 5.0, 5.1, 7.5, etc. That means the software has been improved and continues to be constantly updated. Why is that? Because it was never perfect to begin with! It had bugs. Omissions were found that had to be addressed later. More features were added or poorly executed features taken out. But the software was sold anyway and later fixed and updated.

As you keep improving your product, you will also keep raising your standard. But many guitarists don't get their career going, their CD released, or their video finished because they are constantly, endlessly perfecting the product. There has to come a time when you say, "Okay. This is very good. This is me. It's not perfect, but the quality is exceptionally high. I need to close it and get it out to the market and move on to my next project." Moving on will certainly result in better career growth and personal development as opposed to working on the same songs forever. Plus, delaying the introduction of your work into the marketplace can mean missing major opportunities that may never present themselves again.

That's not to say you want to produce or release unprepared or unpolished, mediocre products. That would go against your values as an artist and possibly tarnish your reputation and damage your credibility. At the same time, however, you can't wait for your work to be perfect—that just isn't going to happen. As French poet and philosopher Paul Valéry wrote, "An artist never really finishes his work, he merely abandons it."

chapter 13

RELIABILITY AND HONESTY COUNT

RELIABILITY COUNTS

Being a reliable person is not just for traditional business types. Music industry people have to deal with an assemblage of flakes— nutty, crazy, on-the-edge artist types. Dealing with a relatively down-to-earth musician is a breath of fresh air for non-musicians. I can't tell you how many times "normal" people have said to me or implied, "Wow, you actually returned my call or email." Or they were amazed that I actually showed up for an appointment on time and prepared.

Establishing a reputation for reliability is very important for the future of your career. Don't ever forget that you are involved in the music *business*. Business thrives on obligations, schedules, and reaching goals. Time is money—your own and that of the people with whom you work. The artist who can complete a job on schedule generates income. He can then move on to the next job, generating more income. When you show up on time, keep commitments, and meet contractual obligations, you generate respect. People will want to continue to work with you and depend on you for future projects.

In the mix of hustlers, poseurs, and pretenders in the music business, someone who actually does what he says he will do, keeps promises, and meets or exceeds expectations shines like a gleaming jewel apart from the riff-raff. People are drawn to a person they can rely on. They will risk far more time and money on a reliable person than an undependable, kooky, or unstable "artiste."

Test yourself. Monitor your behavior as is—don't try to change it yet. Just do your regular thing. For one week keep track of how quickly you return phone calls and emails. Keep track of how often you are late for appointments. Do you sometimes miss them altogether? How often do you lie or tell half-truths? How often do you do what you say you will do? Then, the following week, begin to make changes in your behavior. Choose one or two things to improve. Perhaps concentrate on returning all calls or emails within 36 hours. Make a list of some relatively easy tasks and then do them. Get your act together. Don't use the excuse, "Well, I'm just a crazy disorganized musician–creative type." No, you are a screw-up. Being unreliable and irresponsible is just another bit of hype artists use to justify a screwed up or chaotic life. Don't go there.

Some creative artists find it difficult to grasp the significance of some of the following words:

Punctuality
Reliability
Responsibility
Dependability
Commitment
Consistency

A list of words guaranteed to help a creative artist achieve success:

Punctuality

Reliability

Responsibility

Dependability

Commitment

Consistency

HONESTY AND INTEGRITY ALSO COUNT

The "H" word—honesty. The "I" word—integrity. Both are important to your future. Many people think it doesn't hurt to lie now and then or skim a little money here and there. They can make themselves a little extra money and get by with it. The problem is, that kind of behavior affects your reputation. A bad reputation can follow you forever. You will be working directly with other people: possibly with other musicians in a group, definitely with business associates and advisers. All these people must remain loyal to you and trust you. Be an honorable person with whom to work.

Paraphrasing American author Hunter Thompson:

The music business is a cruel and shallow money trench,
a long plastic hallway where thieves and pimps run free,
and good men die like dogs. There's also a negative side.

Be that as it may, if you think lying, stealing money, cheating on your taxes, and libeling others is just part of the entertainment biz, then you will be living in a world where no one trusts you. You will have to watch your back all the time. Any successful person and any formerly successful person now in prison can tell you it just isn't worth it. It may take a little longer to succeed with honorable behavior, but you will sleep better at night. People will want to do business with you. Others will say good things about you. As you become more successful, no one will be able to bring you down because of a dark element in your past. You will always be able to breathe freely.

Integrity can cover many things. Here are a few directly related to music:

1. Do not burn copies of CDs you don't own.
2. Observe copyright laws. Don't photocopy copyrighted music you haven't purchased. Ask for permission to use any copyrighted material whether printed text, printed music, or recorded music.
3. Don't cancel a gig at the last minute because a better or higher-paying one suddenly pops up.
4. Always pay mechanical royalties or fees when recording copyrighted music.
5. Always give credit to others' work (including photo credits).
6. Don't ever try to cheat the IRS.
7. Be sure your email lists are opt-in. Do not send people email they have not specifically given you permission to send.
8. Make good on any defective merchandise you sell.
9. Volunteer your talent now and then. Do a freebie for a charity. Do a favor for a total stranger.

As many have written, "Integrity is doing the right thing even when no one is watching."

QUITTING?

The thought of quitting my pursuit of the guitar as a career has never entered my mind. I couldn't imagine doing anything else. I couldn't imagine anything else giving me the pleasure, happiness, and contentment that playing the guitar provides. I love the freedom of setting my daily schedule the way I want it. I enjoy the independence of not having to work a real job or of working for someone else. I enjoy earning money by, of all things, playing the guitar. I enjoy feeling that I have made and continue to make a contribution to the world.

Throughout history, people have done horrendous things to each other. In today's world, the news media tend to emphasize the horrific and the negative—that's what sells newspapers and holds viewers glued to television screens. But what the world needs is a constant reminder of the *best* that humanity has to offer. I believe that works of artistic creation display humanity at its best. I am proud to be a small part of that. The thought of giving it up has simply never occurred to me.

For many others, however, the door is always open to quitting. Quitting is easy when your idea for a project has been rejected thirty-five times. Quitting is easy when you're out of money, or owe money to everyone you know. Quitting is easy when a concert goes bad, or you just can't seem to get out of a creative rut. Quitting is easy when people whose opinions you respect tell you your music isn't any good. You will find hundreds of reasons to throw in the towel at almost any given time in your career when things aren't going well.

Before success comes, you are certain to lose many battles, some small and some huge. You will make mistakes and suffer failures. When confronted with defeat, the easiest thing to do is to quit. That's what most people do. When Napoleon Hill, author of *Think and Grow Rich*, interviewed more than 500 successful people, *all* of them told him that *success came just a few steps beyond the point at which defeat had temporarily overtaken them.*

An excellent example is Patrick and Barbara Kavanaugh's story of two young failing songwriters:

> *In the late 1960's two young men in England began to write songs together. After months of work they actually wrote a musical. The response to the musical was terrible—it was never even performed. But they continued to write songs. They got nowhere with that either. No one liked what they were writing.*
>
> *After a few years of constant rejection, they were ready to give up. One day the principal of a small school in London (who knew one of the boys) asked them to write a "religious work" for an end-of-the-year school concert. Looking into the Bible, the boys chose to base their music on the story of Joseph and his brothers. Eventually, they turned the small project for the small school into a full musical,* Joseph and the Amazing Technicolor Dreamcoat.
>
> *If Andrew Lloyd Webber and Tim Rice, both in their early twenties, had given up just a week earlier, before the school*

principal called, they would have missed their boat to be-
coming arguably the best writers in history for the musical
theater. Just imagine—after trying and trying, when they
were going to give up, when the school principal called,
they had no idea what was just around the corner.…

In *Success Built to Last,* Jerry Porras tells this great story:

The fellow asked the bearded sage he met on the path,
"Which way to success?" The monk said nothing and ges-
tured down the path. The seeker was elated by the prospect
that success was so close and so easy, and rushed ahead.

Suddenly, there comes the sound of splat. In a little
while, the seeker, now tattered and stunned, limps back,
assuming he must have taken a wrong turn. He repeats
his question to the guru, who again points silently in the
same direction.

The seeker nods, turns, and heads back in the same
direction as before. This time, the sound of splat is deaf-
ening. When the seeker crawls back, he is bloody, broken,
and angry. Screaming at the monk, he demands to know
why he was sent off in the direction of disaster. "No more
pointing. Talk!"

Only then does the guru speak. "Success is that way," he
said. "Just a little past splat."

You have no idea what could be right around the corner or a little
way further down the path. Sometimes you have to wait years, maybe

decades, for the fulfillment of your vision. I believe a timetable exists for all our lives. If you are a Christian, you know God has His timetable for your life and knows best when you are ready to be used for His glory.

Yes, the time will come when you will have to cut your losses, look reality squarely in the eye, shut a project down, or change directions. If the first plan you painstakingly put together didn't work, replace it with a new plan. If that one doesn't work, try another. This is where many people meet with permanent failure. They don't have the persistence to keep creating new plans or altering plans to take the place of those that fail. Remember, temporary failure is not permanent failure. It means your plan was unsound. Make another one. Start over. But quit? That word doesn't exist in the vocabulary of the true entrepreneurial guitarist.

chapter 15

YOU'RE A FAILURE— CONGRATU- LATIONS!

A guitarist's career may fail for many reasons. Two have to do with failure itself:

1. Fear of failure
2. Not failing enough.

FEAR OF FAILURE

Some guitarists are so afraid of failing that they simply freeze and do nothing. They come up with excuses for not even getting started. We saw the list before, but if you have forgotten, here is an encore presentation:

1. "I don't have the money."
2. "I have a family to support."

3. "I don't have any contacts."

4. "I don't play well enough. I don't read music. My songs aren't any good. I get stage fright. My technique isn't good enough…"

5. "I'm not smart enough."

6. "I don't have enough time."

7. "I can't find anyone to help me."

8. "This is going to take too long and take too much time and effort."

9. "I'm afraid of poverty." Or any other noun that applies to your situation.

10. "I'm shy. I don't like dealing with people, especially business types."

11. "I'm too old." Or, "I started too late."

12. "I'm not good at asking people for things."

And then the infamous "ifs and whens" list:

1. "If I wait until tomorrow, circumstances will be better."

2. "I'll do it when the perfect opportunity appears."

3. "I'll do it when the time is right."

4. "I'll do it when I have more time."

5. "I'll do it when I find the right partner."

6. "I'll do it when the kids are out of school."

7. "I'll wait to see if I get another promotion. If I don't, then I'll do it."

8. "If I take some classes first for a few years, I'll be better prepared."

9. "What happens if I fail?"
10. "If I fail, I'll be embarrassed."

No one wants to fail, so we come up with no end of excuses to avoid taking actions that might lead to failure. If we don't take the first step, we're safe. But that in itself, of course, is failure. In fact, avoid people who play it safe. They can't help you. In a rapidly changing world, the false stability of playing it safe leads to extinction.

YOU AREN'T FAILING ENOUGH

The second reason careers falter is that the guitarist doesn't fail often enough! You must be willing to go down many avenues and take many risks to develop your career. Many of these will be dead ends or result in failure. You will experience a great deal of failure. In fact, if you have reached your mid-twenties and haven't had difficult times in your life, you're either not fessing up or you're not passionately engaged in life.

My take is that if you aren't failing *throughout* your career, you aren't exploring all the possibilities that lie before you. You aren't looking at enough opportunities. You have become stagnant or complacent. If you're not making mistakes, you're not taking risks, and that means you're not going anywhere. When things stagnate or plateau, pursue new opportunities. In other words, take new risks (which may lead to failure) in order to keep your career moving, or to get it moving again. The key is to recognize that making mistakes is okay. Making mistakes means you will have more chances to learn. The more you learn, the better your progress will be toward achieving your goals.

Others will judge you by the number of times you succeed. But the number of times you succeed will be in direct proportion to the number of times you fail and pick yourself up, dust yourself off, and try again. After all, you don't drown by falling in the water; you drown by staying there!

Mistakes will be made, but you will correct them quickly and completely. Ironically, you will usually succeed through failure. As basketball great Michael Jordan said, "I've failed over and over and over again in my life and that is why I succeed."

LEARNING FROM FAILURE

We all want to know the answer to the question, "What is the secret to success?" General Colin Powell said, "There are no secrets to success. It is the result of preparation, hard work, and learning from failure."

Your success will largely be determined by 1) your willingness to explore and pursue opportunity, and 2) your willingness to risk and learn from failure. *The more mistakes you make, the smarter you become,* IF you are *willing and able to learn from them.* If you are an employee in a real job, making too many mistakes can get you fired. In the music business, as a self-employed entrepreneur, it can be a key part of your success.

If you went to college, you paid tuition—a rather large sum of money for instruction and enlightenment. In the music business, you pay tuition to experience failure. Then, if you're smart, you get your money's worth by gathering the fruits of learning from the experience.

Look at mistakes as opportunities to learn something about yourself and your career. Think of a mistake as being like a stop sign telling you, "Wait. Stop and think about what just happened. You're missing something." In other words, a mistake is a signal to you that you should step back and examine the problem. Glean every bit of information you can, so you can do better next time and avoid a similar outcome. You want to come out of it having learned something new. If you don't do that, you may be doomed to making the same or a similar mistake again.

If you are fully engaged, you will be in a constant state of trial and error. Take good notes as you proceed. Review your notes often, because when you make mistakes, you only want to make *new* ones. And while we're at it, remember that feedback and learning are gained from both failure *and* success. You are not doomed by failure. Nor does success entitle you to rest on your laurels. Analyze both and use the lessons learned as feedback to determine your next move.

The great Thomas Edison, founder of General Electric, was once criticized for his endless failures in attempting to develop his version of the electric light bulb. His reply to his detractors was "I have not failed. I've just found 10,000 ways that won't work." If Edison had been a guitarist, he would have had a great career!

IF YOU'RE GOING TO FAIL, DO IT THE RIGHT WAY

Edison shows us that whether something can even be counted as a mistake is a matter of perspective. Part of the essence of being a successful entrepreneurial guitarist is to try new things, or try old things in a new way, particularly things that other people tell you are unlikely to work. Remember, few rules can be found on how to succeed in the music business. Because you will often need to follow untraveled paths, the chances of making mistakes are high. Recognize and accept that.

But one can make mistakes in such a way that negative outcomes are minimized. Do not pursue opportunities mindlessly or recklessly. Experiment, but do it responsibly. Take *calculated* risks. Study and evaluate the opportunity. Think through the potential consequences (both intended and unintended) of taking an action. Find a way to minimize likely adverse consequences. Use your past experience of making poor choices to increase your odds of making the right choice this time. Then proceed with the experiment. Not all experiments work, as Edison intuitively knew. Sometimes you do the wrong thing. But is it a mistake to have tried the experiment, to have taken the calculated risk? Of course not. Losers call making the wrong choices failure. Winners call it learning. Your judgment will improve over time.

Don't be afraid of looking stupid. Don't be afraid of what others think. Do what your heart and intellect tell you to do. But find the balance. You do have to think about your credibility. If you make too many mistakes, your reputation could be harmed. Fortunately, that is usually the exception.

Let's look at a famous failure in the classical music world:

> For thirty years Richard Wagner experienced more rejection than possibly any other musician in written history. His first opera was rejected, the second withdrawn. After being fired from a conducting job, he went to Paris, where another opera failed. He spent time there in debtor's prison. His marriage was in ruins, more debts mounted, and he became ill, which required large expenditures for medical treatments. His next few operas were total disasters.
>
> In the midst of poverty and rejection he continued to do the work in which he believed. Only in the last twenty years of his life did his unstoppable persever-

ance finally pay off. It took that long for him to become known for his accomplishments. When he launched *Der Ring des Nibelungen* in 1876, even his harshest critics were silenced by Wagner's magnificent achievement.

ANALYSIS PARALYSIS

Too many people, especially those who are highly educated, focus on total avoidance of risk and fall victim to analysis paralysis. They focus so much on gathering information and identifying and eliminating every possible risk that they never feel confident moving forward with their plans and don't get out of the starting gate. Self-development guru Steve Pavlina has a saying that might come in handy to eliminate the problem: "Get ready, go, get set."

Obviously, you do not move forward without regard for the consequences of your actions. Be responsible and do your homework. Have a plan. But recognize the point of diminishing returns. You can analyze and gather information forever. Additional planning is just wasting time or procrastinating. You will never be able to eliminate every risk. Do not fall victim to analysis paralysis. Take a look at the reality of what you are doing, and move forward. The future starts today, for God's sake, not tomorrow.

LOSING IS NOT AN OPTION

The successful entrepreneurial guitarist accepts and even welcomes mistakes. After all, he will make corrections and learn valuable insights from them. But losing is not an option. Vince Lombardi, the famous coach of the Green Bay Packers football team, once said, "Show me a good loser and I will show you a loser." Accepting defeat or taking it lightly means you will keep losing. Saying to yourself "Winning is not that important, it's how you play the game" is nonsense in the world of professional music. You will be trounced and buried. If you lose, it should make you angry. Use that anger to spur you on and inspire you to win the next battle.

You're going to get knocked down; the point is whether or not you get up. For example, if you give a lousy performance, figure out what went wrong and what you should do to make it a good performance the next time. You might need to buckle down and practice much harder. Or it might be as simple as asserting yourself more to the stage manager and insist that the lighting or sound be done the way you want it, if that is what threw you off. Or, learn to deal with bad sound or lighting and rise above it. Or, you might need to aggressively work on your stage personality or controlling your nerves.

If you get rejected for a gig, don't take it lightly. Find out why you were rejected and do something about it. When the next opportunity comes up, your chances of getting the gig will be greatly increased.

Don't accept losing. Let it be a kick in the butt. Let it inspire you to prepare harder for the next battle—and win.

chapter 16

KEEPING YOUR FINANCIAL HEAD ON STRAIGHT

Obviously, this is not a book on personal finance. But unless you have your head on straight financially, all the advice in this book will be for nothing. Yes, you will make a million dollars playing the guitar, but you could still end up living in poverty if you spend it all.

Therefore, in this chapter I will give you a few things to think about, and some advice that is particularly relevant to the entrepreneurial guitarist. Remember, this is only the tip of the iceberg. Do more reading and studying on your own.

ALL HAT, NO CATTLE

Income is not the same as wealth. If you spend all your money as you make it, all you're doing is living high. You aren't accumulating anything to live on in the hard times, which you will inevitably have. You won't have money saved to spend on a creative project you want to do. You don't want to be All Hat, No Cattle.

For a good example of the "All Hat, No Cattle" crowd, take a look at the big-spender entertainment types and sports figures promoted and sensationalized by the media. Contrary to what many believe, many of these people, who live in expensive homes, drive luxury cars, and live high on the hog don't have much wealth. Why? They spend all their money on Bright Shiny Objects—material possessions!

We are bombarded with messages that say you're successful if you own lots of stuff—Bright Shiny Objects. You need to own a fancy, expensive house. You have to have a great car. Wear fashionable clothes. Have the latest and greatest.

For many people, acquisition can be a great motivator. Those Bright Shiny Objects—fancy cars, clothes, jewelry, houses, techno gadgets etc.—can inspire you to work really hard. But be careful—as I found in my own life, they can be tremendous distractions and suck the momentum out of your career. Taking care of them takes time and energy you could be devoting to things that matter more.

You can end up on a treadmill of acquisition. You may think, for whatever reason, that you really do need a certain kind of car or a certain size house. Your wish may be legitimate, or it may not. You may *want* "x," but you should probably ask yourself, "Do I really *need* 'x'?" That's an important distinction for your financial well-being. After all, something else is always available to buy— something bigger, better, or shinier. Remember, *you can never get enough of what you don't really need to make you happy.*

Although we are taught by media hype that the rich spend lavishly, the truth is very different. In the bestselling book *The Millionaire Next Door*, Thomas Stanley and William Danko report the results of their study of American millionaires. They found that most millionaires don't look like millionaires. Few millionaires spend over $500 for a suit, few spend over $200 for shoes, and few spend over $300 for a watch. Many spend much less than those amounts. They shop at Penney's and Wal-Mart, not at boutiques.

Research shows that most wealthy people don't live in expensive neighborhoods or fancy homes, don't drive fancy cars or wear expensive clothes. One reason they are wealthy is they don't spend their money on expensive stuff. They have small hats, but lots of cattle. They save and they invest. Building wealth takes discipline. People become millionaires by budgeting and controlling their expenses. They stay millionaires the same way.

Now let's be clear. I don't want you to lose sight of the purpose of this book. My goal is not to make you a millionaire—to have a net worth of one million dollars. I am only teaching you how to *earn* a million dollars over the course of your career by playing the guitar. But I want you to hold on to some of it—not just spend it mindlessly as fast as you earn it.

And to be honest, I don't have a net worth of a million dollars. The reason I'm not a millionaire is because I didn't follow my own advice, and the constant admonitions of my father to control expenses. Instead, I followed the media template: if you're making money you have to look like a millionaire. I bought an extravagant estate, antiques, and objets d'art. If I had lived more sensibly, I would easily have a net worth of a million dollars today. Not only that; but the pursuit of those Bright Shiny Objects drew me away from the thing that means most to me—the guitar.

I'm a little slow, but I have finally seen the light. Material objects no longer attract me. I live modestly and have no interest in living the lifestyle of the rich and famous. My focus is on the guitar. I am very content. My bank account is growing happier every day as well.

TAXES

Speaking of controlling expenses, what do you think the single largest annual expenditure is for most people? The answer is taxes. Some of you who have real jobs and regular paychecks may say, "Well, no, I don't pay much income tax. In fact I get a refund every year."

Look at your pay stubs. Do you think your pay is what you see on your check? Wrong! That is the *net* amount. That is what you are given *after* the government has stuck its hand in your pocket and taken a big chunk of your money. Look at the actual gross amount you are paid before deductions. Then look at what you take home. You *are* paying income taxes—a ton of them.

Rush Limbaugh has said the surest way to wake up people in America to how much they are paying in taxes would be to pay them their actual gross salary—no deductions. Then, out of that amount, have them write separate checks to the government for all the money they owe for taxes.

For example, let's say you are paid $24,000 a year. That means you get $2,000 every month. "Wow," you say. "I get my full $2,000." No, you don't.

Before you can even spend it, the government will begin demanding "its share." You will receive bills from:

- The federal government
- The state government
- The local government
- The fire department
- The police department
- The school district

Oh. And remember Social Security and Medicare? Did you forget, or did you even know, your employer has been paying half of your Social Security (also called the "FICA" or "SS Tax") and Medicare "contributions"? Well, no more. Now you have to pay what you were already paying (the boxes that say "Fed OASDI/EE" and "Fed Med/EE" on your pay stub) AND the share your employer paid. In other words, *double your old amount.* The total comes to 15.3%!

If you receive other income from self-employment (most if not all of your income as an entrepreneurial guitarist is from self-employment), you will receive another bill from the feds wanting 15% of that.

The typical American family pays more than 38% in federal, state, and local income taxes. At that rate (which doesn't include the 15% self-employment tax), that lovely $2,000 chunk of money you had has shrunk dramatically. You have paid your friendly government at least $760. At best, you are left with $1,240. How does it feel to work hard at what you do and have $760 (probably more) taken away from you every month? This doesn't take into account the additional money you pay in sales taxes, gasoline taxes, and gosh knows what else. Everyone either has their hand out or already stuck in your pocket.

If you are young or in your early career, you may not be in that typical American family tax bracket yet. But it probably won't be long. Remember, as you become more successful, *big government means less money for you.*

Some relief for the self-employed guitarist comes in deductions for business expenses, which I discuss in Chapter 36, "Taxes." But taxes will probably be your largest expense. Plan for it.

SPECIAL IRS GOTCHAS FOR THE ENTREPRENEURIAL GUITARIST

Lucky you. Here you are, trying to get your career off the ground. You have the American entrepreneurial spirit. You are gung ho. Good for you. But watch out. A shadow is lurking in the background. That shadow belongs to the IRS, the Internal Revenue Service.

Don't mess with the IRS. Don't think you can put one over on the IRS. They keep special tabs on the self-employed (that's you), people who operate businesses out of their homes and take the Home Office Deduction (that's you), and they keep tabs on certain professions such as the entertainment industry (that's you).

If you are dishonest, they will hunt you down and crush you. Be well-informed. Do the right thing. Seek professional help when you need it to be sure you are doing the right thing. I am not trying to make you paranoid. Those are the facts.

People much smarter than us have tried to outsmart the IRS. They failed. They ended up in prison or were fined very heavy penalties, or both. Follow the rules and you won't have to wear one of those fashionable orange jumpsuits.

I already mentioned one IRS Gotcha. That is the 15% self-employment tax. You have to pay that on all the income you receive from self-employment. Remember, that tax is *on top of* the regular federal income tax you and everyone else pays.

The other biggie is that you will probably have to file estimated quarterly tax payments. For people who work regular jobs, the government deducts taxes from their paycheck. But you, as a self-employed person, don't receive a monthly paycheck from which the government can take "its" money. Consequently, the government demands you *es-*

timate how much you will owe for the year. You pay that off by making a payment every three months. That is your estimated tax payment. You must set that amount aside. You *have* to. Your estimated payment is due June 15, September 15, January 15, and April 15. But April 15 you get a double whammy. You give them a check for the final payment for the previous year and another check for the first payment for the coming year. Again, *you have to have the money set aside* because if you don't pay it or pay just one day late, they find you. They track you down. You pay penalties.

Isn't this fun? This is why you must do some reading to educate yourself on taxes. Don't depend on the little bit of information I have given you here. Even if you seek professional help with your taxes (and I highly recommend that), learn enough about what's going on to monitor your situation. You don't want anything overlooked.

Do everything you can do legally to lower your tax bills. Everything. It's *your* money, not the government's. They are taking *your* money. Don't let them take any more than they are legally entitled to take. But keep everything aboveboard and accurate. Don't mess with the IRS.

RULES TO LIVE BY

1. **LIVE BELOW YOUR MEANS.** Keep track of how much money you earn. Do not spend more than that!

    If you want to spend more, you will have to earn more. If you can't earn more, cut your expenses. If you aren't keeping up with your expenses, cut every expense possible. Get a cheaper place to live. Move in with a friend. Move back into your parents' place. Shop more carefully to save on groceries. Stop eating out. Cut your utility bills.

In your early career, the amount of extra money you have at the end of the week is determined more by how many expenses you can cut rather than how much you earn. And whatever you do, do *not* spend in anticipation of increased earnings. If you are expecting an increase in earnings, wait until the money is in the bank before you start buying stuff.

2. Begin investing and saving early in your life. Just like beginning to learn the guitar when you're very young pays big dividends later, saving early in life makes a huge difference in wealth accumulation.

3. **LIVE BELOW YOUR MEANS.**

4. Planning, budgeting, and living frugally are essential elements to building your wealth over time, even if you are lucky enough to earn a high income. Because of the vagaries of the music business, you must think about your future. Ideally you want to achieve financial independence. That means being able to maintain your current standard of living for years without earning a paycheck from a job. Even those who earn high incomes must live below their means in order to become financially independent.

A proven correlation exists between financial planning/budgeting and wealth accumulation. People who successfully accumulate wealth and/or have successful businesses have a strong habit of planning and keeping track of their finances.

At the very least, you want to avoid having to eat cat food in your later years (See Chapter 25, "It's a Road, Not a Racetrack"). I warn you. You can be a great musician, have a strong mission, and achieve great success and still end up dirt poor when you're sixty if you don't think about these things now. And yes, I know playing the guitar and working on your mission is far more engaging than working on planning your financial future. But make the time. Take the time. Do it.

5. **LIVE BELOW YOUR MEANS.**

6. Begin tracking your expenses and set up a budget. You are an entrepreneurial guitarist—control your spending. This means personal spending as well as your business spending. If you don't know how much you typically have spent on services or products in the past, controlling future spending will be difficult. Keep an accurate record of every penny you spend. Many books, articles, and computer programs such as Quicken are available for setting up budgets and tracking expenses.

Don't tell me you don't have time to do this. Don't tell me you can't figure it out. Don't tell me you are making good money and don't need to do it. I used all those excuses and ended up spending money unnecessarily. Had I saved and lived more modestly, I could have used more money for creative projects and achieved financial independence by the time I was fifty.

7. **LIVE BELOW YOUR MEANS.**

8. Choose your mate very carefully. In the current legal climate, entertainer types (even classical musicians) are considered easy prey by divorce lawyers. Whether you are Paul McCartney or an unknown, if you are making income from creative projects you will be hit very hard in the courts. Judges seem to think your creative ability is a source of unlimited income, and having over half of everything you own taken away from you and given to the opposition is perfectly fair. After all, you will earn it back in no time. They also seem to think that since you are one of those artistic types, the failure of the marriage is all your fault anyway. Be very careful whom you marry. Have a pre-nuptial agreement drawn up by your attorney. I don't care if you're in love and you are positive it will last forever. I don't care that you're too busy practicing the guitar or in the middle of writing a song. Call your attorney well before the wedding date.

9. **LIVE BELOW YOUR MEANS.**

chapter 17

HOW TO GET ALONG WITH PEOPLE

Why in the world am I devoting a chapter to getting along with people in a book about how to make a million dollars playing the guitar? Because the business of the entrepreneurial guitarist is totally about how to connect with people. If you can't do that, you haven't a prayer.

A FUNDAMENTAL CONCEPT

Want to stir up resentment that will last for years? Then engage in stinging or negative criticism of someone, especially if you are certain they deserve it.

Don't ever forget, in dealing with other people, you are always dealing with creatures of emotion, not logic. People are motivated by pride and vanity. Yes, getting something off your chest, telling a person a thing or two, explaining to someone why they are a failure may very well make you feel better. But the damage caused by such impulsiveness can last a long time and come back to cause you irreparable harm. Benjamin Franklin, though tactless in his youth, later wrote, "I will speak ill of no man...and speak all the good I know of everybody." Any idiot can criticize, condemn, and complain. Most idiots do. But it takes character and self-control to be understanding and to forgive. Instead of condemning or criticizing people for what they do, try to figure out why they do what they do. It can be a very interesting and educational exercise. You will very likely even find a way to profit from it. At the very least it generates sympathy, tolerance, and kindness. If you want to increase the chances of your success, treat others well.

PEOPLE ARE INTERESTED IN THEMSELVES

You are interested in what you want. You are *eternally* interested in what you want 24/7. But no one else is! The rest of us are interested in what *we* want.

If you want to get a person's attention, if you want to get them interested in something you are doing: *talk about the things the other person treasures most.*

For example, if you have a meeting scheduled with some big shot, the last thing you want to talk about is your project. Find out what the big shot is interested in. If his hobby is chicken farming, find out everything you can about chicken farming and talk about that. If his passion is for golf, do some research on golf.

The concept is pretty simple. People are interested in themselves. The great British Prime Minister Benjamin Disraeli said it well: "Talk to people about themselves and they will listen for hours."

If you show genuine interest in a person's likes and wants, they will connect with you and remember you. They will be interested in you in return. Therefore, one of the best ways to influence others is to talk about what *they* want and show them how to get it.

This rule is at the heart of all marketing and selling: give the customer what he wants. Henry Ford once said that the secret to success "lies in the ability to get the other person's point of view and see things from that person's angle as well as from your own." This basic concept is painfully obvious, and its truth is primal. Yet almost everyone ignores it most of the time!

Being in a position to solve others' problems and wants presents a great opportunity. If you can manage to show another person how your service or merchandise will help them solve a problem, you won't need to sell them. They will buy.

The world is full of self-seeking, me-me-me people always looking out for what they want. The rare individual who unselfishly tries to help others has an enormous advantage and has little competition. Owen Young, the founder of RCA, once said, "People who can put themselves in the place of other people, who can understand the workings of their minds, need never worry about what the future has in store for them."

Note that we are not talking about manipulation. Looking at the other person's point of view and figuring out what they want is not to be done solely for your own benefit. Both sides need to gain from the partnership or negotiation. Otherwise, you will be perceived as insincere and untrustworthy and your efforts will result in failure.

GIVE PEOPLE WHAT THEY WANT, AND THEY WILL BE MUCH MORE LIKELY TO DO FAVORS FOR YOU IN RETURN

If you want to influence people, give them what they want. What do they want? John Dewey, one of America's most important philosophers, believed one of the must-haves for all people is the need to be appreciated. He categorized it as one of the deepest urges in human existence. Harvard psychologist and philosopher William James said, "The deepest principle in human nature is the craving to be appreciated." Note that he didn't use the phrase "desire to be appreciated" or "wish to be appreciated." He used the word "craving." This human hunger is constant and consuming. If you can satisfy another person's hunger for appreciation, they in turn will *want* to do things for you. You can use this powerful human need to improve your ability to get along with others.

As a musician, you want to generate enthusiasm and support from those around you. The best way to do that is through appreciation and encouragement, not criticism. Don't be one of those people who criticizes others when they do something wrong, but never says anything when they do things right. People will work much harder for you and give you their support when you treat them with a spirit of approval rather than criticism. Praising others publicly in the earshot of others is better than private praise.

Richard Branson, entrepreneur extraordinaire and founder of Virgin Records, said, "You have to be good at motivating and bringing out the best in people, and make sure that you appreciate those people." The ability to appreciate others' work, talent, and devotion is an important ingredient in staying on the right side of the thin dividing line between success and failure.

BUT, FLATTERY IS NOT THE ANSWER

Flattery and appreciation are entirely different. Flattery doesn't work with intelligent people. Appreciation is sincere; flattery is not. Flattery sounds counterfeit, shallow, and selfish. Flattery is cheap praise. The insincerity is sensed immediately.

We spend about 95% of our time thinking about ourselves. If we would spend some of that time thinking about another person's good points, flattery becomes unnecessary. We can easily find things about the other person we can sincerely and honestly appreciate.

Remember, people thrive on feeling that they matter. They flourish with appreciation and praise. They light up when someone else is interested in them. Be hearty and sincere in your approbation of others, and exuberant but genuine with your praise.

YOU CAN LEARN A GREAT DEAL FROM YOUR DOG

Many of us are familiar with coming home and being greeted by our beloved dog. As soon as the dog knows it's you, he almost jumps out of his skin to show you how thrilled he is to see you. You are the highlight of the dog's existence. This show of affection is absolutely sincere. He has no ulterior motives. The dog doesn't want to sell you anything. He doesn't want to marry you. He "makes his living" by giving you nothing but love and devotion.

Man's Best Friend doesn't need to read books on how to please people or make friends. He instinctively gives unconditional love and exhibits boundless enthusiasm for others.

The lesson from Man's Best Friend is this:

> You can make more friends in a month by becoming genuinely interested in other people, than you can in a year by trying to get other people interested in you.

Many people mistakenly go through life trying to get others interested in them. Let me clue you in. Other people are not interested in you. They aren't interested in me either. They are interested in themselves—morning, noon, and night. Being self-centered is simply human nature.

If you try to impress others, if you try to get others interested in you, it will not result in true, long-term friendships. Human nature just doesn't work that way.

Viennese psychologist Alfred Adler wrote, "It is the individual who is not interested in his fellow men who has the greatest difficulties in life and provides the greatest injury to others. It is from among such individuals that all human failures spring."

I don't know about you, but when I hear a composer's music or listen to a performer, I can tell immediately if that person likes people, is involved with what is going on in the world, or has some type of deep spiritual conviction. Empty uninvolved people produce empty music. The dull, unexpressive quality of the music is immediately apparent. As a person grows older, as they mature, they think less about themselves and relate more to bigger things outside of themselves. They realize that life is not just about them. As such, their music also grows, matures, and takes on greater vision. The classical field has countless examples of older instrumentalists who might lose some of their technical facility as they age, yet produce some of their greatest performances in their advanced years.

For you performers, remember, *your attitude is contagious to your audience.* When you go onstage, the audience knows if you are genuinely interested in pleasing them.

When I perform I am truly thankful that people have come to see me. I want them to enjoy themselves. I want to make them happy and take them to places they have never been. I want to share my personal joy of playing the guitar with them. I want us to be spiritually or emotionally uplifted—to experience the greatness of humanity and human achievement that is present in great music.

WHAT'S IN A NAME?

You know now that most people are interested first and foremost in themselves. And each of them has a name. Remember this: that name, that word, is wholly and singly owned by that person. *Magic* is in that name. The sound of that name is music to their ears. When you make a request of someone or wish to tell them something, *their mind will engage with you when they hear you say their name.* Knowing, remembering, and using the other person's name is a way of letting them know you are genuinely interested in them.

Most people don't remember names. They don't take the time or make the effort to fully catch a name and fix it in their minds. They make excuses about having bad memories or not having enough time to make note of it. Or, horror of horrors, they think, "Oh I'll never see this person again," or, "I have no use for this person. Why bother with their name?" I'm embarrassed to say how many times I did that when I was young, only to find that this "unimportant person" was in a position of great influence or power many years later. Or, many years later, I would be ashamed when they remembered my name but I couldn't remember theirs. People remember you and will be much more likely to cooperate with you when you address them by name. And don't be an idiot like I was. Forget whether you think they will be "useful" to you or not. This is not about you. This is about being genuine. This is about being interested in others. If you don't do this, you are headed for trouble.

YOU'RE A MUSICIAN, RIGHT? WELL, LISTEN!

Listening attentively with genuine interest to another's words is one of the highest compliments we can pay that person.

Most people don't listen attentively. They are too busy thinking about what they will say next and stop hearing the other person's words. If an idea pops into their head while the other person is speaking, they interrupt in the middle of a sentence. They are more interested in their own thoughts or talking about themselves.

Being a good conversationalist often means remaining relatively quiet. Be attentive. Ask questions the other person will enjoy answering. Encourage them to talk about themselves and their accomplishments. Show more interest in the other person than in yourself. Remember, your partners in conversation are far more interested in themselves and their wants, needs, and problems than they are in yours. This doesn't mean they are bad people or thoughtless and uncaring. Again, their behavior is simply human nature.

WANT TO GRAB SOMEONE'S ATTENTION? STOP THINKING ABOUT YOURSELF!

I realize that much of the preceding information may sound like very hollow, insincere, behind-the-back strategies to get things for your greedy little self. Nothing could be further from my purpose.

This is not at all about how to treat a person to get something out of him. This is about looking far beyond you. Something much bigger is out there, much bigger than you scheming to get ahead in your career.

As author Daniel Pink pointed out in his commencement address to the 2008 graduates of the Minneapolis College of Art and Design, "It's not about you. The world does not exist to make you happy, satisfied, and fulfilled. Other people are not on the planet to ensure that you are happy, satisfied, and fulfilled." The best way to achieve that blessed state is to stop looking in the mirror, and begin looking around you at the rest of the world.

Hitch your personal strengths, desires, and passions to your mission. One of the turning points for people who ultimately achieve success is when they realize it's not about them. They discover they succeed by delighting their customers and by providing real value to their clients. Performing artists succeed by enthralling their audiences. The successful person—happy, satisfied, and fulfilled—succeeds at life by asking, "What can I give?" not "What's in it for me?"

Poet Alfred Lord Tennyson wrote, "I am a part of all I have met." Think about how you affect others in your life and how they affect you. Every little thing you say or do has the potential to make a difference in someone else's day or life, whether you realize it or not.

Be a good person:

- Be *un*selfish.
- Radiate positive thoughts.
- Show honest appreciation for others without plotting what you will get out of it.
- Make others feel important and appreciated.
- Do things for others without ever expecting anything in return.
- Do things for others who *can't* do anything whatsoever in return for you.

This is a way of living (perhaps a law of human conduct) that will keep you out of trouble most of your life. Living contrary to it will result in a life of endless trouble and disappointment.

Jesus summed it up very nicely: "Do unto others as you would have others do unto you."

You want the approval of others. You want recognition of your worth. You want to feel like you matter, that you are important in your own corner of the universe. You don't want insincere flattery. You want honest, sincere appreciation. We all do.

How do you get these things? Simple. Follow the Golden Rule. "Do unto others…" Do it all the time and everywhere. It will work magic in your life every day.

chapter 18

AGE HAS NOTHING TO DO WITH IT

I have to admit a lot of this book is directed to the younger reader, perhaps under age thirty. After all, I am talking about earning a million dollars playing the guitar over your lifetime, not overnight, not in a year, not even ten years. Earning a million dollars over your lifetime becomes more difficult to do if you are already forty years old.

But, remember the other side of the equation. The older guitarist is working with the huge advantage of life experience. Experience is priceless. As you age, you learn more. If you had the ability to be twenty again, guess what? You would be an ignorant twenty-year-old. For you twenty-year-old guitarists reading this, that is not an insult. It is fact. Ignorance is not stupidity. It is lack of knowledge as a result of lack of experience and exposure, nothing more.

Let's face it. Aging is decline. But it is also growth. You have learned a heck of a lot about basic human interaction that a younger person simply doesn't know. And I hope you older readers will be patient with me talking about life skills you take as second nature—things like organization, accomplishing one task at a time, focus, responsibility, etc. But many younger readers may not know these things, so I have to address them. If you are an older reader, you are ahead of the game before you even begin. And yes, older folks sometimes say, "Oh, if I were only young again. If only I had started doing *x* when I was younger." But those words "if only" are only a reflection of unsatisfied or unfulfilled lives and missed opportunities. Don't tread there.

For some, the light bulb may suddenly have come on in your life. Maybe you have been searching to find real meaning in your life. Maybe you had an "aha!" moment. You've found something you are dying to do. You're excited. You're totally pumped.

If that is where you are, believe me, you don't want to go back to your younger days. You want to go forward full speed ahead, perhaps more so than the younger person because you are aware of how quickly life can pass you by. You want to do more, work harder, move forward. And you probably know from life experience how to do that more efficiently than a twenty-year-old. I can tell young people where a lot of the land mines are in the music world and in life, but guess what? They will probably step on them anyway! Because of your broader perspective and experience, you will miss most of them. You can envy the young if you want. I never have.

Delight in who you are and where you are. You are a unique being. No one else has your abilities, your insights, your viewpoints, and your life experience. Use everything you have within you to better yourself and to find and follow that path you see ahead of you that gives meaning to your life. Living unhappily is not an option. Even for the most cynical among you, it is never too late or too early to step onto a pathway to happiness. Age has nothing to do with it.

PART TWO: This Is How You Do it

chapter 19

GO FOR GREAT

I n his excellent book, *Good to Great*, Jim Collins details how major US companies such as Gillette, Kimberly-Clark, Kroger, Walgreens, Wells Fargo, and others transformed themselves from good companies to great companies. In his five-year study, he sought to find timeless, universal answers that any organization could use to improve its stature and performance, possibly to the point of becoming great. Many of the topics covered in the book are applicable to the entrepreneurial guitarist as well. These principles apply not just to the big picture of your overall career, but to turning a good CD into a great CD, a good performance into a great performance, a good song into a great song.

Let's look at the phrase "good to great." Collins explains that good is actually the enemy of great. In our country we have a good educational system, but is it great? No. We manufacture some good automobiles, but for the most part they aren't great. Few of us have great careers or great lives, because we tend to be happy with, and settle for, the good life. Most of us count ourselves as lucky when we can say, "I have it pretty good."

Becoming great is not easy. Statistically, by definition, not everyone will be great or even above average. But if you're going to put considerable effort into your career, why not go for great? Why put energy into mediocrity? That will only drain and demoralize you. Aiming high and demanding abundance and prosperity is far more pleasant than accepting mediocrity, misery, or poverty. W. Somerset Maugham wrote, "If you refuse to accept anything but the best, you very often get it."

The poem "My Wage" by Jessie B. Rittenhouse, says it well:

I bargained with Life for a penny,
And Life would pay no more,
However I begged at evening
When I counted my scanty store.

For Life is a just employer,
He gives you what you ask,
But once you have set the wages,
Why, you must bear the task.

I worked for a menial's hire,
Only to learn, dismayed,
That any wage I had asked of Life,
Life would have willingly paid.

The poem says exactly what your father, mother, uncle, teachers, etc. told you over and over when you weren't applying yourself or making an effort. Don't you remember? You rolled your eyes when they said it: "You get out of life what you put into it." Ouch. They were right.

I am trying to teach you how to make a million dollars playing the guitar. But remember, I'm using the phrase "playing the guitar" very loosely. Depending on the area of the music business on which you plan to focus, you don't actually have to be a great guitarist or the best guitarist. As long as you maintain the attitudes detailed in my book, you will accomplish the goal of earning a million dollars. *But you do have to be very good or great in whatever niche of the guitar or music world you choose to compete.* You or your product will be a nichebuster, not a blockbuster.

Let's face facts. Music and the guitar are what we love. This is our life passion. We feel in our hearts that what we do is meaningful to ourselves and to others. Be mediocre? Unthinkable. We always try to do our best because we are artists. Producing the best we can is in our souls. Is it even possible for you to imagine *not* trying to make your work great? I doubt it. Regardless of the mission you pursue, the quality of your life will be in direct proportion to your commitment to excellence.

That's what the next few chapters are about—how to turn good into great. Good may earn you a passable living. But great will produce your million dollars.

chapter 20

THE RIGHT
PEOPLE

The great artists who work with other artists in bands, duos, string quartets, and the like, or have others who do significant business work for them (managers, producers, promoters, etc.), make it a point to choose the right people with whom to work. The great pop bands gathered people together who somehow meshed and created magic. Think of the Beatles, U2, and the Rolling Stones. In the classical field, think of the Juilliard String Quartet and the Beaux Arts Trio. In the classical guitar world, think of Presti and Lagoya. On the business side, many times the artist stumbles upon the right people. Or the right people find the artist (Colonel Parker and Elvis, Sol Hurok and Segovia).

Those of us who work as solo artists often extend the solo attitude into other areas of our life. We have always "worked alone" relying on our own talents and thoughts to produce our art. But, to accomplish our big goals, especially making a million dollars playing the guitar, we need the help and cooperation of other people. We must face the fact that we alone do not have sufficient experience, education, and knowledge to do everything necessary to succeed. Perhaps those who work in musical groups are already more in tune with this way of thinking.

In general, people who became highly successful assembled the right people who worked together to drive them to greatness. Inevitably, few started out with all the right people. But, they got rid of the wrong people before the bad apples could do significant damage to their careers. Interestingly, they didn't determine a destination and then choose people they thought would get them there. Instead, the right people were gathered first and the wrong ones gotten rid of. Only *after* the right people were assembled did they decide where they were going to go, what they were going to do together, and what their strategy would be.

Collins, in *Good to Great*, describes it in terms of a bus ride. If people get on the bus primarily because they like the destination, what happens if a few miles down the road, things change or you encounter an obstacle and you have to change direction? You have a problem. The people got on the bus because they thought they were going to a certain destination, but now it has changed. They may not want to continue on the trip. They may want to get off. On the other hand, if the people riding the bus are there because of the other people and not a specific destination, then changing direction as conditions change becomes much easier. They're all in it together regardless of where the bus goes.

Therefore, if you begin with "who" instead of "where" or "what," you can adapt to changing conditions. That is very important in the music industry. Also, if you have the right people, the problems of motivation and long-term commitment melt away. The right people are self-motivated by the common inner drive to produce or create greatness.

Who are the right people? They aren't always the ones with specialized knowledge or skills. Many times they're the right people because they have certain innate abilities, personality traits, or strong character.

When you have the right people, compensation will not be an overriding motivator. If they are in a group with the right people, most musicians give little thought to compensation, especially in the exciting early days of growth and development. They are excited about each other, what they are producing, and the potential they see in each other. That's what drives them.

Understand, though, the picture is a little different for those who are not in the immediate circle of creating the product. They will probably not want to work very long without compensation. Not even the musicians can work indefinitely without some form of pay. And any reasonable person wouldn't expect others to work without compensation. Fortunately, the compensation doesn't always have to be in the form of money.

The business side has countless examples of high-powered producers, agents, etc. taking smaller percentages, fees, or even no compensation at all in the early years of an artist's development, because they recognize his potential greatness. They will do the right things and produce the best results they possibly can because of their inner commitment to building excellence for excellence's sake, not because they think they will get a bigger percentage or a larger fee out of their efforts.

For the less altruistic people with whom you work, all kinds of deals can be struck in terms of shares of future profits and products in order to get things off the ground in the early years. You can negotiate deals with a recording studio owner as simple as "Our band will play at your daughter's wedding if you give us six free hours of studio time." With a little thought and imagination, you can come up with all kinds of barter and trade deals. Many times you just have to ask for a favor. As Rush Limbaugh's father once told him, "The class acts are the people who will do things for you without a second thought as to what they will personally get out of it."

What if you suspect you are associated or working with the wrong people? Act.

You know the feeling. You are working with someone and they just aren't meeting your expectations. You think, "Well, I'll just give them a little more time. I'll give them other alternatives. I'll give them a third or fourth chance. Things will get better. I will just have to do my part differently to compensate for their shortcomings."

But things don't get any better and resentment builds. You end up spending way too much energy on their problems and shortcomings when you could be spending time and energy with the right person producing greatness. If you're lucky, much to your relief, they eventually quit on their own. Or, you finally take action and get rid of them (much to your relief). Meanwhile, everyone around you says, "What took you so long?"

Keeping the wrong people on your bus is not good for you and is unfair to the right people on your bus. The right people have to pick up the slack for the subpar work of the wrong people. It could possibly drive away the right people. The best people are accustomed to results and excellence, and don't want their work impeded or bogged down by second-rate people around them.

Don't wait too long to get rid of the wrong people. Letting them hang around too long is unfair to them as well. You know in your heart that things are not going to work out. Don't hold the seat on the bus for them—you're stealing time from their lives. They could be out spending time finding a better place where they can flourish and succeed. Don't hold on for your convenience or because you don't want to have to deal with it. Dealing with it will probably be a hassle, painful, distasteful, stressful, and possibly more. You've made the mistake. Face it, admit it, and deal with it so you can get on with great work and they can get on with their lives. You will be greatly relieved—and that's an understatement.

If some doubt remains in your mind, ask yourself, "If I had to do it all over again, would I choose this same person?" If the person came to tell you they were leaving, would you feel disappointed or relieved? Ask yourself those two questions and your choice of action will be very clear. If any lingering doubt remains, you may have the right person, but you have put them in the wrong seat. Perhaps they are languishing because you have placed them in a position that is not using them to their potential. Or maybe you have placed them in too high or demanding a position. If you change their seat, they might flourish and become a fantastic member of the team.

Let's also be clear that the right people are not always people who will agree with you. They may disagree with you on many things and argue about everything. They will fight you to the finish.

Disagreement is good when the people are arguing to discover the truth. However, if a person is arguing just to prove the other wrong, then you have a problem. The focus must be on issues, not each other. In the end, no matter how vicious the argument, when a decision is made, when you have the right people, they will line up behind that decision. They will unify. They know it was made for the common good and is the best decision for the end goal on which everyone agrees.

Finding the right people is important not only to your career but your entire life. If you aren't spending time with people you love and respect, you won't have a very enjoyable, let alone great life. As Collins says in *Good to Great*, "But if we spend the vast majority of our time with people we love and respect—people we really enjoy being on the bus with and who will never disappoint us—then we will almost certainly have a great life, no matter where the bus goes."

chapter 21

THE BRUTAL FACTS OF REALITY

CONFRONTING THE BRUTAL FACTS OF REALITY WITHOUT LOSING FAITH

Let me clue you in: things are not always going to go well. In fact, at times things are going to get very bad. Then they're going to get worse. This tends to be especially true for musicians in general. One of the essential things you must do throughout your life is to confront the brutal facts of reality and deal with them. In difficult times, if you continually make an honest effort to determine the truth of your circumstances, the right decisions to get you back on the road to success become obvious. If you aren't confronting reality, you can't make good decisions to get yourself back on track.

Think of finding answers to alarming problems in the same way as turning over rocks to find out what is under them. You will find yucky, squiggly things underneath. You can either scream in fright and throw the rock down, or fearlessly look at the yucky stuff up close—you might even have to touch it!

The entrepreneurial guitarist will look under one of those rocks and may realize:

1. I don't sing as well as I thought.
2. I have a personality problem.
3. I don't relate to other people well.
4. I am a terrible salesman.
5. I am terrible at marketing.
6. Our CD is terrible.
7. My guitar playing is sloppy.
8. The mixing I did on my recording is very muddy.
9. My girlfriend/boyfriend/spouse's ability at _____ is inadequate.
10. My lyrics stink.
11. My harmonic structures are too simple/complex.
12. I get too nervous performing in public.
13. Our drummer/lead guitarist, violist, singer, etc. just isn't cutting it.

You get the idea. The list could go on and on. But the wonderful thing is that when you confront the brutal facts, no question will remain about what you must do to fix the problem. Once corrected, you will be a much better artist. You will be stronger and more confident, not weakened or discouraged. After you face up to the hard truths, you will feel exhilarated and encouraged to never give up. You will always find a way to prevail.

In *Good to Great*, Jim Collins tells us that in studies of people who suffered serious adversity, "they found that people fell generally into three categories: those who were permanently dispirited by the event, those who got their life back to normal, and those who used the experience as a defining event that made them stronger."

To help you deal with adversity in your career, a very powerful tool may be used, called the Stockdale Paradox. In *Good to Great*, Jim Collins describes how the concept evolved.

> *The name refers to Admiral Jim Stockdale, who was the highest-ranking United States military officer in the 'Hanoi Hilton' prisoner-of-war camp during the height of the Vietnam War. Tortured over twenty times during his eight-year imprisonment from 1965-1973, Stockdale lived out the war without any prisoner's rights, no set release date, and no certainty as to whether he would even survive to see his family again.*
>
> *He shouldered the burden of command, doing everything he could to create conditions that would increase the number of prisoners who would survive unbroken, while fighting an internal war against his captors and their attempts to use the prisoners for propaganda. At one point, he beat himself with a stool and cut himself with a razor, deliberately disfiguring himself, so that he could not be put on videotape as an example of a 'well-treated prisoner.'*
>
> *He exchanged secret intelligence information with his wife through their letters, knowing that discovery would mean more torture and perhaps death.*
>
> *He instituted rules that would help people to deal with torture (no one can resist torture indefinitely, so he created a stepwise system—after x minutes, you can say certain things—that gave the men milestones to survive*

*toward). He instituted an elaborate internal communi-
cations system to reduce the sense of isolation that their
captors tried to create....*

You get the picture. He was one tough cookie. In his research for *Good to Great*, Collins asked him how he survived. Stockdale replied, "I never lost faith in the end of the story. I never doubted not only that I would get out, but also that I would prevail in the end and turn the experience into the defining event of my life, which, in retrospect, I would not trade."

Definitely a member of group number three as outlined above—those who use an adverse experience as a defining moment that makes them stronger. Collins then asked Stockdale, "Who didn't make it out?" Stockdale replied, "Oh, that's easy. The optimists."

But wait a minute. Wasn't Stockdale an optimist? He goes on to clarify.

*The optimists. Oh, they were the ones who said,"We're going
to be out by Christmas." And Christmas would come, and
Christmas would go. Then they'd say, "We're going to be out
by Easter." And Easter would come, and Easter would go.
And then Thanksgiving, and then it would be Christmas
again. And they died of a broken heart.*

False hopes are quickly swept away.

Then Stockdale sums up with what Collins calls the Stockdale Paradox:

"You must never confuse faith that you will prevail in the

*end—which you can never afford to lose—with the disci-
pline to confront the most brutal facts of your current reality, whatever they might be."*

Imagine telling your fellow prisoners, "We *are* going to get out of here. But we're not getting out by Christmas. Probably not by Easter, probably not by Thanksgiving. Deal with it."

All this relates directly to the entrepreneurial guitarist. This is how you will hang in there during the bad times and emerge stronger and better. Not only that, but always seeking out and facing the brutal facts will continually smooth and refine your path to success and perhaps greatness.

What separates people, what will separate you from other guitarists and musicians, is not the presence or absence of difficulty. Difficulty in life is a given. The difference is how you deal with your difficulties. As UCLA basketball coach John Wooden (possibly re-quoting Art Linkletter) says, "Things turn out best for the people who make the best of the way things turn out."

Your band broke up, your singing partner was killed in an accident, your CD you put your heart and soul into sold 42 copies, and you got booed last night at a gig. You must keep your faith that you will eventually prevail in the end, regardless of your difficulties. The end may be nowhere in sight at the present time. You must confront the brutal facts of your current reality in order to seek solutions (which will usually be very apparent) so you may move ahead. Hit the difficulties of your situation head-on. You will emerge from adversity a stronger person, better able to deal with what lies ahead.

Collins believes the Stockdale Paradox is a signature of all those who create greatness, either in their own lives or in leading others. In his studies, no matter how bleak the situation, no matter how insurmountable the difficulties appeared to be, the people who sought success all maintained unwavering faith that they would not only succeed at attaining their immediate goals, but would move on to greatness. At the same time, they were relentless in confronting the brutal facts of their current reality.

As an individual artist, you must courageously turn over those rocks that are blocking your path and look under them. But if you're working with others in a band, group, duo, or in business relationships, another dynamic enters the picture. Coming up with answers all by yourself, and motivating the others to follow what *you* think is right, will not lead to greatness. Work *with* the others.

Also important is to create a climate in which the truth can be heard. If you want to face reality, you don't want people around you telling you what you *want* to hear. Instead, involve the others.

The key is to ask questions. Keep asking "why" to gain understanding and gather information. Members of some of the great classical chamber groups describe many of their rehearsals as being raging battles over how to interpret one measure of Beethoven. They yell and argue, sometimes to the point of being ready to whack one another with their bows! "Loud debate," "heated arguments," and "intense disagreement" are some of the phrases you will hear mentioned when groups describe their rehearsals. It can get heated, but it's okay because the right people are gathered together who are all completely on board to search for and find the best answers to any question. They are committed to greatness and don't mind facing the brutal facts. They don't mind engaging in dialog and debate. They don't make it personal. The arguing is for the good of the ensemble.

When things go wrong, figure out what went wrong, but do it without blame. Conduct an autopsy without blaming others so you have a climate in which the truth can be heard. It can be tricky, but when you have the right people in your group, you should rarely have to put blame on anyone. Indeed, some will voluntarily take the blame. The important thing is to search for and find understanding of what happened and *learn from it.*

Collins says his research showed the key elements to achieving greatness to be deceptively simple and straightforward. The great were able to strip away clutter and noise and focus on the few things that would have the greatest impact.

They were able to do so because they worked both sides of the Stockton Paradox. They never let one side override the other:

A. They maintained faith (not false hope) but didn't lose sight of reality.
B. They faced the brutal facts of reality but never lost faith.

If you can use this every day in your own life, you will dramatically increase the odds of making the right choices at the right time—a key to success in the music industry.

chapter 2 2

FOXES, HEDGEHOGS, AND SUCCESS

"The Hedgehog and the Fox," by Isaiah Berlin, is an essay about Russian author Leo Tolstoy's view of history. The title references a literary fragment attributed to the ancient Greek poet Archilochus: "The fox knows many things, but the hedgehog knows one big thing."

Although scholars disagree about the interpretation of the phrase, on the surface it sounds like a Looney Tunes cartoon adventure. The cunning fox, hiding behind a tree, waits for his prey. The hedgehog waddles past. The fox darts out: "Aha, I've got you this time!" The hedgehog looks up, sees the fox, and thinks, "Oh no, it's that stupid fox again. Will he ever learn?" The hedgehog rolls up into a ball with his sharp spikes pointing outward in all directions, impervious to attack. The fox screeches to a halt, realizing he is foiled again and lopes off to plan a new attack for tomorrow. Each day another version of the battle takes place. Although the fox is cunning and clever, the hedgehog always wins.

In his essay, Berlin uses this Looney Tune-esque adventure to divide people into two artistic and intellectual personalities: foxes and hedgehogs.

The foxes pursue many things at the same time, things often unrelated and even contradictory, related to no central moral or aesthetic principle. Berlin describes them as "scattered or diffused, moving on many levels." They don't organize their thinking into an overall concept or unified vision.

In *Good to Great*, Jim Collins tells us that "hedgehogs, on the other hand, simplify a complex world into a single organizing idea, a basic principle or concept that unifies and guides everything. It doesn't matter how complex the world, a hedgehog reduces all challenges and dilemmas to simple (indeed, almost simplistic) hedgehog ideas. For a hedgehog, anything that does not somehow relate to the hedgehog idea holds no relevance."

Freud and Einstein were hedgehogs. Being a hedgehog doesn't mean one is ignorant, unaware of the many elements around them, or narrow-minded. On the contrary, these individuals and others like them understood the power of simplicity. What could be simpler than reducing the unconscious human mind into the id, ego, and superego? What could be simpler than $e=mc^2$?

Collins elaborates, "No, hedgehogs are not simpletons; they have a piercing insight that allows them to see through complexity and discern underlying patterns. Hedgehogs see what is essential, and ignore the rest."

He points out that the hedgehog mindset has a large role in making the transformation from being just good at what you do, to great. In the business world, those companies that developed a Hedgehog Concept for their company became clearly focused on one concept that drove their decision making, producing spectacular results.

The hedgehog mindset works in the music business world as well.

Bands and individuals who developed a clear personality or style (think the Beatles, Rolling Stones, Chet Atkins, Andres Segovia, Barbra Streisand, Eric Clapton—the list goes on and on) went on to huge success. The style of each of these examples is easily described and recognized. They do it better than anyone else. Each had a concept or vision and relentlessly pursued it. They succeeded brilliantly by executing that concept with excellence and imagination.

You might ask again, "But Doug, I thought you said I didn't have to be a great guitarist or the best guitarist to earn a million dollars playing the guitar. You said if I maintain the attitudes detailed in the book, I will succeed anyway." Yes, that's true. We're not talking about being the best *guitarist* in the world or a great *guitarist* per se. I will tell you things to keep in mind that just might turn your career from good to great, though not specifically as a guitarist. Furthermore, even though being great at your niche talent isn't necessary to make a million dollars with the guitar, it will definitely help! Besides, I will repeat what I said earlier. I believe that because we all love the guitar and music so much, very few of us ever settle for pretty good or good enough. We have pride in what we do and are always working toward great. Making our creations the best they can be is a vital part of our artistic spirit.

Let's delve more deeply into the Hedgehog Concept. The magic of the Hedgehog Concept only comes about from a convergence of all three of these key elements:

Element #1: The thing that you can be *the best in the world at* (and, equally important, understanding and facing up to what you *cannot* be the best in the world at).

Element #2: What will drive the flow of money into your bank account? Figure out what single denominator (profit per *x*) will have the greatest positive impact on your financial bottom line.

Element #3: Focus on what you are deeply passionate about.

Now, let's look at each of these elements in detail.

ELEMENT #1
The thing that you can be *the best in the world at* (and, equally important, understanding and facing up to what you *cannot* be the best in the world at).

This is more than being competent or really good at what you do. We are talking about being *the best in the world*. The entrepreneurial guitarist asks himself, "If I can't be the best at it, why do it at all?" That may sound harsh, but if you think that way, you won't waste energy and money pursuing the wrong activities.

Element #1 of your Hedgehog Concept will not be that you will be the best guitarist in the world. Nor will your concept depend on that.

We are not talking about a goal or a strategy to be the best at something. The hedgehog doesn't decide what he *wants* to be the best at. He discovers what he *can* be the best at.

The distinction is crucial. Your chances of success are far better when you choose a goal that is right for you. Succeeding or trying to succeed at the wrong goal is a colossal waste of time and money, not to mention unnecessarily risky. Look at your strengths and weaknesses and seek goals that use your strengths but sidestep the weaknesses.

The thing you can do best may have little to do with actually *playing* the guitar. It will be a particular gift you have that is probably somehow related to the guitar, or a particular niche you see that no one else does, that you will identify and cultivate. It will be within that niche, possibly a very narrow area, that you will indeed be the very best. I'm generalizing, but it could be playing particular types of pieces in altered guitar tunings, playing a particular kind of music on a particular kind of guitar, or with a particular technique. It could be writing songs about aliens, about childhood, about a political issue. If you are a music store owner, it could be selling a particular type of merchandise or targeting a particular niche market. If you are a performer, it could be something about your live presentation, where you perform, or how you book performances. It could be something way out there, or very obvious— so obvious (perhaps with a unique twist) that no else has ever done it. It may be as simple as doing a common thing in an uncommon way. Take the mundane and turn it into something new—something with style, life, and excitement. Find a way to give people something they didn't know they were missing. As with everything else in music, the possibilities are truly limitless. Here are some examples of Hedgehog Concepts in the music business:

> The Vic Firth Company is the world's largest manufacturer of drum-sticks and mallets. It was founded "by accident" according to founder Vic Firth, a drummer and percussionist. Firth had been a percussionist with the Boston Symphony Orchestra for twelve years. Firth found that some of the BSO's repertoire demanded

higher-quality drumsticks and mallets than those that were being manufactured at the time. Firth decided to design a set of his own sticks. Firth says, "It came out of necessity, not of imagination or my ability to start a company." Today, the Vic Firth Company manufactures 12 million sticks a year.

You electric guitarists who have used "Slinky" strings know this guy:

Ernie Ball grew up in a musical family. His father was a car salesman and taught Hawaiian steel guitar on the side. Ernie played the steel guitar for a while, got bored, and gave it up. But in his early teens, he took a renewed interest in the instrument and began practicing three hours a day. He soon began to play professionally.

When he was around 24, Ernie opened a teaching studio. While teaching his students, he noticed the difficulty they had bending strings and fingering guitar chords with the relatively thick-gauge strings of the time.

In his late twenties, he opened one of the first music stores to sell guitars exclusively. He was told repeatedly that a guitar store would never succeed and that he would go broke. Though he did go broke many times, Ernie always managed to pay his bills and move on.

Thinking back to his teaching and his students' difficulty playing on guitars with medium and heavy-gauge strings, Ernie approached several manufacturers with the idea of developing custom-gauge strings. After being scoffed at and rebuffed by Fender, Gibson, and others, Ernie Ball soon brought out Slinkys himself.

Ernie Ball did not really create anything new. He simply saw a demand and improved upon existing products. He found ways to better fulfill market demands, creating products that helped shape the sound of rock-n-roll. Endless hit songs have been played on Ernie Ball Strings since the 1960s. By the time Ernie Ball passed away, the company was grossing $40 million per year.

All this resulted from an idea that came to him from teaching his guitar students!

Look at Derek Sivers, founder of CD Baby, as detailed on the oreillynet.com website:

A full-time musician since the age of eighteen, he started CD Baby in 1998 knowing nothing but basic HTML, and taught himself just enough PHP and SQL to get by as the site grew. A hopeless learning addict, endlessly fascinated with the technical/programming/design process, Derek spent much of his time inventing and re-inventing the code behind his growing company's websites.

He eventually sold CD Baby to Disc Makers, netting $22 million for his foundation, The Independent Musician's Charitable Trust, which will fund music education after he passes away.

Or, look at Michael Laskow at Taxi. Think about the countless developers of music hardware and software. Think about the people who developed Pro Tools or Finale. Be a music attorney instead of a real estate attorney. Use your imagination, look at your abilities, and connect them to your love of music.

Psychologist Dr. Joyce Brothers once quoted Professor Paffenberger of Columbia University as recommending that one should "concentrate on one small part of one subject and become the world's greatest authority on it." That may still be commendable advice for some. But Dr. Brothers updates the professor's statement. She emphasizes the importance of being unique. Although one can be unique by knowing more about one subject than anyone else in the world, one can also be unique by knowing more about a small *cluster* of subjects than any other person. I think that can be a key for many entrepreneurial guitarists.

As an educator, I have come to realize that every person has unique abilities and gifts. The abilities may not be obvious. It is often unclear which abilities will be a determining factor in the person's ultimate success. Being extraordinarily talented or exceptionally smart certainly are not necessary to achieve success. Usually a combination of many traits is needed, some of which will not be obvious at all. Author, journalist, television commentator Bill O'Reilly advises, "Identify what you're good at, and then try to make a living doing it. It's as simple as that." He says that one reason he believes in God is that he has observed that every single person on earth has a unique ability. O'Reilly calls it a gift—"something unique to them that they can do better than other people."

Jerry Garcia of the Grateful Dead went a step further. He said that you do not merely want to be considered the best at what you do. You want to be considered the only one who does what you do.

Over and over again I come into contact with students at the University that other professors or other students think will never succeed at anything. In working with these students I see that yes, they may not succeed at the university. But then I see the unique viewpoint or unique ability they have that, if cultivated, will possibly take them on very exciting life paths and probable success.

Winston Churchill's teachers once wrote a note to his parents, stating he would never amount to anything. Those teachers were so insular and isolated in their own little world they were unable to see young Winston's unique qualities and abilities. They could not understand that his unique qualities were something to be capitalized upon, not suppressed or criticized.

You may find that playing "second fiddle" to someone else is your strength. Arrigo Boito was a great librettist. He wrote the libretti (the words and story) to Giuseppe Verdi's great operas *Othello* and *Falstaff*. When you hear about either opera, you only hear the name Verdi. Few remember or know of Boito. Yet Boito, standing in the wings, not the spotlight, made Verdi's success with these two great operas possible.

When you begin to look at yourself with brutal honesty, you may realize you are not the best at anything and never have been. But if you use the Stockdale Paradox discussed earlier, you can confront the brutal facts of what you *cannot* be the best at (so you don't delude yourself) but maintain faith that you *will* find what you *can* do better than anyone else—you will find it no matter how awful things look right now.

Lifestyle entrepreneur Frederic Fekkai doesn't believe one must be "gifted" to succeed. He says, "I think it's baloney. I mean, obviously there are some geniuses, but for me, it was not such a thing. Because I'm ambitious, I became talented." He studied and practiced what he learned. He literally taught himself to be talented. *He absorbed the best from the best because he wanted to become the best.*

It's important to acknowledge and face another brutal fact: your current pursuit may not be what you can be the best at. You will need to identify this and not waste time on things you are only pretty good at. Even though you may have already spent months or years pursuing a certain goal, if you can't be the best at it, that pursuit can't form the basis of your Hedgehog Concept.

If you're playing blues guitar like a hundred thousand other blues guitarists, you need a slap upside of the head. The world doesn't need another competent blues guitarist. But if you can find an angle, something no other blues guitarist in the world does as well as you, then you're on the right path. If you can't, however, you may need to forget playing blues guitar and look at something else entirely. Everyone wants to be the best at something—the best guitarist, the best singer, the best band—but not very many people can understand with egoless clarity what they truly have the potential to be the very best at, and again, with equal clarity, what they *cannot* be the best at. Don't fool yourself.

The Hedgehog Concept requires a severe standard of excellence. If you think like a hedgehog, you don't think about building on the strengths or competence you currently have. Instead, you work at understanding what you, your band, your duo or trio truly has the potential to be the very best at in the world, and sticking to that one thing. It could be something in which you have no current competence!

Yes, you could pursue something you are reasonably good at, not worry about being the best, make money, and over time make your million dollars if you follow the rest of the advice in this book. But if you use the Hedgehog Concept, focusing solely on what you can potentially do better than anyone else, and combine that with the rest of the concepts in this book, you will embark on a path that possibly will lead to greatness. If not to greatness, your path will most certainly be smoother and quicker to making your million dollars playing the guitar.

ELEMENT #2

What will drive the flow of money into your bank account? Figure out what single denominator (profit per *x*) will have the greatest positive impact on your financial bottom line.

Good news! Collins' studies showed that a company didn't need to be in a great industry to become a great company. In fact, many became great in very unspectacular industries. Some were in terrible industries. The secret to success was to attain profound insights into their own company's economics.

The lesson for us entrepreneurial guitarists is to not be discouraged about the never-ending talk about the imminent demise of the music business. Yes, CD sales are declining, profits are down, and piracy is up. Doom and gloom. Ignore it! You can succeed in spite of it all. In fact, you may succeed *because* of one of those elements if you find a unique angle to get around them. Look at Steve Jobs at Apple. CD sales were plummeting. Jobs came up with an angle: iTunes. Enough said.

All of this means that even though many characterize the music business as a terrible industry, it doesn't matter. You can make money in niche and fringe areas of the music business. But the key is to understand the economics of your situation and capitalize on that knowledge.

In his studies, Collins noticed "one particularly provocative form of economic insight that every good-to-great company attained." That insight was the single economic denominator. Think of it in terms of a fraction or ratio:

$$\frac{\textbf{Profit}}{\textbf{X}}$$

Or, you could describe it in words as profit per x.

Ask yourself: *If I could choose one ratio to increase over time, what x would have the greatest and most sustainable impact on my economic engine, my financial bottom line? What x will pump the most money into my banking account?*

The denominator may not be obvious. It could be very subtle. It could be profit per each CD sold, profit per each CD released, profit per concert appearance, profit per song, profit per customer visit to your website (or brick-and-mortar music store), profit per geographic region or local population (focusing on regional or local touring, CD distribution, radio airplay, promotion), etc. The key is to use the answer to the question to gain insight into where to focus your energies to maximize financial gain.

Interestingly, especially in the music business, the main source of your income may not come from what you would first think of as your core business. For instance, profit from CD sales might be negligible. Profit from merchandise sales or tour income might trump CD profits by far.

Take computer printers for example. These days you can buy excellent printers for $40–$100. The manufacturer makes zilch on the sale of the printer. But the ink cartridge replacements sometimes cost as much as the printer and must be purchased again and again. The profit is in the ink cartridges, not the printer itself.

Collins goes on to say you don't have to have a single denominator. But, trying to come up with one denominator produces better insight than diffusing your thoughts into three or more denominators. Identifying the key drivers in your economic engine is important. The point is not just to have a denominator. The point is to gain understanding into what will make more money and, very importantly, *sustainable* earnings from your efforts.

ELEMENT #3
Focus on what you are deeply passionate about.

Focus on the activity that ignites your passion or that drives your life. The great pedagogue Nadia Boulanger routinely announced to her new music composition students (who included Aaron Copland and Leonard Bernstein among others), "Either you devote your whole life to music, or you abandon it now!"

In his commencement address at Stanford University Steve Jobs, founder of Apple Computer, related how devastating it was to be fired from Apple:

> *I'm convinced that the only thing that kept me going was that I loved what I did. You've got to find what you love, and that is as true for work as it is for your lovers. Your work is going to fill a large part of your life, and the only way to be truly satisfied is to do what you believe is great work, and the only way to do great work is to love what you do. If you*

> *haven't found it yet, keep looking, and don't settle. As with*
> *all matters of the heart, you'll know when you find it, and*
> *like any great relationship it just gets better and better as*
> *the years roll on. So keep looking. Don't settle.*

Not too many actually know what they want in life. A study by the Ford Foundation cited by Peter Spellman, Director of Career Development at the Berklee College of Music, found that:

- 23% of the population have no idea what they want from life, and as a result they don't have much.
- 67% of the population have a general idea of what they want, but they don't have any plans for how to get it.
- Only 10% of the population have specific, well-defined goals.

Ask some of your friends. Few will be able to give you a specific answer. It's unlikely they have given much thought to how to achieve their desires.

A desire doesn't happen through wishes and hope. It must be obsessive. A desire can only be fulfilled with definite plans that are in continuous action, through never-ending persistence.

Napoleon Hill, in his classic book *Think and Grow Rich*, describes your obsessive desire as your *definite major purpose*. Hill believed that focused thought is a driving force. If mixed with purpose, unrelenting persistence, and passion—burning desire—it can result in great riches. His research showed that successful people pursued their purpose with burning desire. They pursued it with the right people around them, knowledge, and *persistence that did not recognize defeat.*

Successful people have a single-minded devotion and total commitment to their definite major purpose or mission. Some people refer to overachievers and totally dedicated people as workaholics. That implies illness. Nothing could be further from the truth. If you are a totally dedicated person, you are pursuing what you want to do more than anything else in the world. How lucky you are. Naysayers around you may say you should cut back on spending so much time and effort on achieving your dream. Wait a minute. These are the things that make you happy. Cut back so you don't enjoy your life quite so much? That's ridiculous. Full speed ahead, my friend.

Some of you may worry that you have some self-doubt lingering in the deep recesses of your mind. You may be having difficulty truly believing that all this will really work—that you can really achieve what you want. This is where your burning desire will come to your rescue. Knowing precisely what you want is crucial. You must want it with white-hot desire. You must want it so badly that it becomes an obsession (in a good way). Only then will you honestly and totally believe you will get it. Once you believe, you are well on your way to making it reality.

Richard Branson, the colorful entrepreneur behind Virgin Records, Virgin Airlines, and many other endeavors, points out that the dividing line between success and failure can be very thin. He reminds us that many people who start with nothing and set up a business fail. In order to succeed, "You just have to throw yourself wholeheartedly into what you're doing. You have to passionately believe in what you're doing. You have to make sure that all the people around you passionately believe in what they're doing and what you're doing.... Then at least you have a chance of staying on the right side of that dividing line."

Passion cannot be manufactured. You can't motivate people to feel passionate about something. You can only *discover* what ignites your passion and the passions of those around you, be they family members, business associates, band members, songwriting partners, whomever. You can't say to your band members, "Okay, let's get passionate about what we are doing." And you most certainly can't say that to yourself.

Let's review. The Hedgehog Concept is a combination and clear understanding of three elements:

Element #1: The thing that you can be *the best in the world at* **(and, equally important, understanding and facing up to what you *cannot* be the best in the world at).**

If you aren't the best at what you do, your progress will be lackluster or your career may fizzle.

Element #2: What will drive the flow of money into your bank account? Figure out what single denominator (profit per *x*) will have the greatest positive impact on your financial bottom line.

If what you do isn't making economic sense, you might have loads of fun doing it, but the end result may be costly or unrewarding financially.

Element #3: Focus on what you are deeply passionate about.

If you lack passion about what you're doing, you may be able to make some money and achieve success, but you won't be able to stay with it in the long run. Longevity is essential in the music business.

To remain great, to maintain a robust music career, to keep the money flowing into your bank account, apply these three fundamental principles for the duration of your career or you will slide backward.

Most of you currently reading this book are probably in the "pre-hedgehog" state. You're looking to find what direction to go. Things may be a little foggy. You're slowly marching along trying a path here, a path there. You come to forks in the road and are unsure which road to take. Your career isn't really going anywhere and very little money if any is coming in. It looks like making your million dollars playing the guitar is way off in the future if it's there at all.

But once you become a hedgehog, you'll find yourself in a clearing. The fog will disappear and you will see clearly what's up ahead. As a hedgehog, you will actually be running along, and decisions as to which roads to take will be made quickly and decisively—decisions you could never have made when you were still in the pre-hedgehog fog.

Without a Hedgehog Concept, musicians change their focus from one thing to another. Out of desperation or lack of patience, they travel down the wrong roads, listen to the wrong people, listen to people making empty or ridiculous promises, and make unwise decisions. Then they have to back up and reverse course, wasting precious time and money. Some of those wrong roads can have deep potholes that damage your career or may even send you careening off into a ravine.

The hedgehog maintains a clear picture of the three elements of his Hedgehog Concept. Therefore the hedgehog stays in the clearing and out of the fog, traveling on the right roads. He asks the right questions, is able to discern the right answers, and is able to set goals and strategies based upon clear understanding of his Concept.

Because of its vital importance, sitting down right now to come up with your Hedgehog Concept in the next thirty minutes is not a good idea. It will take months or even a few years to really clarify your Hedgehog Concept. It can be very difficult to craft a clear and simple Concept. It will have to cook and simmer. Getting a handle on your

Hedgehog Concept will be an ongoing, constantly questioning process for a while. Forming your Concept is not an event. Its development is best done over time.

You can work on it yourself if you are an individual artist. Or you might want to include trusted advisers, family members, or knowledgeable members of the music world. If you work with someone else or are in a group, you will include them as well.

Collins recommends you assemble a group whose purpose is to gain understanding about where your career is headed, within the framework of the three elements of the Hedgehog Concept. All members should argue and debate for understanding—not for the purpose of personal gain or protecting one's turf. Members should have a range of perspectives but all should have a deep knowledge of the aspects of your career and the music world. The group should meet as often as once a week or as little as once every three months. Don't seek consensus—that often results in mediocrity or produces bad decisions. The responsibility for the final decision is with you or the leader of the band, trio, etc.

The group charged with developing the Hedgehog Concept must ask questions, debate, and argue. Make some decisions, try them out, autopsy the results. Learn from it all. Each time you meet, do it again— over and over, *all within the context of the three elements that form a Hedgehog Concept.*

Eventually your Hedgehog Concept will take shape. It will materialize. But it won't be accompanied by a trumpet fanfare. When the day arrives and someone says, "Yeah, we can be better at that than anyone else," it will be stated as a matter-of-fact recognition of truth—not much different than saying the grass is green or the guitar has six strings.

The words in your Hedgehog Concept will not contain hype, wishful thinking, or PR baloney. They will be observations of fact, though backed by passion. It will be a statement that you *could* be the best in the world at what you are attempting to do. It will be recognition that being the best in the world is in the realm of possibility, not a delusion.

You don't know that you *will* become the best. But you know with confidence and certainty that you *could* be with perseverance and determination. That distinction is what makes all the difference. Knowing what they *could* be the best at is what separates those who become great from those who do not.

chapter 23

THE "D" WORD: DISCIPLINE

You already know about discipline. You use it when you decide to practice the guitar every day for several hours come hell or high water. You use it when you turn down offers to go to a party or to socialize so you can stay home and practice. You use it when you rearrange and reschedule distracting outside activities to give yourself more time to practice.

I personally get up in the morning at 4:00 am so I can practice four to six hours the very first thing in the day, before everything else hits the fan. The rest of the day can go well or horribly—it doesn't matter because I got my guitar time in ahead of everything else. The guitar is numero uno. Listen up: it cannot be any other way.

Live by the Principle of Priority which states 1) Learn the difference between what is urgent and what is important, and 2) *Do what's important first.* What is important is *playing your guitar or working at your music and attending to your career.* Read that principle several times until you really get it. I don't think I need to dwell on this aspect of discipline. Your passion for the guitar and music certainly already drives your life, and discipline is almost an afterthought. But for those few who may have a problem with it, I highly recommend the book *The War of Art* by respected author Steven Pressfield. He mainly speaks to the discipline required for writing, but the book relates directly to any art, especially music.

Discipline is at the crux of everything: perseverance, preparation, research, and focus. But discipline in itself will not carry your career forward and put one million dollars in your bank account. Use your discipline for specific purposes.

Now that you understand the Stockton Paradox, you can use disciplined thought to face the brutal facts of reality, but maintain absolute faith that you can and will succeed—that you will absolutely make a million dollars playing the guitar and possibly move on to greatness.

Use disciplined thought to formulate and adhere consistently and almost fanatically to your Hedgehog Concept. Once your Hedgehog Concept has materialized, it will be time to apply disciplined action to bring it to life. Remember what you've decided you could be the best at, and direct your energies and your focus to that one thing. Because that one thing is your core passion, the discipline required to focus on it will come naturally. Next, remember your economic denominator. Discipline yourself to direct your energies and your focus to feed that.

A key for many of us is to also know what NOT to do. Anything that doesn't fit into your Hedgehog Concept, you simply will not do. You won't waste your time or money on it.

Look at the legendary gospel singer Mahalia Jackson. She held audiences spellbound around the world with her rich, deep contralto voice. Elements of blues and jazz are in her music, but she insisted on only singing gospel music. She turned down opportunities to sing secular music that could have made her millions of dollars. She knew her core values and she knew what she was absolutely the best at. She didn't waste time trying to perform music that didn't fit into her Hedgehog Concept.

Making "to do" lists is very helpful. I do it sometimes two or three times a day. But equally important is to make "stop doing" lists. Discipline yourself to stop messing with extraneous activities and distractions.

As a creative type, some red flags may be waving in your head. "Doug, it sounds like you're boxing me in. You're setting limits." The paradox is that if you stay within the three elements of your Hedgehog Concept, the number of positive opportunities for growth will increase. You are focusing on what you do best, what drives your economic engine, and what ignites your passion. It's a no-brainer—*of course* your creativity and career will take off like a rocket; *of course* many (and the right) opportunities will spring up all around you. And, you will have the clarity to see when "once in a lifetime" opportunities are bogus. You will have the discipline to easily pass them by. You will be able to just say no to all kinds of distractions, hangers-on, and bad influences.

Because we have a definite purpose or mission in life, that purpose totally dominates our thoughts and actions. Our thoughts and actions become magnets that attract us to the forces, knowledge, people, and circumstances of life (being in the right place at the right time over and over again) that serve and harmonize with our purpose. We do the right things and make the right choices that drive us to success. Even the inevitable mistakes we make and failures we suffer are positive lessons that lead us closer to achieving our purpose. I have found it to be an amazing and mysteriously wonderful phenomenon.

I am a fairly rational and sensible person. I don't mean to get mystical on you, and I know it sounds crazy, but I honestly believe that when you have a strong mission or purpose in life and are passionately committed to it deep down in your soul, invisible forces in the universe—God, a Muse, perhaps your Guardian Angel—come to support you. People you never met and circumstances and opportunities you never could have imagined join together to help you, if not for the money, certainly for the mission. I have experienced this phenomenon far too many times for it to be coincidence.

Back to earthly delights, let's look at how disciplined thinking affects budgeting. Traditionally, a budget exists to decide how much money to apportion to a variety of activities and expenses. In the world of the hedgehog, disciplined thought is used to decide which areas should be fully funded and which *should not be funded at all*. The hedgehog doesn't give a little money to this and a little to that. He determines which activities support his Hedgehog Concept and fully funds those, and eliminates the rest entirely. Say you have a daughter, cousin, or niece named Suzy. Does little Suzy want a new pair of shoes? Does buying little Suzy new shoes support your Hedgehog Concept? No? Then tell little Suzy to get a job and buy her own shoes! Just kidding, but do you get the idea?

Sometimes it will take guts to focus your resources, financial and others, on one thing. The most effective investment strategy is a *non*-diversified portfolio *when you are right*. "When you are right" may at first sound a little iffy and dangerous. But knowing when you are right isn't that hard when you have all the pieces in place. You are likely to be right on the big decisions if:

1. You have your Hedgehog Concept
2. You have the right people on the bus
3. You confront the brutal facts of reality while maintaining faith
4. You make decisions based upon understanding (not false hopes or bravado)
5. You make your decisions and focus your activities and time in the framework of your Hedgehog Concept

Once you know the right thing to do, use your discipline and courage to do the right thing and *stop doing the wrong things.*

Once you have adopted this discipline of thought in your activities, others around you may see you as dull, no fun, or boring. But if they look a little deeper, they will see a person filled with passion, excitement, and stunning intensity.

Unfortunately, the world abounds with unhappy people. Those people (and many of them will be around you) don't like people who *are* happy. It makes them uncomfortable and envious. "Why are *you* so happy? What makes *you* so special?"—said in a sarcastic tone.

When they see you immersed in your work, they will notice your newfound energy and enthusiasm. And, much to their annoyance, they will see a very happy person having more fun than a human being should be allowed to have!

chapter 24

TECHNOLOGY MAY *NOT* BE THE ANSWER

If you read music and recording magazines or cruise musicians' sites on the Internet (as you absolutely should be doing every day to learn, learn, learn), you may be led to think that technology is everything these days. Buy this, buy that. You need the latest and the greatest. But the fact is, technology may *not* be the answer to finding success in the music business.

As a quick example, let's look at the Internet. How many people, how many bands, are selling boatloads of CDs on the Internet just because they have an Internet presence? The answer is zero. You can have thousands, even millions of people listen to your clips on MySpace.com or watch your videos on YouTube. But guess what? That alone is insufficient to sell thousands of CDs. A great deal more has to be present than just a strong Internet presence to actually *sell* CDs and see money flowing into your bank account.

But don't misunderstand. Technology is great and can be a crucial ingredient to your success. However, don't spend time and money on it just because everyone else is using it or because you are afraid of falling behind the pack. Develop your Hedgehog Concept first. Then tie your use of technology to your Concept. Let your Hedgehog Concept drive your use of technology, not the other way around. Don't let the glamour, glitz, and inflated promises of high tech cloud your vision. Use carefully selected technologies to fuel your economic engine. Don't jump on the bandwagon with everyone else because the media say this is the latest and greatest. The media are usually wrong. Those who tend to buy the latest and greatest usually find the technologies buggy and difficult to use. Only after the dust has settled over time do they begin to work properly.

If the technology isn't directly applicable to your Hedgehog Concept, you may not need it at all. If the technology is somewhat applicable, you may only need the bare essentials or a basic system. You may not need the most advanced system.

For example, spending a hundred grand on recording equipment may be great fun, but it won't make you a great guitarist. And, the cost of the equipment will set you back a hundred grand on your goal of making a million dollars playing the guitar.

People don't purchase the CDs of Madonna, U2, Mariah Carey, and other best-selling artists because of the recording equipment they use. Not that the equipment is unimportant, but it is secondary.

The hedgehog asks himself, "Will this purchase feed the fire of my economic engine? Will it pay for itself and then some in terms of how much money it puts into my bank account?" If the expense doesn't measure up, he rejects it.

Here is an entertaining but probably apocryphal story from the Internet that illustrates these points very well:

A jobless man went to apply for a job at Microsoft as a custodian cleaning lavatories. The manager there arranged for an "aptitude test." After successfully completing the test, the manager told him, "You're hired. You'll be paid $50 a day. Let me have your email address, so I can send you a form to complete and advise you when and where to report for work."

But the jobless man confessed he had neither a computer nor an email address. The Microsoft manager replied, "Well, to us that's like saying you don't exist. Sorry, we can't use you."

The man left. He had only $10 in his pocket. He went to a supermarket. He was looking around and suddenly an idea came to him. He bought a small crate of tomatoes. He found a spot near the supermarket and began selling his tomatoes, one at a time. In less than two hours he sold them all at a 100% profit. He did that three times that afternoon and returned home with $60. The jobless man had discovered capitalism. He wondered if he might be able to earn his living selling tomatoes.

Soon he bought a cart so he could transport several boxes of tomatoes at a time. After outgrowing that, he bought a pickup truck. Before he knew it, he owned a fleet of trucks and was managing a staff of formerly jobless people, just like he had been.

As his success grew, he thought about the future of his wife and children. He decided to buy some life insurance. He called an insurance broker, and selected a plan to fit his new circumstances. At the end of the telephone conversation, the broker asked him for his email address so he could forward the documentation for the policy.

You guessed it. Our tomato entrepreneur replied that he didn't use email. Stunned, the insurance broker said, "How can you not have email? How on earth have you managed to put together your operation without the Internet, email, and e-commerce? Do you know where you would be now if you had been computer savvy from the very start?"

After a moment's silence, our tomato tycoon replied: "Yeah, I do. I would've been a lavatory cleaner at Microsoft."

Moral of the story: the Internet, email, and e-commerce do not necessarily need to rule your life.

On the other hand, if a technology fits into your Hedgehog Concept, then yes, absolutely become a pioneer in the application of that technology. Once you identify which technologies are relevant, you will become fanatical and creative in applying those technologies to your Hedgehog Concept. But always keep in mind that your talent, your special gift, and what you can do better than anyone else in the world will be the most important things driving your career. You won't want to be a slacker in the use of technology, but for most people it will not be the primary driver on their road to making a million dollars playing the guitar. Indeed, thoughtless reliance on technology can be a liability, sucking up dollars, time, and energy.

The key is to avoid tech fads and bandwagons. Instead, be a pioneer in the use of *carefully selected* technologies. If a technology fits directly into the three elements of your Hedgehog Concept, go for it. If it doesn't, you can settle for parity with the rest of those in your field or ignore it entirely. Don't react to technological change and advances out of fear of being left behind or to stay up-to-date. In fact, "crawl, walk, run" can be a very good strategy when it comes to the adoption of technology. Respond with careful thought; pause, reflect, ask questions, gain understanding. And for you technophobes out there, you may have to face the brutal fact of reality that technology is indeed an important ingredient in your Hedgehog Concept. You will have to conquer your fear and reluctance to get into the tech arena. Just be sure to seek out the expertise of people who know what they're doing.

The point of this short chapter about technology is about perspective. Neither the Internet nor glitzy high-technology equipment will help you face the brutal facts of reality or instill resolute faith in yourself. No technology will help you shape your crucial Hedgehog Concept. No technology will help discipline you to adhere to your Hedgehog Concept. Technology might *accelerate* the progress of your career and the flow of money into your bank account, but technology itself will not create it.

Advances in technology can bring change, disruption, and unknown or unintended consequences. But we don't respond to the unknown with fear of being left behind or looking like a primitive Neanderthal. We don't react to what others around us are doing. We don't lurch about, desperately trying to keep up, hanging onto the technological bandwagon looking for the magic elixir. Instead, the hedgehog remains true to his fundamentals, gaining momentum, scooping up only what will feed that momentum, moving faster and faster with few stops or detours on his path to success.

chapter 25

IT'S A ROAD, NOT A RACETRACK

Time for another **REALITY CHECK:** The phrase is "road to success," not "racetrack to success" for a very good reason. Looking for a fast track to success in any field is usually a bad idea. Infomercials on television use the words "fast track" again and again. Does that tell you anything? Remember, your focus is on making your million dollars *over the course of your career.*

Don't be misled by commentators speaking about the overnight success of this artist or that artist. What might seem like overnight success to the casual observer is far from it. Over and over again you will hear the top artists in the music industry who have achieved phenomenal success (not the flash-in-the-pan types) say, "Oh yes. It took about ten years for me to become an overnight success." And the number ten is usually conservative.

One must also think about long-term financial returns. Typically, a young musician will struggle for years and then perhaps achieve significant success in his twenties or thirties. A pop artist might make an income of six or seven figures. But then musical tastes change, the artist ages, the fan base loses interest and wanes in numbers. The artist finds himself at age thirty or forty living on dwindling royalties and income after the go-go years. If he isn't careful, he may find himself in "The Cat Food Years." The career is gone, the money is gone, and all he can afford to eat is cat food.

Of course it doesn't have to turn out that way if the artist thinks ahead and prepares for the inevitable changes in his fan base. He will still have that bubble of success, but he can keep income coming in the rest of his life at a steady (albeit lower) rate. Simon Cann has a very good discussion on how to do this in his book, *Building a Successful 21st Century Music Career*.

Although I tend to marginalize it, it certainly *is* possible to become a real (but temporary) overnight success. A savvy marketing person or producer sees a singer (with negligible real talent) who has the right look or the right song, and turns him into a tremendous overnight success.

Unfortunately, that success has no foundation. The performer has no real talent or has just one song. The overnight success vanishes in a puff of smoke. If a person finds himself in this situation, careful management of the money he made could carry him through the rest of his life.

But historically, what happens most often is the person blows the money in a short time or mismanages it. He gets caught in a severe downward spiral of disappointment.

In happy endings, he is able to dust himself off, regroup, and work on developing a career with a real foundation (often not as a performer). In sad endings he drifts off into drugs, alcohol, or other means of self-destruction.

Achieving overnight success, and having it taken away from you just as quickly, is difficult for even the strongest to endure. Sound like I'm being overdramatic? The back alleys of the music world are littered with these unfortunate souls. And they come not just from the genre of pop music but the jazz and classical fields as well.

Enough doom and gloom. Let's stay off the racetrack. Instead, let's talk about flywheels. Yes, flywheels.

Imagine a huge metal disk (like a tire) mounted on an axle. That contraption is called a flywheel. Our disc is massive, weighing thousands of pounds. This flywheel is *your career*. Your job is to get the disc to move faster and faster and keep it spinning as fast and long as possible. Remember, the disc weighs thousands of pounds.

With great effort, you get it to move a few inches. Then you move it a few feet. After a while you actually have moved it a full turn. You keep pushing and pushing consistently in the same direction. You've moved it two turns. Then three, four.... You notice it beginning to gain a little momentum. It builds speed. Now you've turned it ten times, forty times, eighty times, a hundred. Eventually you feel the wheel working for you. Its momentum carries it along. You are pushing just as hard as on the very first turn, but the flywheel actually moves faster and faster. Each time the flywheel turns, it builds momentum on the effort you already put into it, seemingly compounding your investment of effort.

Suppose a reporter from a newspaper or television or radio station comes along and asks, "What was the one push that really got this thing moving?" You couldn't possibly answer the question. It was your cumulative, never-ceasing effort in the same direction that got it going and kept it going. Even if some pushes were more forceful than others, they were only a fraction of the overall effort that got the wheel moving and kept it moving.

That is exactly how your career will feel to you. There will be no single event, lucky break, CD, concert, competition, video, or killer innovation that you will identify as the thing that made everything happen for you. It will be a cumulative process. There will be many things, thousands of little pushes, that will move your flywheel slowly at first, then faster and faster.

To an outsider, your live appearance on "The Late Show with David Letterman" may look like overnight success. What they don't know is that you have been putting an unimaginable amount of effort into getting your flywheel to move, and have kept at it constantly to keep it moving, rotating it thousands and thousands of times before you arrived at the television studio. Of course for most of us our "overnight success" will not be as glamorous as a national television appearance. We will be very lucky if we are noticed by the national media at all. Fortunately it won't matter.

But regardless of what level you are on or shooting for, all your effort must be unceasing. Keep stirring the brew. Every action you take will produce a reaction. The action of promotion causes the reaction of interest. Creating interest over a period of time inevitably opens up opportunities and builds an audience. You may be a great singer. But if people don't know about you, if you don't build an audience, you will only be singing in the shower.

Let's recap. This is about the long haul, not about "The Big Break" or a few "Aha moments." Within the framework of our Hedgehog Concept, we will quietly and deliberately do what needs to be done to get the best results. We will plan, grow, evolve. Consistency and coherence are very important to the entrepreneurial guitarist. All the pieces will interlock, building upon one another. There may be a few big pushes on our flywheel, but they will be just that—a few. What will count are the thousands of additional pushes in a consistent direction over time that will keep our flywheel spinning and accumulating energy. That is what will send those million dollars into your bank account. Expect difficulties along the way. But, by maintaining strict adherence to your Hedgehog Concept and values, you will bounce back and emerge stronger after passing through those difficult times. Your flywheel will keep turning through it all.

chapter 26

WHAT EXACTLY AM I GOING TO DO TO EARN A LIVING?

MULTIPLE STREAMS OF INCOME

If you are lucky, by now you might have your Hedgehog Concept figured out and be engaged in mapping out your life strategy. But most of you are probably still in a fog. You know that playing the guitar or some part of the music world is your passion and you know it has to be your purpose in life. You can't imagine yourself doing anything else.

But you don't know yet what specific thing relating to the guitar and music is the one thing you can do better than anyone else on the planet (Part 1 of your Hedgehog Concept). That's okay. You are working on that. The fog will lift in the next several months. If you are young, it may take a year or two.

Right now, you must start bringing in some money. Look at your strengths and figure out what you can do right away to start pulling in income. You will earn that income from multiple sources. Even if you have formulated your Hedgehog Concept, you will need multiple streams of income to survive. This is especially true in the early stages of your career. One or two musical activities will probably not generate enough income to support yourself.

Most musicians should not think of a music career in terms of these general statements:

1. I will be a performer (doing performances and recording)
2. I will teach at a university
3. I will be a recording engineer
4. I will be a producer
5. I will be a composer
6. I will be a music teacher
7. I will be a record company exec
8. I will be a music publisher

Even if you have top-notch training in your field and are really good at it, chances are a record label, publishing company, or artist management/agency is not going to call you and say they want you on their label, or they want to have Reba McEntire record your songs, or they want to put you on a sixty-concert US tour.

After you get your doctoral degree in music, a university will not suddenly call to offer you a job. Any job opening at all will probably attract hundreds of applicants.

If you go to a recording school or get a degree in music production, jobs will not be waiting for you as soon as you hit the street. You might get a job as a "gofer" or receptionist at minimum wage or worse. Justin Timberlake isn't going to call you to produce his next CD.

If you are a pop composer, no one is going to call back after you've left them a message that you just wrote two dozen potential #1 hit songs. Film production companies aren't going to call after you've submitted your portfolio.

If you have a degree in music and master of business administration degree, you might be able to find an entry-level job at a publishing company or record company.

Get the idea? You won't find music biz types at job fairs. They won't be out there recruiting college graduates. This isn't like planning to be a doctor, lawyer, accountant, or other such profession. Those professions have fairly clear paths. The students do four years of undergraduate general studies in college. Then they get their masters and/or doctorate degrees. Perhaps they will do residencies or internships. They move on into their job. Musicians don't have the luxury of that type of clear career path. No job is waiting for them after their university and advanced studies. You, as a musician, will have thousands of potential paths you can take, all with different results.

You will have to send out feelers in many directions and figure out how to *build* your own career ladder, let alone climb it, to even get started. Unless you have a relative or good friend already working for a company in the music industry, it will be difficult to even get a grunt office job.

I WILL BE A PERFORMER

Let's look at "I Will Be a Performer" for example. In both the classical music field and popular music field, the number of people who can earn a living solely by performing and recording is infinitesimally small. Out of that number, few of them can sustain a career over their lifetime. On the pop side, most build their career over several years, then "hit it big." That lasts for a few years. Then their fan base and career go into decline fairly quickly. It takes quite a bit of skill and business acumen to maintain a career in popular music past the first big bubble of success.

But even the big-name performers (especially in the pop field) who produce a successful CD on a major record label, selling hundreds of thousands of copies, are lucky to break even on their CD and download sales. Most end up *owing* the record label significant amounts of money! I talk in detail about how that happens in Part Three, "Recording and Selling Your Own CDs."

But, by doing loads of gigs (they *have* to concertize to fuel CD and merchandise sales), selling other merchandise, and having other sources of income, they end up with enough profit to support themselves. The CD sales alone don't do it. If they only depended on CD sales, many would be bankrupt.

Therefore, not even big-name performers depend on one source of income. They will have income from:

- CD sales
- Downloads (iTunes, Rhapsody, and many others)
- Merchandise sales
- Songwriting royalties (which include mechanical royalties, performance royalties, synchronization fees)
- Live performances
- Sales of videos on DVD
- Sponsorships and endorsements
- Commissions from CD and DVD sales on Amazon.com (many artists receive more income here than royalties

from their record label)
- Ringtones

Then, each item above will produce multiple streams of income. For example, merchandise sales would include multiple streams of income from:

- Clothing such as T-shirts, sweatshirts, caps, jackets
- Calendars, souvenir books, programs, posters, photos, cookbooks
- Stationery, notebook covers, rulers, pens, pencils
- Coffee mugs, glasses, plates, decorative china
- Buttons, tote bags, mouse pads, coasters, refrigerator magnets, key chains
- Whatever you can imagine!

Many of the streams of income listed above will only be available to rather big-name performers. It will be up to you to figure out and develop your own multiple streams of income from your talent. Some of those streams may not directly relate to performing. You might have income coming in from teaching guitar lessons or working at a music store. You might be lucky enough to work a few hours a week in a recording studio as a "gofer" for minimum wage or less. But even if the pay is next to zero, it could be tremendous experience and generate valuable opportunities down the road. That is true of almost any job in the music biz. Just getting your foot in the door is a great step.

I WILL TEACH AT A UNIVERSITY

This is a big one for classical types. I teach guitar at the University of Missouri—Kansas City. In my discussions with students about what they want to do, many performance, theory, and composition majors say they want to teach at a university. That's fine, but unfortunately, thousands of students graduate every year from music schools around the country wanting to teach in universities. Very few full-time teaching positions are available. Even part-time positions are difficult to find.

If you are lucky enough to secure a part-time teaching position at a university, it won't pay enough to earn a living. Even if you get a full-time position, the entry-level pay may barely get you by. Music programs, and the performing arts in general, are at the bottom of the totem pole in university budgets. Depending on the school, sports teams are usually near the top of the list of priorities, along with the medical school, law school, technology programs, business schools, etc. Therefore, the pay scale for teaching positions is quite a bit lower in the music departments of universities than other departments.

All of this means that you will want to supplement your university teaching income. You will seek out multiple streams of income:

- If you are a performer, do some concertizing, make and sell CDs
- Teach privately in addition to university teaching
- Write and sell publications. You could write textbooks, books, teaching materials, or computer software programs for ear training, music history, or composition.
- Sell lectures on DVDs or for download

- Develop online courses for sale
- Open an online consulting service

These examples are very general in nature and by no means the only possibilities. And for the most part, these are activities you will pursue just to generate income on which to live. Your ultimate goal is to develop your Hedgehog Concept and come up with income-producing activities that fit your unique abilities. Then things will really start to click.

I AM GOING TO BE...

My point is that no matter what you think you want to do, especially until you develop your Hedgehog Concept (and perhaps afterward), you will most likely earn your living through multiple streams of income. Don't pigeonhole yourself into one category.

This is not a new concept. Christoph Wolff, in *Johann Sebastian Bach, The Learned Musician*, tells us that, as a child, Johann watched his father and big brother Balthasar engaged in all sorts of musical activities. Life "consisted not merely of teaching, practicing, rehearsing, and performing, but also of collecting and copying music, repairing and maintaining musical instruments, and other endeavors related to an extended music-business establishment."

One of the great things about today's new music industry is that the influence of the major labels, publishing companies, and entertainment conglomerates has been greatly reduced. For the small independent artist like yourself, that means far more opportunities are available for you to get your music or your products out to your audience. The big problem, of course, is that you have to know who your audience is and where they are. Books in the Recommended

Reading List on my website, MillionDollarGuitarist.com, will tell you more about that.

But these changes also mean your income will not come from just one or two sources. It will come from many sources. Some will pay well, others very little. But when you add them all together, suddenly you are actually earning a good living in music. With no or little overhead or middlemen, you will do quite well, especially when you keep those streams flowing over a long period of time.

Remember your insatiable thirst for knowledge? It was one of the Nine Questions to which you had to answer yes to have a good chance of success in the pursuit of your million dollars playing the guitar.

Well, the time has come for you to put that drive for knowledge to work. As you continue to hone in on your Hedgehog Concept, begin researching the fields in which you are interested. Start figuring out:

1. What you *want* to do
2. What you *can* do
3. How you will do it
4. What your strengths and weaknesses are
5. What potential streams of income can be tapped

Your Hedgehog Concept will eventually dictate all this to you. But until it crystallizes, think about what you can do right now to begin bringing in multiple streams of income.

Begin mapping out your goals and the steps necessary to achieve them. Keep adding to your lists of things to do, and opportunities to explore and pursue. Keep adding to and adjusting your plans as you learn more and hone your skills. Have your long-term goals, monthly goals, weekly goals, and daily goals written down and pursue them with persistent, ferocious resolve.

It's hardly ever too early to get started. I began teaching at the YWCA in St. Louis when I was thirteen. I started teaching privately the following year. I started playing gigs in bands around the same time. I started doing classical guitar gigs when I was fifteen.

If you are older, plunge in and get your feet wet as soon as possible. Enroll now in the school of hard knocks. The only caveat is not to try to take on something for which you are obviously unprepared. You don't want to make a fool of yourself and potentially temporarily damage your career. But begin learning right now from the greatest teacher of them all—experience.

This book does not discuss the various general fields of the music business. Other books survey that quite well. Check them out in the Recommended Reading List on my website, MillionDollarGuitarist.com. You will have to do the intense, detailed research into your area of interest on your own. The possibilities are endless. Few rules will get in your way. A prescribed career ladder to climb does not exist. You build your own ladder and decide where to place it. You start climbing. You may have to move your ladder several times. You may have to rebuild it.

Keep the right mindset. Maintain a positive mental attitude, go deep for knowledge, pursue every opportunity, and learn from failures. Keep your multiple streams of income (both short and medium-term) coming in to support you while you pursue your bigger career goals. Relentlessly pursue your dream with white-hot desire. You should be fine.

PART THREE: Recording and Selling Your Own CDs

chapter 27

DO-IT-YOURSELF VS. COMMERCIAL STUDIOS

I want to offer what I think is valuable advice about recording, and the production and selling of CDs. This information is not generally found in other books. Although I think my information will be helpful, by no means is it comprehensive, so don't depend on my information alone. These are just a few of my thoughts and opinions.

Before we begin, let's be clear that just because you produce a CD, even a great one, doesn't mean you will have a music career. Also, keep in mind that for many, producing a CD may not be relevant to your Hedgehog Concept. But if it is, keep reading.

At one time, the only option for a musician wanting to make a CD was to use a commercial recording studio. But things have changed dramatically. Today with computer-based recording software, you can set up a high-performance studio in your home.

You can record at home at your leisure. What convenience! And, you have total control over everything. Plus, you know your music better than anyone. You know the sound you want. At home, you can do take after take, fuss over everything as much as you want. You can take all the time you want to experiment with mics and mic placement. You can spend hours tweaking an effect. The extra time won't cost you a dime. When you pay by the hour at a commercial recording studio, time goes so fast, it feels like you are flushing money down a toilet. You also are paying for overhead and for services you don't use or really need. Why would you go to a commercial recording studio and pay thousands upon thousands of dollars when you can do it at home for a fraction of that, and end up with an equally good if not better-sounding product? And once you've invested in the equipment, the cost of recording each CD goes down, down, down.

Sounds good, doesn't it? Well, as with many things, most issues have two sides. Here are some more things to consider.

I am a classical guitarist. When I record, I'm the only one in the studio. Recording a solo classical guitar is much simpler logistically than a production with singers or several instruments, especially percussion. You may need more physical space than you have at home.

Your space at home may be comfortable and quiet, but is it isolated from outside noises? Most commercial studios have excellent sound isolation. Basements work well if you turn off the AC or furnace while you record. Some musicians remodel their garage to serve as a studio, but that can get expensive since you need heat/AC and sound insulation.

You will also need a way to isolate the computer and any other noise-producing equipment from the recording area. Put the equipment somewhere behind a wall or in a cool (cool as in temperature) closet or separate room. Run the cables into the recording area. You can buy extension cables for your computer monitor, mouse, keyboard, etc.

Your room at home must also be superb acoustically. Commercial studios invest many thousands of dollars to make their rooms acoustically perfect for recording. Controlling reflected sounds such as standing waves, flutter echoes, and low-frequency room modes is the key to turning the worst-sounding room (which is what most people start with at home) into a room good enough to yield world-class sound.

Sound is controlled by the use of sound absorption and diffusion. Auralex Acoustics (and other companies) produces room acoustical treatment products to fine-tune your studio. The great thing about Auralex is that you can send them a diagram of your space with your written details about the wall, floor, and ceiling construction and they will send back a free analysis. They will recommend acoustical treatments to make it a viable recording studio. Or, for $250, you can use their Room Analysis Plus. You record a frequency sweep in the room and send the wave file to Auralex for them to do an in-depth analysis of your space.

Another downside to recording at home is that you don't have outside input (although you can get others' opinions later). If for some reason you *aren't* a good judge of your sound and style, you might not end up with a good recording if you do it yourself. Nor will you have that buzz of working in a "real" studio. Another downside is the danger of overperfectionism where you just keep futzing with the recording at home and never quite finish. In the commercial studio, you will usually have a certain amount of time during which you *must* complete the project.

A home studio requires that you deal well with the tech side of music and computers. Even though I had no clue about any of it when I started, I am fascinated by tech stuff now and deal quite well with it. I even actually enjoy reading the manuals to all the hardware and software. I'm probably one of the few people on the planet who finds reading a tech manual as compelling as a novel by Vince Flynn. When I get stuck with a problem, I also actually enjoy calling tech support.

You will experience the phenomenon of left-brain/right-brain conflicts when you record. The left side of the brain deals with the tech side of recording and the right side deals with the creative part of performing and making music. Some people have a tough time during the recording session going back and forth between the two. But it really isn't difficult. Just get everything set up in advance and when it comes time to record, hit the red button and immerse yourself in the music. You don't need to worry about the computer and equipment. They will function fine on their own. Just let go.

But some people really struggle with it. They would rather leave the tech stuff to the professionals. They prefer the commercial studio where all they have to do is perform.

Commercial studios are not a waste of money or a thing of the past. Far from it. The good ones do a fabulous job. But I have found that many have staff that know their equipment and the tech side, but really can't hear. They are engineers, not musicians. At worst, they are failed, incompetent, or untalented former musicians. They are unable to hear or discriminate between subtle details. Or, their idea of what you should sound like is very different from yours. When that is the case, you are in for an uncomfortable session of tension, dissatisfaction, and arguments. You will be paying a great deal of money for headaches and frustration.

From the money standpoint, if you get good equipment and know how to use it, putting together your own home studio can be a good idea. If you crank out several CDs over a period of time to amortize the cost, the costs of production will be next to nothing, and your profit per CD exceptionally high. If you do it right, all the money you spend on equipment and setting up your studio will soon be flowing back into your own wallet.

chapter 28

BUYING EQUIPMENT

As I have mentioned, I teach the classical guitar at the Conservatory of Music and Dance, University of Missouri—Kansas City. In the late 1990s, we faculty were given computers for our offices. I had no interest in computers at all. People would continually tell me about all kinds of things you could do on a computer. My standard response was, "Shakespeare and Beethoven didn't have computers. They did just fine." In fact, I don't think I turned it on for at least a year or two. I used it to stick those yellow Post-It notes on.

One day Rick Abate, one of my students, said, "You know, Doug, you can record on your computer." My eyes lit up and I said, "Really?" He went on to explain how it worked and how easy and fairly basic it would be to record just a solo guitar. And he told me about Cakewalk Pro Audio 9 (now Sonar) and Pro Tools recording software. I went to the bookstore and started reading audio recording magazines and computer magazines. I learned to access the Internet.

I had another former student, Scott Gregory, who worked in the recording studio at the Conservatory. He advised me on my first purchases of an audio interface and headphones. And, he told me about

a company called Sweetwater. Sweetwater is one of the premier suppliers in the world of serious audio recording equipment. They have
knowledgeable staff (they call them sales engineers) and stand behind
their products.

Scott's telling me about Sweetwater cost me thousands of dollars
in equipment purchases. But it was money well spent. It resulted in a
payoff of many more thousands of dollars from the sales of the CDs I
recorded on that equipment.

Let me tell you a little side story that illustrates a good way to shop
for equipment:

> From the age of thirteen, I dreamt about one day own-
> ing a Neumann microphone. All the great classical gui-
> tarists and other musicians from the 1950s on seemed to
> use Neumanns. I loved how they looked—so serious and
> professional. But they were expensive and far out of my
> price range. With my money from teaching guitar classes
> at the YWCA in St. Louis, the best I could do at the time
> was to buy a Shure SM-57. Back then, the 57 probably cost
> about sixty dollars.
>
> But many years later, and enjoying a much better in-
> come than I had teaching at the YWCA, I was holding the
> Sweetwater catalog in front of me. There were pages and
> pages of microphones. There were at least two pages of
> nothing but my coveted Neumanns. Which one should I
> get? How could I possibly decide?
>
> Easy. I asked my sales engineer to send me one of al-
> most every Neumann they carried—tens of thousands of

dollars' worth of microphones. I charged them to one of my credit cards.

I was able to test all these great mics, record with them, and do A/B comparisons. It took a couple weeks and hundreds of tracks. I kept the Neumann TLM 170 R's and returned the rest. No problem, no restocking fees. My credit card was fully credited for the value of the mics I returned.

A couple years later, I did the same thing with mic preamps and studio monitors. You *have* to try the stuff out in your own space to know how it sounds. You certainly can't go by catalog or magazine or Internet hype.

Personally, I would invest more money on the analog components of your system: mics, mic preamps, speakers, and analog-to-digital converters. The quality of those components can significantly elevate the quality of your recording. Over time, their manufacture and engineering will change very little and they can be used for many years. On the other hand, computers, digital work surfaces, and recording software change and are upgraded by their manufacturers frequently. But, they don't significantly affect the quality of your sound. Spending money on them results in far less improvement of your recordings.

One word of caution: don't overdo the equipment thing. Spending a hundred thousand dollars on equipment will not make you a great guitarist. In fact, the more talented someone is, the less they need the latest and greatest. Author Hugh MacLeod (*Ignore Everybody*) quips, "Meeting a person who wrote a masterpiece on the back of a deli menu would not surprise me. Meeting a person who wrote a masterpiece with a silver Cartier fountain pen on an antique writing table in an airy SoHo loft would seriously surprise me." He goes on, "A fancy tool just gives the second-rater one more pillar to hide behind. Which is why there are so many second-rate art directors with state-of-the-art Macintosh computers."

Having cooled your acquisition fever somewhat, let's return to outfitting your studio. You can spend an endless amount of money on electronics. In general, the first one to three thousand dollars per item are well worth it for good mics, preamp, studio monitors (speakers), analog/digital converter, etc. Beyond that, however, an extra thousand or two will get you a better piece of equipment, but it will only be a *little* better. As you spend more and more, the improvement in your final recording becomes incrementally smaller and smaller. Spend what you must to get the job done, but don't overdo it. Otherwise, it will take much longer and many more CD sales to turn a profit. You won't make your first million dollars if you spend all your money on fancy equipment.

Be certain to insure your recording equipment too. Because you are using it for your business, it probably won't be covered under your basic household or renter's insurance policy. Shop around for the best rate but be sure the policy offers solid coverage without a bunch of loopholes. The insurance premiums you pay to cover your business equipment are tax-deductible on Schedule C of your tax return.

You may have a spouse, parent, boyfriend, girlfriend, or other doubting Thomas who may have a big problem with your spending $2,000 on a microphone. A strategy around this is to explain that the new microphone is an *income-producing asset.* "No, honey, we can't afford to buy you those new shoes today. I need to get that Avalon mic preamp. It will give me a better sound for my vocals and we will sell more CDs. The Avalon is an investment, an *income-producing asset*. When the money starts to come in from the CD sales, we can buy all the shoes you want." Or for you female artists out there, "No, sweetheart, we'll have to wait on that hunting/fishing gear or big-screen HDTV, or Jet Ski. I need to get that Apogee converter to clean up the high end on my guitar. My recordings need to be high quality to sell commercially. Remember, the Apogee will be an *income-producing asset*."

Don't you love it? But actually, this is a financially sound philosophy. Boats, fashionable clothes, furniture, appliances, hunting gear, dirt bikes—yes, they are all very nice but they don't directly produce income. If you are going to spend money, spend it on something that will *produce more money*, not eat it up. The entrepreneurial guitarist doesn't spend money unless he must. He doesn't buy anything until he knows where the money is coming from to pay for it. But when he does make a purchase, he makes certain the money spent generates much *more* money in return.

You may be thinking, "But Doug, if I get on a good record label, won't they set me up in their own state-of-the-art studio or send me to an independent top-notch studio and pay for the cost of the recording? Why not do that and skip buying all my own stuff?"

Read on, my friend...

WHY YOU DON'T WANT TO SIGN WITH A MAJOR LABEL

First, let me repeat that this book is directed toward those who are driven by a guitar- or music-related mission, and want to earn a million dollars over the long haul. My advice is not targeted at those whose lives are driven by a need for superstardom. My recommendations are not directed to those whose self-worth and self-image are determined by their having to be on a major label or represented by major management.

Not that anything is wrong with those goals—if that is what you want, by all means go for it. I had those goals for many years when I was young. But as I grew older, I realized I didn't really have the "right stuff" for that kind of career. I also realized there were ways to succeed financially that were better suited to me. If you are going for broke to fill huge arenas and sell millions of CDs, all power to you. I don't want to turn you off to the idea of getting a major record deal if that's what you want and really believe you can get. Don't let me or anyone else tell you that you can't do it.

However, in case the major record label deal doesn't work out, I want to show you viable alternatives to achieve success. These alternatives will lead to success on their own, or in tandem with an audacious goal such as record label stardom.

The guitar can be used to achieve success in ways that provide tremendous satisfaction with few strings attached (sorry). Your friends and family may never see your face on *People* magazine or the Letterman show; but if your guitar playing provides you a good, steady living, you may find that achieving fame isn't as important as you thought it was. Regardless of whether you become famous or not, making a living with the guitar is a beautiful thing.

For reasons I will explain, 99.9% of us will receive far better financial rewards by recording our own CDs and promoting and selling them ourselves. Our goal is to sell a high volume of CDs *over a long period of time*, not to try to have a blockbuster, overnight, mega-hit CD.

Getting involved with a large label will usually result in your forgoing tens of thousands of dollars in net income just so you can impress people by being on a major label. If you decide to go that direction, you must understand the label's mindset. When an exec talks about a "good CD," he is talking about one that has mass appeal, sells hundreds of thousands of copies, and therefore will make a bundle of money for his company. Unless you can translate it into dollars, he isn't interested in art or your creative freedom and process. Record labels think and speak "money," and you have to speak their language.

One of the best books about the music business, especially the nitty-gritty of contracts, fees, licenses, royalties, and just how everything really works, is *Music, Money, and Success* by Jeffrey and Todd Brabec. One of the most enlightening and sobering chapters is the one titled "Music, Money, and the Recording Artist." If you have any thoughts about going for the big deal, you absolutely have to read that chapter or you could get into big trouble.

Major labels use high-priced attorneys to draft recording contracts that run from 20 to over 100 pages. The contract is written for one purpose: to protect the record company at all costs. Depending on how the contract is written, it is not unusual for two different artists to each sell one million CDs and reach #1 on the charts, with one receiving royalties of over a million dollars and the other less than $10! An artist with identical sales can even end up with a debit balance—owing the record company over $100,000.

If you sign with a label, yes, they will foot the bill for all the costs of recording, graphic design, photography, packaging, manufacturing, marketing, promotion, distribution, etc. You won't have to come up with any money up front. They might even kick in several thousand dollars for living expenses. Sounds great, doesn't it? It's called your "advance."

But guess what? You have to pay it back. And, you don't pay it back gradually, or when it's convenient for you. All of those costs (and many more) are recouped by the label out of income from CD sales *before* you receive a dime. Only about 5% of artists releasing a CD on a major label will earn enough money from CD sales to reimburse the record label for the advances. That means 95% see absolutely no income from their work—not one penny—and will actually owe the label a sizable portion of the money the label advanced to record and promote the CD. Because of the accounting methods they use, if and when any profit comes rolling in, you will see little of it make its way into your checking account. It may be years (if ever) before you will see a dime of income from your efforts.

In addition to the financial side, artistic considerations must also be taken into account. The label will probably dictate what you will record and how you record it, and have final say on the overall design, title, layout, and content of your CD.

REALITY CHECK: You will probably not be signed by a major label. If you do get signed, the chances are very slim that you will make any money from your CD.

Contrast that with producing and marketing your CD yourself. No one will tell you what songs you can record and how they should sound. You will be responsible for the final appearance and content of your CD. With even moderate success, you will likely make a very nice profit from your efforts. This profit will be in the form of dollars in your checking account within days, not years after the release of your CD. You will not have to worry about being stiffed by complex contracts and entertainment lawyers. In fact, unless you become a "name" artist, you won't need to deal with agents, managers, or lawyers—yours or theirs, except on a very minimal basis. In the end, you will likely make at least five to ten times more money doing it yourself as being with a label.

Granted, plenty of people believe you aren't a real recording artist unless you are on a label. Let's face it: if someone asks your wife or girlfriend what you do for a living and they say you're a musician, the assumption is you are just another starving artist without a real job (or probably delivering pizzas at night). They probably assume your wife or girlfriend is supporting you while you're at home all day watching TV and playing your guitar. If you do begin to achieve some success, the friends will say, "Oh wow. Maybe now he can get on a real label and get his CDs in stores." They may even think that since your CD isn't in stores, it must not be very good. Those people are just ignorant of the modern music business.

If you are a professional in today's music business, you're intent is to make money. Unless you are a household name, you won't make money having someone else (a record label) release your CD or even distribute it. You will not make money having your CDs sold in stores on consignment, which is essentially what even the big labels do—the record company receives no payments until the CDs are actually sold. Sure, you might get lucky and have Wal-Mart or Best Buy carry your CDs nationally. Sure, you can ship out 5,000, 10,000 or 50,000 of your CDs so all the stores across the country have your CDs. Jeez, your wife's or girlfriend's friends will really be impressed. *Your* friends will be impressed. Just don't tell them six months later that 4,900, or 9,000, or 45,000 of those CDs didn't sell and were returned to you (at your expense, of course) and are now sitting in a warehouse. And hope that no one asks why you no longer park your cars in the garage—yes, your garage is now filled floor to ceiling with those unsold units! Remember, the same thing would likely happen if the CDs were shipped by a major label. The only difference would be that they would be sitting in the major label's warehouse, not yours. The "Returns Clause" in contracts with major labels is a work of art in itself. See *Music, Money, and Success* for the details of how it works.

I can't emphasize enough that in many instances, the pursuit of recording for a major label is an exercise in vanity—a pursuit of missing self-esteem and status. Yes, artists such as Britney Spears and Madonna are raking in the dough through their royalties. Good for them. I sincerely congratulate them on their success. But, for the vast majority of recording artists on major labels, the royalties are a joke. The pittance of money most artists receive from their label is outrageous and scandalous. The music and movie industry use "Hollywood" accounting to determine the royalties payable to their artists. They manage to define "net profit" in such a way that rarely does any remain to divide up.

Keep in mind that huge changes are shaking up the traditional music business. CD sales in general are plummeting and many brick-and-mortar stores have closed, leading to more downturns in sales. That is all the more reason not to split your CD's sale price with middlemen, distributors, and retailers. Unless you are the next Michael Jackson, Bono, or Madonna, producing and distributing your CD yourself is a great way to go. Making a CD isn't that difficult or complicated. You have a real chance to actually make real money doing it. And you can start today.

Another possibility to consider is to sell single tracks via services such as iTunes, instead of a complete CD. The major labels are experimenting with a variety of strategies. Some offer digital singles only. Some launch a pre-release campaign, offering singles before the official CD release date, to generate buzz. Some big-name artists offer complete CDs only; no singles, no digital downloads.

The results suggest that any of these strategies has the potential to produce good sales. The best strategy depends on the music and the artist. Obviously, an unknown artist or one with a small following will use a different strategy from the name artist with a large, loyal fan base. Keep your mind open to the various options.

Spending considerable money and time to record and manufacture a complete CD, with beautiful artwork and your lovely countenance on the cover, may *not* be the best way to go. Instead, selling individual downloads may be the most economical and profitable way to distribute your music.

Many books and articles are available about how to record your own CD or tracks. I have recommended several in my Recommended Reading List on my website, MillionDollarGuitarist.com. Recording your own tracks will require some ingenuity on your part. We have already discussed investing in your own recording studio versus renting a professional studio. You could possibly find a friend, or friend of a friend, who has top-notch equipment to do the recording for you. If you are attending a college or university, you could probably use their recording facility fairly inexpensively.

One way or another, recording the CD will cost you a sizable amount of money. But keep in mind that all costs of producing the CD (recording, graphic design, photography, packaging, manufacturing) are tax-deductible and will be amortized over the total number of CDs manufactured. In other words, if you spend $10,000 to produce the CD and have 2,000 CDs manufactured, the cost is only $5 per CD. If you sell that batch and manufacture more, the cost per CD continues to decline. Producing a CD for well under $5 per unit is not difficult. You will sell it for at least twice that and all the profit will be yours! Sell just 1,000 CDs per year for a measly $10 per CD. At $5 profit per CD, you have made $5,000. No, you can't live on that, but the money from your CD sales is another stream of income that, when added to others, will enable you to make your million dollars playing the guitar. Plus, your profit per CD will rise with each reprinting, until the cost per CD is $3 or under. If you price it at $12.99 you will make a $10 profit per CD! You will *never* make $10 per CD in royalties from a commercial label.

One more time: if you have the potential to be a household name and hit it big, a major label will certainly be worth everything it can provide for you, the good far outweighing the bad. But if you aren't going to be the next Michael Jackson or Sting, the pursuit of a major label deal just isn't worth the trouble and aggravation. Go the independent route and actually earn some money.

PART FOUR: Good Business Procedures for All Musicians

NUTZ 'N' BOLTZ BUSINESS BASICS

This is not an in-depth discussion of operating a music business. This is some basic, valuable information of particular interest to the entrepreneurial guitarist.

WORKING OUT OF YOUR HOME

As a guitar entrepreneur, you will probably work out of your home. These days, depending on where you live, homes associations can be a real annoyance. Read your homes association bylaws about operating a business out of your home and comply with the rules. Things such as the number of deliveries, number of visitors per day, parking, etc. are sometimes regulated. To ward off potential problems, getting a business license from your city is a good idea. Usually, they cost less than $50. You may not have any problems, but if a neighbor complains about a truck delivery or two, you can tell them you are licensed by the city to operate your business out of your home. Same thing if you are teaching students.

You will be using a home office. Space dedicated to your home office is deductible on Schedule C of your tax return. Measure the square footage of your home office space and the total square footage of your dwelling. Figure the percentage of space devoted to your home office. This is done by dividing your business-use square footage by the total square footage of the dwelling. For instance:

600 sq. ft. business use ÷ 1700 total sq. ft. of dwelling
= .3529 = 35% business use

In this example, your home office is 35% of your total square footage. Therefore, you can deduct 35% of your rent or mortgage on your tax return. You can also deduct 35% of your utility bills and other expenses associated with your residence.

Just remember, the portion of your dwelling you are calling your home office *must be used exclusively for your business.* The space you use does not have to be a separate room. If you are using part of your bedroom, the space in square feet occupied by your bed or bedroom furniture cannot be figured into the equation. Closing off the non-business space with a partition is unnecessary. Just don't count it in your business square footage.

In a former home, almost my entire basement was used as a recording studio, the dining room as my teaching room, a bedroom as a practice/warm-up room for students, and another bedroom as an office/computer room. I figured all of those spaces into my home office deductions. I was able to deduct nearly half of all my house expenses!

Sometimes the tax code is a beautiful thing. Just remember to be accurate and honest. Don't mess with the IRS.

You may need to collect sales tax on various items that you sell. Contact your state agency (usually a division of the department of revenue) about what you should do.

YOUR BUSINESS NAME

You can operate under your own name or come up with a company name. I once thought (and in the back of my mind must admit I still do) people wouldn't take me seriously if I just operated under my own name. Today, since everyone seems to be in business for themselves on the Internet, operating under your own name carries no stigma. But if you want to use a company name that doesn't include your real name, you will have to register your company name with your state (usually the office of the Secretary of State). You will fill out a form with your real name and address and the name of your new company or your fictitious name. It usually costs less than $200 (in Missouri, where I live, it costs less than $20). Some states don't even require it. But check to be sure.

Some guitarists just starting out pick some grandiose-sounding name. You will probably look foolish, or possibly attract lawsuits because your name sounds like you are a large, anonymous company with loads of money. Some people don't think twice about cheating a large corporation. But rarely will they try to take advantage if they know you are just an individual trying to earn a living. This can be important if you take credit card orders or accept checks. If you want to use some sort of company name instead of your own name, be certain it has not been trademarked. Also be certain the name is not being used by someone else, especially within the music business.

YOUR BUSINESS ADDRESS

What address should you use for your company/business? This is actually kind of tricky. Your initial thought will be to use your home address. It's convenient. The problem is, you must be very careful about putting that address on your CDs or other merchandise. If you move to a different address, the old address will be on your merchandise forever unless on the next merchandise order you have the address corrected. That's a pain and expensive. I recommend you include contact information on your merchandise, but maybe use just your website and/or email address—those are unlikely to change.

As a physical address for your general business dealings, a post office box is probably the best solution. Assuming you stay in the same city, it won't change. It also gives you a bit of anonymity to prevent kooks from coming to your house. Be sure *you* are the renter of the post office box so you have total control over it. If for some reason you hire someone to do your fulfillment of orders (which is usually a bad idea), do *not* allow them to rent a post office box or use their company post office box to receive *your* orders. If the box is in their name and you fire them, unless they are cooperative, you can't get the post office to forward your mail (all those customer orders) to a different address—you are stuck if things get nasty. Rent a post office box in your name and give them a key.

INC. ??

The sole proprietorship is the cheapest and easiest way to run a business. Most self-employed people choose it to operate their business. The biggest drawback of the sole proprietorship is its lack of legal protection. Sole proprietors have unlimited liability, which means if your business is sued, your creditors can come after both your business assets *and* your personal assets: your home, your car, your guitar…everything!

For that reason, many small business owners are using a business structure called the Limited Liability Company or LLC. In most states, an LLC is fairly easy and cheap to set up. Its tax treatment is very flexible. Most importantly, an LLC will protect your personal assets from most claims against the business. In addition, the LLC has a second layer of liability protection that shields the business from any personal lawsuits launched against you.

For most entrepreneurial guitarists, incorporating is not necessary or desirable. A corporation doesn't have the built-in liability protection of an LLC. Most self-employed guitarists would pay more taxes under a corporate structure than as an LLC or sole proprietorship. Setting up a corporation and maintaining corporate records is also much more complicated.

As with everything else, do your research. Check out my Recommended Reading List on my website, MillionDollarGuitarist.com, and then meet with an attorney to discuss your options.

YOUR TELEPHONE

Always return emails and telephone calls the same or next business day. Do *not* put stupid messages on your cell phone or business answering systems. If I call someone with an opportunity and their cell phone "I'm not here" message is an impersonation of some character, awful music, or inarticulate rambling, I hang up and call someone else. You want to give the impression you're a professional and have your act together. I assume you practice your guitar skills in order to get the best results possible. Do the same with your telephone talking skills as well.

Try to keep a permanent phone number so you don't have to change your promo materials every time your phone number changes. Also, if someone calls you a year or two later with an opportunity, and your phone number has changed, you lose the gig—it could have been a very important gig. They probably won't spend time trying to track you down. In addition, you don't want a phone number answered by your little brother or sister, grandmother, or hung-over roommate. Get a separate number with an answering service, voicemail, or answering machine. A cell phone is great if it works with dependable service and reception. You don't want to miss a single call.

BUSINESS STATIONERY

Thirty years ago, having business stationery with a good letterhead and even a logo was important. Most correspondence was handled by snail mail and your letterhead said a lot about you and helped communicate your image. Today, most communications are done by phone and email. But you still need adequate company stationery. You can make it on your computer. You don't need some silly logo. Keep it simple. Spending time and money on fancy stationery is like using a grandiose company name. You are probably operating out of your basement or your bedroom closet, right? Focus on turning out professional work. If you are going to be a professional, be real. Don't pretend to be professional by imitating others or spending your money on window dressing. Yes, looks are important, but if your money is limited, spend it on the look of your CD, not your stationery.

EMAIL ADDRESS

You will probably have a website. Most website hosting services provide you with a nearly unlimited number of email accounts. The addresses will read as JohnDoe@Widgets.com or Info@Widgets.com. Use these accounts for your business email. They sound more professional than John@hotmail.com.

Also, use an email "signature" for all outgoing mail. This signature is not the handwritten kind. It is a few lines at the end of your message stating your company name and contact information. You can also include a line, "Visit my website at www.Widgets.com". You can even include a graphic of a company product or logo. Or, you could include a short line about your new CD. Keep the signature as short and concise as possible so that people can read it at a glance. Don't make it a press release!

chapter 31

YOUR WEBSITE

Just as thousands of marketing wizards are pitching countless schemes for selling your products, thousands of website designers/optimizers are on the web ready to help you part with your hard-earned dollars. They all guarantee instant success if you follow their advice or use their services. Some of what they offer may work for you; much of it won't. In truth, no surefire methods exist to optimize your website and guarantee astounding, instant success.

But, knowing a variety of basic principles will at least get you on the playing field. First, you do *not* need a fancy website to have a successful website. In fact, complex websites take longer to load, and can have difficulty displaying properly on all browsers. They are also more difficult to maintain and update. I recommend that you keep things simple enough that you can regularly update it yourself and can easily add important content. Be sure visitors don't get frustrated or sidetracked by complex graphics. Keep navigation simple and straightforward.

And, do *not* listen to friends or your kids telling you your site isn't cool enough. "Cool" will probably not be too important for most entrepreneurial guitarists. Your goal is not to have people leave your website thinking, "Wow, that was a cool site. Neat graphics." What you want is a site that will sell your stuff. That's the whole purpose: to sell your stuff. Don't distract your visitors. Motivate them to buy your stuff.

As I mention in the next chapter, "Selling Stuff on the Internet," you will probably want to use your own website to sell your product directly to your customers. Any time you involve a middleman or use a service, it will cost you money, thereby reducing your profits. For example, even though Amazon.com provides reliability and good service, it takes a big cut out of your sales. Therefore, you probably won't want to use them as your main sales outlet.

You do not have to pay someone thousands of dollars to build your website. Do it yourself! Hundreds of companies such as Network Solutions and Yahoo provide template websites. They can have a bit of a cookie-cutter appearance, but are good for beginners because they require little expertise to construct, run, and maintain. They charge anywhere from $18 a month to well over $100 a month depending on the features you need and the space required. Keep in mind that sample MP3s from your CDs or video clips take up a good chunk of website space (although you can put your videos on YouTube.com if you like). Microsoft offers FREE websites on OfficeLive.com (but they put ads for other products on your site). They also offer site options without advertising and with more features, for which you pay a monthly fee.

I am certainly no expert on website design. I do not intend to tell you how to create one. Thousands of books and web articles about website design are available, all of which need to be updated hourly (!) to be totally helpful. (Most books and articles having anything to do with computers have a very short shelf life.)

Having said that, even though it was published back in 2005, I strongly recommend a book titled *Call to Action: Secret Formulas to Improve Online Results* by Bryan and Jeffrey Eisenberg.

They cover many basic principles that do not change by the hour.

Their main point is that driving traffic to your site in large numbers is not the important thing. The number of visitors is irrelevant. What you want are sales. You want income. You want to increase your *conversion rate*. "Conversion" is the process by which a visitor is induced to take action: to buy products, subscribe to newsletters, contact the business, sign up for a mailing list, etc. For us entrepreneurial guitarists, it means getting visitors to buy our products, not to admire our cool website. Having a cool website with fabulous graphics and doodads may look great and may generate a large number of visitors. But again, that does not translate into making money. Conversion alone translates into making dollars flow into our bank account. Conversion is a separate animal and must be tamed on its own. For that reason, *Call to Action* is an important book to read, have in your library, and reread every few months.

We know the cool factor is not that important. Many books address the usability of a website. But even that is not as important as getting your visitors to *take the action* you want them to take. *Call to Action* gives you practical advice that produces results. Overstock.com increased their conversion rate by 5% by fixing just one thing the authors recommended. You should be able to recover the cost of the book in just a couple days by following one or two of its simple, practical suggestions. Here are just three small examples from their book.

EXAMPLE #1:

Focus on helping your visitor get in, buy, and get out quickly:

- Make it obvious which button to click.
- Be sure each button or link is made up of as few words as

possible that complete the sentence "I want to ____."
• Don't make them "Click Here"

Have the button specify:

"I want to listen to ____."
"I want to read more about ____."
"I want to see a sample of ____."
"Order CD now."
"I want to ask a question."
"Sign me up for your mailing list."
"Sign me up for your newsletter."
Visitors don't want to hunt for things. "Order CD now" is
   not pushy. It's a clear message for those busy visitors who
   want clarity, ease, and efficiency.

EXAMPLE #2:

Hundreds of things can be done to improve your website and conversion rate. Many are obvious and can be made immediately. And
they cost nothing! Others are more subtle and need to be tested. The
best strategy is to change only one parameter at a time. If you change
a bunch of things at once, and you have an increase in sales, you will
be very pleased with yourself. But unfortunately, you won't really know
which changed parameter had the most impact. If sales go down, likewise you won't know precisely why. Plus, in making several changes at
once, a few negative changes could have diluted a change that on its
own would have been very positive. But you won't know it! So, make a
change and analyze the results. If sales go up, make another change.

Analyze. If sales go down, undo that second change and try something new. That way, you are always improving your conversion rate. And again, all this costs you nothing if you have a simple site that you can tweak on your own, rather than paying another person or service to do it for you.

Remember, *results* are what count. What you think *ought* to work doesn't matter. You simply have to do more of what produces sales and less of what doesn't. What *should* work is not important. What *does* work is what you use.

EXAMPLE #3:

Watch people navigate through your site to purchase an item. Sit next to them and watch—don't say anything to them, help them, or give them guidance of any kind as they go through the shopping process. If you do this with three or four different people, you will be amazed at what you learn, and will come away with a long list of things you should change. You created the site, so you think everything is quite obvious: how to navigate through the site, what to click on, how to find items, etc. But believe me, others will not move through the site as you would expect them to. Time and time again, you will watch in disbelief as they take routes you never would have anticipated, and in so doing, they will get lost or discouraged.

Another topic the book strongly emphasizes is testing and metrics. The Eisenbergs admonish us that all of the basic elements of a website such as buttons and background colors are important. Every word is important. Most people think of these as small design decisions. But you cannot ignore anything. All of these elements are part of what the Eisenbergs call your persuasion architecture. No detail is too small. Everything on your site and every part of your shopping cart either adds to or detracts from its ability to convert your visitors. They recommend testing everything. Measure, test, and optimize for conversion.

How do you measure and test a website? You can pay a service hundreds of dollars a month to do it for you. They will report on single page visits, entry pages and exit rates, traffic analysis, shopping cart analysis, etc.

Or: *You can sign up for a Google account and get a service called Google Analytics for free for your website.*

This tip alone will pay for the price of my book. You will not believe the wealth and depth of information you will receive, which is updated daily.

The main Google Analytics display contains number of visits, pageviews, pages/visit, bounce rate, average time on site, and percentage of new visits. Each can be displayed over various time periods. Visitors can be analyzed according to language, network location, browser, what type of connection their Internet service uses, operating system, screen resolution, whether they have Java and Flash installed, and more. You can see how many visitors you had from each country. You can see what keywords they used to find you, what sites they visited to come to your site, and what search engine they used. You can see what pages they viewed, where they entered the site, and where they left. And much more.

The amount of information Google will collect for you is absolutely astounding. Again, Google Analytics is free! Don't miss out on this. Once you have a Google account, you can sign up for their Gmail email service, their calendar, Docs and Spreadsheets (an online Microsoft Word-type program you can access from any computer, anywhere), and much more. This is *all for free*. Using Google Analytics is a great way to learn what is working and what is not working on your website. Using Google Analytics correctly will make it easier for more money to flow into your bank account.

chapter 32

SELLING STUFF ON THE INTERNET

FIRST, A FEW THOUGHTS

We all know the Internet has become a powerful force in the advancement of human knowledge and has produced a tremendous shift in many areas of commerce, including music. No one has any idea how the Internet will ultimately change the music industry. For you, the entrepreneurial guitarist, it remains a *potentially* very valuable resource. By itself, it probably will not produce all of your million dollars. But it certainly will contribute significant streams of income toward it.

Countless wild promises and expectations have been made over the past few years about the Internet. Many thought the Internet would be the indie musician's salvation. So far, those dreams and expectations have not been met. Michael Laskow of TAXI sent the following email out to thousands of TAXI subscribers in 2006:

> *Dear Passengers,*
> *People always ask me if I think Internet exposure will*
> *translate into actual sales of their music. "Not necessarily,"*

is always my answer.

When the band, Ok Go's "A Million Ways" video was featured on VH1's show, "Best Week Ever," it got more than 3 MILLION online views. They performed on Good Morning America, *and they played live on* Jimmy Kimmel Live.

The band released their second video, "Here It Goes Again" on the Internet and got one million views in its first week and THREE Million by the end of August.

But the band's CD isn't doing that well. Sales are slim enough that the music press is talking about how poor they've been. Ouch!

I've heard that the band is GREAT live. I've seen them in a TV commercial and thought they rocked. But with all that exposure on the Internet, you'd think they'd be doing big numbers.

But I meet people all the time who say things like, "Somebody from Finland bought my CD because they found me on the Internet." Cool, but did a LOT of people buy your CD because you're on the Internet?

That's the question I've got for you. If you have sold more than 5,000 copies of your CD in the last year as a direct result of being on the Internet, I'd like to hear from you. One of the topics I'm thinking about covering in the book I'm working on is "Real World Sales on the Internet."

Please let me know your name, the band name (if any), how you sold your product online, what genre of music it

is, and how I can confirm your sales.
Thanks for your help! I look forward to hearing from you.
Talk to you soon,
Michael

That says it all. Widespread exposure on the Internet does not necessarily translate into dollars in your bank account. Think of the Internet as just one of your multiple streams of income, not as your primary source of income. The Internet is another marketing medium, just like radio, TV, newspapers, etc. The difference is its instant interactivity. It enables you to deliver marketing messages quickly, cheaply, and easily. Another advantage is that you can easily and continually tweak whatever message you have, to maximize its effectiveness. But as Laskow alluded to in his email, just having a presence on the web won't necessarily produce income. Having a cool site means nothing. What counts is how much spendable cash your presence on the web generates.

One can find literally thousands of books in print about marketing and Internet sales. Many of them were written by academics and many by "marketing gurus." (Interestingly, some of the gurus ended up in jail after their "success.") I am certainly no expert on marketing, but want to touch on a few basics.

Any marketer must address three questions:

1. Who is my target audience?
2. What do they want?
3. How can I motivate this target audience to act *now* (especially important on the Internet)?

As an entrepreneurial guitarist, don't spend all your time practicing and endlessly perfecting your music with no time left for figuring out who your audience will be. After spending so much time on it, don't just throw your music out there and wait and hope for the crowds to appear at your website or concerts. They won't. Your music and creative efforts deserve much more than that.

You must spend a significant amount of time and energy finding your audience. You must find customers hungry for what you have to offer. Then, create a feeding frenzy.

Think of selling your product in the same way as feeding a pride of hungry lions. If they're hungry, and you show them food (showing them is the advertising), they will do anything they can to get it. The food doesn't have to be presented in any special way to hungry lions. They will wolf it down regardless of how it's presented (in other words, your advertising can be written by an amateur).

To create or find hungry customers doesn't mean you alter your core values or define your Hedgehog Concept to align with the current whims of the marketplace. Plan and think. Find your hungry customers and create a feeding frenzy all within the framework of your Hedgehog Concept.

Here are a few other website marketing basics:

1. **Entice your visitors to give you permission to contact them again.**

   This is one of the most important things your website should accomplish. By gathering email addresses, you are creating a private reserve of potential customers. This reserve is your nest egg—a source of long-term income.

Offer something free on your website, for which visitors will leave their email address. These are willing recipients of your messages who have opted in—what you send to them will not be unsolicited spam. Make the freebie easily seen and accessible. Write a few enticing sentences on the value of your freebie. You only have 3–5 seconds to make your customer stick to your site before they head off into cyberland. The freebie could be a download, video clip, newsletter, coupons for discounts on your merchandise, sheet music, or tips—whatever you can think of. Make your site "sticky"—make it feel like a treasure trove of cool, interesting stuff.

2. **You must hit the hot button of your customers.**

   Find out what that is—ask them. Don't assume that what you want is what they want. You must satisfy their reason for visiting your site.

3. **Be credible.**

   The web is full of bad information and dangerous, unsubstantiated opinions. Don't add to that morass. Don't try to fool or trick your customers. Don't oversell—be straightforward.

4. **Don't try to be a mass marketer.**

   Traditional mass marketers send out millions of emails and spend big bucks on advertising. Huge companies spend thousands and thousands of dollars on their websites. Don't try to compete with that. The same goes for price. Someone will always be cheaper than you.

5. **Be the best at what you do.**

This goes back to your Hedgehog Concept. Be the expert at what your customers want. Don't just sell products— feed your customers. Provide your customers with value. Satisfy their hunger. Marketing is about creating satisfied customers.

Countless marketing tactics and methods of driving traffic to your site are ballyhooed by various marketing experts. All you can do is investigate; accept or reject. Try them or pass them by. Your Hedgehog Concept will tell you if they might be useful to you.

SELLING STUFF—THE BASICS

Many of you will be selling CDs. Some will sell books, DVDs, sheet music, or software. You might be selling CD-related merchandise such as T-shirts. Or you might develop some other physical product to sell.

Many of your sales as an entrepreneurial guitarist will be over the Internet. Brick-and-mortar stores are certainly not out of the question for some products, but using the Internet is generally the most profitable. Those who sell CDs and CD-related merchandise will sell them at live concerts and gigs as well.

Your customers should be able to purchase your products by credit card and through PayPal directly from your website. You will make far more money per unit sold selling it yourself than having a middleman such as Amazon sell it. Use services such as Amazon as secondary sales outlets. Remember, the entrepreneurial guitarist eliminates middlemen as much as possible. You want to squeeze out as much profit as possible from each item you sell.

Many website hosting services are available. These services not only host sites but also usually provide tools and templates for building websites too. Do a Google search for "web hosting services" and start researching them. I used to use CityMax, which, like many others, is template-based. I know little about computer code and, when I started out, wanted something easy to use. They also offer an integrated shopping cart and merchant interface with Authorize.net, a leading credit card transaction processing company.

In other words, with a website service such as CityMax, an idiot like me can put together a website from which customers can easily order my products, using virtually any credit card or PayPal. After a few years, I outgrew CityMax. It started to get sluggish and page loading became too slow. I have since read a number of bad reviews from their customers.

I switched over to Yahoo Store. Yahoo offers an excellent integrated website/online store with several options and features. They have excellent tech support by phone. They are reliable, and large sites don't bog down.

Microsoft offers a free basic website service called Office Live that is excellent. But you would have to integrate a store into it, or send your customer to Amazon, PayPal, or CD Baby for them to order and pay for your products. Also, as noted previously, they display advertising for other products on your website.

A tremendous number of options are available for setting up and running your website. They are changing every day. You will have plenty from which to choose.

Just remember, anytime you research a company or service on the Internet, some malcontent will trash the company and say they are the worst ever. Don't depend on one or a handful of reviews. Look at many.

Do you also want to sell your CDs at Amazon.com? If you only sell small quantities of CDs, you will probably use their Advantage program. It is not very profitable—you may make a dollar or two per CD. But I suppose it does give you legitimacy. I do it for that reason, and because some people are reluctant to buy merchandise off an individual's website but do trust Amazon. Also, people may run across your CD at Amazon rather than your own website. Or, if you are doing a radio or TV interview, people may not remember your website name, but can remember to find you on Amazon.

If you think you will sell a healthy number of CDs, look into Amazon's Pro Merchant Plan. They charge a monthly fee plus fees on items that are sold. But your profit per item is much higher than the Advantage program. If you want Amazon to handle everything, you can use this service in tandem with their Fulfillment by Amazon program. For a fee, Amazon stores your products in their warehouses, collects your customers' payments, and ships your products to your customers. It's very convenient, but you are paying them to do the work for you.

CD Baby is an excellent place to sell your CDs. They are musician-friendly and very efficient. They offer the convenience of handling the processing and shipment of your orders, but still pay a sizable royalty to you. CD Baby is also great for getting you digital distribution (iTunes, etc.). In addition to all the above, they are a superb resource for information for independents like you. *Do not overlook CD Baby.*

This is obvious, but if you aren't selling much product, selling from your own website won't pay off. You have to sell enough merchandise to pay for the site and pay for the credit card processing service. You will also find out that the credit card processing company deducts various small fees and percentages of each sale that passes through it. Until your sales pick up, you might want to use both Amazon and CD Baby. Be careful not to compete with yourself. If you are selling your CDs on your own website, be sure your price is better than the price on other sites such as Amazon (or retail stores). The last thing you want is for someone to see your CD on your website and then order it cheaper or for the same price at Amazon where you will barely make any money off of it!

Many Internet merchants do not recommend accepting checks or money orders. Sometimes checks bounce. Or, they may be written for the wrong amount. In that case, you must take the time to contact the customer to send additional money. Or, if they overpaid, you will have to make an adjustment and send a refund check. Some customers deliberately leave off sales tax or shipping, thinking you won't bother to risk losing the sale over such a small amount. The bottom line is that fixing these problems requires your time. You don't want to lower the profit on an order because the customer has screwed up or is deliberately trying to short you. But you know what? I personally have never had a problem with mail orders. They do take extra time to process, but I have never been ripped off.

You may or may not want to take phone orders. I started out with an 800-number. But the number of phone orders I received didn't justify the cost. You pay a setup fee, a monthly fee, *plus all calls are billed as collect calls to you.* You must be there to answer the calls or have an answering service or at least a good answering machine. Even when speaking live with the customer, taking down his information accurately can be difficult. Some people are hard to understand because they have strong foreign or regional accents. Sometimes you get the information wrong and have to call them back. Sometimes the customer ends up wanting to talk to you, or asks for advice. That can be fun and you may make some good contacts or gain beneficial information. Speaking with customers is certainly good customer relations. If the customer is paying for the call, fine. But if they called your 800-number, your profit for that order slowly dwindles as the seconds tick by.

If you use an answering machine or service, I recommend telling the customer to just leave their name and number and that you will call them back. If you leave it up to them to leave credit card information, etc., they will leave something out, or a syllable or number will be garbled and you will have to call them back anyway. Make it simple and call them back for all the information. Be sure you have a form in front of you, or are in front of your computer entering the information. You must write down a long list of information: name, billing address, shipping address, phone number associated with the credit card, credit card number and expiration date, verification code on the back, email address, what they want to order, the shipping charge, tax, etc. You don't want to leave anything out.

chapter 33

HOW MUCH IS IT WORTH?

A product can be developed, marketed, and sold as the lowest-priced product, the middle-priced product, or the highest-priced product.

The trouble with the lowest-priced category is that inevitably someone will find a way to undersell you. You will earn less and less money and will have to deal with cheap customers who will haggle with you to reduce your price even more. Nonetheless, winners can be found in the lowest-price category. Generally they develop a way to drop their prices by cutting their overhead or production costs. If you choose to compete at the low end of the market, you almost have to be a better businessman than the one who competes at the top. Anyone can drop their price and go broke or make marginal income. It takes brilliant business skill to make money on small margins. Wal-Mart is the quintessential example of this kind of strategy.

At first glance, middle-of-the-road pricing looks like a good bet. The problem is, everyone thinks that. Therefore, this is by far the most crowded market, making competition stiff.

Sometimes it makes sense to go for broke and hit the high-priced world. Creating a competitive advantage based on quality can result in larger profit margins and quality customers. Design your projects and price them for special niche customers who are looking at the value of what you have to offer, not the price. You will attract better and more loyal customers. But you have to be able to give your customers something your competitors cannot. Distinguish yourself from your competition. Make that distinction attractive to the customers you are trying to reach.

Do your research. To get a feel for how high-end businesses operate, visit a high-priced auto dealer, then a cheap one. Study what a high-priced luxury hotel offers compared to a cheap motel. How do they run their businesses? How do they advertise? Who are their clientele?

Use this knowledge to identify your customers and to decide how you will design, tweak, and price your products to reach them. Remember, the higher your prices, the fewer customers you will have. Your marketing must be very precise.

Don't ask for opinions from the wrong people. Marketers from Lexus and Mercedes don't visit Billy Bob's Used Car Corral to ask Billy Bob's customers how to design cars and advertise. Seek out the opinions of people who have a feel for the unique quality and value of your products. And don't forget the ego factor. As much as people love to brag about their bargains, others boast when they've bought something few can afford. Note that the same product can be offered in different versions, at different prices, and for different customers. Again, consult marketing books to guide you down this path.

Not only do you want to focus on the right customer from a pricing standpoint. Be sure you focus on the right customer, period. Your potential market will be a typical bell curve with three sections. One small section of the curve will be potential customers who don't like you. Another small section on the other side will be potential and current customers who adore you. The largest section in the middle will be potential customers who have neither negative nor positive opinions about you, or who simply don't know you exist. Don't try to be all things to all people. You will never satisfy everyone, especially in music. Forget the people who don't like you. They either can't afford what you have to offer, don't need it, or simply don't want it. Instead, focus on those on the other side who do like you. Turn those customers into fans who will give testimonials for you, who will talk you up to everyone they know. This is called viral marketing and can be especially powerful on the Internet. It can also grab some of that middle group who have yet to know you.

SHIPPING

I'm sure you would figure out this information about shipping procedures on your own. Much of it you would learn by trial and error. But I will try to save you a little time and grief and go over some basics.

Right off the bat, do *not* allow anyone to come to your home to pick up their order. Nutcases are everywhere these days.

If you can find the space in your house, try to set up an area devoted to your "shipping department." (For several years, the "shipping department" of DouglasNiedt.com was on the ping-pong table in my basement.) Have everything you need within easy reach in one compact area:

- A couple boxes of your merchandise
- Packing tape gun
- Address and/or return address labels
- Empty boxes/envelopes
- Postal scale/meter
- Computer/printer
- Packing material (old newspapers are best—bubble plastic, peanuts, etc. are pricey)
- Stamps

Filling an order should involve as little moving or walking around as possible. In other words, organize your shipping department as an efficient assembly line.

Tempted to watch television or listen to the radio while filling orders? Be careful. Mistakes are surprisingly easy to make. Maintain focus. Common errors I have made are:

- Not noticing the shipping and billing address are different.
- Not noticing that someone wanted two copies of a book or CD instead of just one.
- Forgetting to include an item when a customer ordered four to six different items.
- Forgetting to put the packing slip in the box before sealing it.

I have found that shipping by the United States Postal Service is generally cheaper for smaller items such as CDs. But UPS and FedEx both offer excellent services as well. My discussion here will focus on shipping by the USPS.

For shipping out sold merchandise, you can get free USPS plastic bins at the post office. Use them to make it easier to carry your packages to your car/truck and into the post office. Or, you can arrange to have the packages picked up at your house by your mail carrier—save yourself time and gas money.

In addition to your "shipping department" you need a "warehouse." If you sell CDs or books, you will probably be storing them at home. Just remember, boxes of CDs or books are very heavy. Be careful about stacking hundreds or thousands of CDs or books in your attic or a second-floor room. Be sure the floor can support the weight. I prefer to store mine in a basement with a concrete slab floor. A garage works well too. In any storage area, be sure the temperature range is not too extreme. If your home or apartment doesn't have a basement or floor beneath it, and is built directly on a concrete slab, the ground floor is fine. But don't set the boxes directly on a concrete floor. The cardboard will wick moisture from even a seemingly dry floor and eventually deteriorate. Elevate the boxes with plastic PVC tubing laid on the floor, or plastic pallets. Don't use wood or brick—they also will wick moisture into the cardboard boxes. Don't stack CDs more than 3 or 4 boxes high—if the CDs are in plastic jewel boxes, the ones in the bottom cardboard box could crack. Steel shelving works well because it allows you to stack a lot more boxes in a given vertical space. It also helps to keep multiple products organized. But don't set the steel shelving on a wood floor. All the weight (anywhere from a few hundred to a couple thousand pounds!) will be on the four small L-shaped feet of the shelving. That can leave deep marks in your wood floor.

Let's also talk about stocking your warehouse. Most of the time, deliveries of your merchandise will arrive by UPS. But once in a while, shipping large or heavy items or large quantities of CDs or books is too expensive by UPS and will require delivery by truck—eighteen-wheelers! You will probably want to avoid dealing with a huge truck stopping in front of your house or apartment, and the driver hopping out with his clipboard saying, "Hey bud, I have four pallets of CDs—where do you want them?" He will also probably tell you, "I can't take them up or down stairs—has to be ground level."

Some residential areas are simply inaccessible to an eighteen-wheeler. The driver may say, "I'll drop the pallets in the lot over at Price Chopper. You can ferry them back to your house." Well, no.

When you place your order for your CDs or other merchandise, be sure that the supplier/manufacturer knows they are shipping to a residential area or apartment. Be sure the trucking company calls you in advance before the day of delivery. They often assume a shipment this large is going to an industrial park or company with a loading dock. They will also assume people will be there from 8:00 am till 5:00 pm to receive the delivery.

Set up a specific delivery time. Tell them you don't have a loading dock. If no room exists for an eighteen-wheeler to maneuver or turn around, let them know that too. Most trucking companies will have no problem transferring the shipment to a smaller truck once you explain the situation.

The truck driver will usually unload a shipment on pallets with a pallet jack. He can wheel an entire pallet at once with little effort into your garage or to your front door. But if any part of the route from truck to your door is on a slope, using a pallet jack could be dangerous or impossible. In that case, the pallet will have to be "broken down" (usually all the boxes on the pallet are shrink-wrapped with plastic that must be cut away) either inside the truck or on the ground by the truck. The merchandise will have to be transported with a hand truck (some people mistakenly call this a dolly) three to five boxes at a time to your door or garage.

Be sure the driver takes the pallet and plastic wrapping away. Believe me, you don't want to deal with having to get rid of a heavy wood pallet. *Nobody* wants them.

Be cooperative and friendly with the delivery guy. If you are physically able, help him unload. He has the power (especially if he is a union member) to refuse to do extra work, or to impose additional charges on you. Offer him a cool drink or a free CD or book. Be nice.

Finally, make sure you carefully inspect your delivery. Count the items. Check *every* individual box for outside damage. If the outside is damaged in any way, chances are the merchandise inside is damaged too. Sometimes the driver will intimidate you into hurrying to sign the shipping receipt before you have thoroughly inspected everything. *Don't do it.* Inspect first. Then sign. If you find damage, be certain to specify the damage in detail on the receipt and make sure you get a legible copy. You won't be the one to deal with the problem of damaged merchandise. Just call your supplier/manufacturer to let them know about the damaged shipment. They will file a claim with the trucking company and take it from there. You won't have to pay for damaged merchandise.

All this having been said, what if your living situation makes it impossible to receive/store large amounts of merchandise? Order smaller amounts—it will cost more per item, but at least you can deal with the logistics of shipment and storage more easily.

Companies such as CafePress.com will manufacture your products one at a time as orders come in. They will even process and ship the order and then pay you a small profit. They produce all kinds of merchandise such as CDs, books, T-shirts, mugs, etc. These services are very convenient and you aren't stuck with 2,000 CDs or coffee mugs sitting in your basement. But you pay for that convenience. You don't make very much money per item sold. It might make sense for you, though, in the beginning. Some CD manufacturers such as Disc Makers offer short-run orders in small quantities. The CDs are actually CD-Rs, but can be a good way to go if you can only handle storing small quantities of CDs at your residence.

Again, one of the services I recommend for selling your CDs is CD Baby. Although they handle order fulfillment, they only keep a half dozen of your CDs on hand in their warehouse at a time. When they run out, they email you to send more. So, you will still have those unsold cartons of CDs sitting in your basement or garage.

Of course, friends or relatives might have some extra space—just keep careful track of who has what and how much.

If you are successful and shipping out increasing volumes of merchandise, renting a small space at a storage/warehouse facility might be cost effective. Or, as I mentioned, use Fulfillment by Amazon and let them warehouse and retail your product. But again, the convenience will cost you. Go to the Amazon.com website for the latest information on how the program works.

The Amazon Advantage program can be used by those who own the distribution rights for their products (which is usually the case for the entrepreneurial guitarist). But once again, using Amazon's services will cut deeply into your profit. Go to their website for the latest terms and conditions.

If you do a search on Google to check out people's satisfaction with these various services, you will see comments ranging from "Amazon is run by a host of benevolent angels" to "Amazon is owned and operated by Satan." My personal opinion is that Amazon works very well, but you pay dearly for their expertise.

If you use an outside fulfillment service, don't give the outside service exclusive rights to sell your stuff. You still want to have the option of selling your products directly.

If you are shipping out CDs, DVDs, or books, you will need packaging materials. Shipping supplies can be expensive, believe it or not. If your profit margin on a CD is $5, it hurts if you have to pay $1 or more on the box to ship it.

One of the best suppliers I have found is Pack It USA. Prices are good and service is fast. Many other good suppliers are available. Disc Makers, the CD manufacturer, offers excellent prices on their CD mailer boxes. If you ship merchandise by US Postal Service Priority Mail, one of the best deals is to use the cardboard envelopes, Tyvek envelopes, and boxes the post office supplies for free. They will even deliver them to you. The only catch is that the postage is a flat rate—if what you are shipping is very light, you may be better off using your own box and purchasing the exact postage required. If you are shipping a heavier item, it could definitely save you money.

For packing material to cushion your merchandise so it doesn't rattle around in the box, I recommend scrunched-up newspaper. It costs you nothing to save old newspapers (have a friend or relative give you theirs), and your customers will appreciate the ease of disposing of newspaper rather than sifting through peanuts or shredded paper that gets all over their floor when they open the box.

Unless you are processing a large number of orders, one of the easiest ways to do postage is on the US Postal Service website, USPS.com. You cannot do first class, but just about everything else is available.

Of most interest to us is Parcel Post, with free delivery confirmation. First, you will need to set up an account with a credit card number. You will also need to order labels specifically formatted for the USPS website. They can be ordered directly on the USPS website or from a company called LabelUniverse.com. You will also need a good scale to weigh your packages. These can also be ordered directly on the USPS website. Unless you're shipping heavy items that weigh more than ten pounds, you shouldn't have to pay more than $40 for an accurate scale.

To send out an order, weigh the package. Then log in to your account at USPS.com. You will enter all the information for the package. It will automatically charge your credit card and you will print out an official label (that you purchased from LabelUniverse.com) to stick on your package. Within a few hours you are sent an email confirmation of your postage purchase. When filling out the shipping information, you can also check a box to have them email you when the package is delivered (no extra cost).

But the best thing is, with the package all ready to go, your postal carrier can pick it up at your home. You don't have to go anywhere. Stay home, save gas money, and practice your guitar. Or, just walk into any post office and, *without standing in line*, hand the package to a clerk or throw it in the large package bin (if available) and walk out. This easy-breezy method is especially fun at Christmas time, when the lines are going out the door. If the post office personnel weigh the package and figure the postage, not only will you stand in line, you will be charged an additional fee for delivery confirmation (which is free on the Internet).

If you receive hundreds of orders, I would recommend looking into leasing a postage meter from a company such as Pitney-Bowes. Postage meters are pricey but well worth it if you are generating numerous shipments.

If you are very successful and end up with hundreds of orders coming in every week, you could use Fulfillment by Amazon. Or, you may be tempted to use a fulfillment house. The difficulty will be finding one that is dependable. Horror stories abound about companies that missed orders, didn't fulfill orders, refused customer complaints/inquiries, and gave merchandise away.

If at all possible, to maximize your profit, do the order processing yourself. Enlist the help of friends, your spouse, your children, relatives. It can actually be fun when done as a group. Hiring someone you know and can depend on is an option. Hiring people you don't know or hiring temps is asking for headaches. Ask any business person what the biggest headache is in their operation and they will invariably answer, "Employees."

CUSTOMER SERVICE

These days you constantly hear about customer service (mostly the lack of it). No one is ever around to wait on you in stores. Live people don't exist to speak to you on the telephone. Clerks (if you can find one) are lazy or uninformed.

You are a budding entrepreneurial guitarist. My advice to you is actually to not offer extraordinary customer service. Offer normal service and nothing more. Here's why.

Extraordinary customer service costs money. That is one reason Amazon.com lost so much money their first seven years. They cut their profit too much by providing extraordinary customer service. The better your service, the higher your service costs. Before you know it, extra services lead to diminishing returns to the point of wiping out your profits. Order tracking, allowing people to call to check on the status of their order, taking phone orders, mail orders, shipping to foreign countries, doing rush orders, volume discounts—all these will cost you in time and money. If you want to maximize your profit, don't offer these services. Or, charge more for them.

Don't misunderstand. You don't want to provide bad service. A good rule of thumb: decent customer service = common sense. If anything, err on the side of under-promising and over-delivering.

By law, you have to provide a certain amount of customer service. The Federal Trade Commission specifies how quickly direct mail companies must ship orders and under what circumstances they must give refunds. On your website order page (or for that matter in an email or on the phone), never say anything about when the order will ship or when the customer will receive it. Refuse to answer those questions. It will seem unreasonable and rude to your customer, but here is why. The Federal Trade Commission has rules that make anything you say about shipment time an iron-clad guarantee! You are violating the law if you fail to deliver your merchandise in the time frame you specify.

Does it ever make sense to offer extraordinary service? Yes. I get extraordinary service from my Lexus dealer. They offer it, so why shouldn't I? It makes sense for them because a Lexus costs roughly 5,000 times the price of my CD! Anyone selling an expensive product will bend over backwards to get your order and give you superior service. They have toll-free numbers with live people answering the phones 24 hours a day. They take MasterCard, Visa, American Express, Discover, PayPal, checks, money orders, C.O.D. traveler's checks, livestock—anything to close the deal!

On my website, I admit that I provide above-average customer service. Yes, I go against my own advice. I do it because I can't stand the lousy service I receive nearly every day from other vendors (mostly brick-and-mortar stores—not on the Internet). I take foreign orders, which are always losers. The postage is a killer. I have to fill out customs forms, and have to wait in line at the post office to have them figure the postage. But I like the idea that my CDs are being heard all over the world. I take phone orders. But, as I said, I dropped the 800-number because it was not cost effective.

Not many people order by phone so it doesn't take much time. The same is true with mail orders. Rush orders (FedEx overnight) at Christmas time are definitely a huge pain. But Christmas is important to me. I want people to get my CD before the holiday. I also accept checks and mail orders—haven't been burned yet.

The level of customer service you decide to offer is certainly your choice. I'm not saying you should offer abysmal or rude service on your website. Just offer the minimum level of customer service necessary to comply with the law and fulfill reasonable customer expectations. After all, the customer is shopping at your website, not Neiman Marcus.

One ruse I have fallen for is the line from a fellow guitarist, "I have a CD too. I will send you mine free if you'll send me yours free." What happens? You lose $10 of profit and receive a CD you can't stand to listen to for more than 8 seconds.

Here is the list of "do not"s to help you maximize your profit, spend less time coddling customers, and have more time to play your guitar:

- No checks or money orders
- No orders by fax
- No orders by email
- No phone orders
- No mail orders
- No in-person orders or pickup
- No C.O.D orders

308 How to Make a Million Dollars Playing the Guitar

- No foreign orders, including Canada and Great Britain
- No rush orders
- No volume discounts
- No "I'll give you a free copy of my CD if you will give me one of yours"

chapter 36

TAXES

As an entrepreneurial guitarist, you will most likely be self-employed. The self-employed are hit hard by taxes. We pay an additional 15% self-employment tax above the usual federal and state tax. There will be no withholding on your income so you may need to make quarterly tax payments. It can all be a killer. Be aggressive in attempting to reduce your tax burden, but don't cheat. As I have stated elsewhere, don't mess with the IRS. They will pursue you and crush you. They are very serious about taking as much of your money as they can!

The good news is, as a self-employed individual, a ton of your expenses are tax-deductible. In other words, you will subtract these expenses from your income, therefore lowering your taxable income. You are taxed on the income that remains, *after* the deductions. Note that some of these deductions must be prorated according to business versus personal use. Others must be prorated according to the percentage of business use of your residence. The rest are deductible in full. Here are a few:

1. Office supplies (paper, printer cartridges, pencils, paper clips, etc.)
2. Computers
3. Computer monitors (you should be using dual moni-

tors—you won't believe how much they will improve your work efficiency)

4. Computer peripherals (cables, thumb drives, routers, speakers, earbuds)

5. Printers

6. Fax machines

7. Software

8. Blank CDs and DVDs

9. Furniture, lamps, file cabinets, bookshelves, CD shelves

10. Instruments and equipment

11. Strings

12. Insurance for your instruments and equipment

13. Instrument and equipment repairs/maintenance

14. CDs, sheet music, and books you purchase

15. Internet access fees

16. Credit card processing services

17. Website hosting services

18. Online storage services

19. Concert tickets

20. Music magazine subscriptions

21. Business postage

22. Advertising

23. Licenses, fees

24. Dues

25. CD production costs

26. CD manufacturing costs (must be figured on Schedule C as "Inventory–Cost of Goods Sold")

27. Printing costs of promotional materials

28. CD player, DVD player, television set (if for business use only)
29. Property taxes
30. Trash collection
31. Cleaning services
32. Renters or homeowners insurance
33. Repairs to dwelling
34. Long distance business phone calls
35. Homes association fees
36. Touring expenses including airfare, gas/toll, motel, food (these are limited by many special rules and limitations)
37. Concert wardrobe

Just a note about your CD manufacturing costs. As I mention in the list, those costs must be entered on Schedule C as inventory costs, which is on page 2 of Schedule C, and is called Part III Cost of Goods Sold.

You cannot deduct the amounts on the invoices from the CD manufacturer for all the CDs you ordered during the tax year. You can only do that if you sold *all* the CDs from the invoices in that one tax year. Instead, you must do a cost-of-goods-sold calculation. That is the amount you are allowed to deduct from your gross income.

Each year around New Year's Day, do a count of all your unsold CDs sitting in your closet or garage. That number, multiplied by the cost of manufacturing each CD (not the retail cost) is your year end/beginning of the year inventory figure. To figure your cost of goods sold, take your beginning-of-the-year inventory plus your purchases of additional CDs manufactured during the year, minus your end-of-year inventory.

Let's say you ordered 1,000 CDs that cost $3 each to manufacture.

That is $3,000. You didn't order any more that year. Say you sold 400 CDs during the year. You would now have 600 unsold CDs left at the end of the year multiplied by $3 each = $1,800. Taking your beginning inventory valued at $3,000 minus your end-of-year inventory valued at $1,800, we are left with $1,200, which is your cost of goods sold. That is the number deductible on your Schedule C, not the entire $3,000.

Let's do another example. Let's say you did really well and ordered an additional 1,000 CDs at $3 each = $3,000. You add that expenditure to your first $3,000 = $6,000. Say you sold 1,300 CDs. You would have 700 CDs left at the end of the year multiplied by $3 (cost to manufacture each CD) = $2,100. Beginning-of-the-year inventory ($3,000) plus purchases of additional CDs during the year ($3,000) = $6,000. Then subtract your end-of-year inventory figure ($2,100). That equals $3,900, which is your cost of goods sold, which is the number you deduct on Schedule C, not the entire $6,000 you paid to have all 2,000 CDs manufactured.

In general, the IRS doesn't want you to be able to deduct expenses within a short period of time. They like to drag it out as much as possible. That is where depreciation comes in, and you have to deduct your expenses over a period of three or more years. For the entrepreneurial guitarist, we usually want to deduct as many high start-up costs as possible to lower our tax liability. This is where first-year expensing comes in. Unless you spend an extraordinary amount of money in business purchases, you will usually be eligible for Section 179 first-year expensing, which means you can deduct the total cost of your purchases in one year and get the maximum benefit as quickly as possible.

Even if you use an accountant to do your taxes, I highly recommend that you thoroughly familiarize yourself with the basics of the tax code and with the mechanics of filling out tax forms. Read *J.K. Lasser's Your*

Income Tax and try using H&R Block's TaxCut or TurboTax software on your computer.

Just remember, the only catch with general business deductions is that the expense must be business-related. Physical items must be used exclusively for business purposes. Do *not* attempt to deduct personal expenses—that is fraud. If you are audited, be prepared to defend your deductions. If your deductions are taken honestly and sincerely, they are usually allowed. If they are disallowed, your taxable income will be higher and you must pay the extra tax due on that income. Possibly, you may have to pay a small penalty. But you won't serve time at Club Fed! As long as you're being reasonable and honest, most of your deductions will be allowed—you won't go to jail for being aggressive in your business deductions. Do *not*, however, understate or ever attempt to hide income. That is a definite no-no and can lead to heavy fines or an extended stay at Club Fed.

I'm sure many of you are already eagerly thumbing through catalogs or browsing music equipment websites, thinking about purchasing that new guitar you always wanted, or that new amp. Wouldn't you like to buy an HD Pro Tools system? After all, it's deductible! Yes, those things are deductible, and in effect you will be acquiring them at a 20–40% discount (depending on your other income/expenses and tax bracket). But you're still spending money you probably don't have. Don't go crazy. Buy only what you need. Be frugal. Spend your money wisely. As an entrepreneurial guitarist, operate on a shoestring budget as much as possible. You've probably heard, "It takes money to make money." Baloney. Ignore that worn-out phrase. *The sweetest financial success comes when you make money without spending a dime to do it.* Pure profit has a taste like no other.

OF COURSE YOU HAVE A DATABASE... RIGHT?

How will you keep track of all your business expenses, sales, and dozens of other things? You will use a database. In their simplest form, databases organize items and information into lists. They are searchable, so you can find absolutely anything in your lists. A database is essential for organizing information important to the development of your career. The database program I use and strongly recommend is FileMaker Pro. The basic program is $300, which is not high-priced considering the power of the software and the benefits it provides. Microsoft Office Access ($229) is also powerful and is included in some versions of the Microsoft Office suite. Other programs can be found, but for the small to medium-sized business (that's you), FileMaker and Access are probably the premier solutions. Don't limit yourself with a spreadsheet program such as Excel.

I use FileMaker in several different ways. I maintain a list of several hundred performing arts series/concert presenters with contact names to drum up concert bookings. If I want to let all the presenters know about my new CD, with a few mouse clicks I can send a mass email to all of them (or a select group) to tell them about it. If I want to do a mass US snail-mail mailing, I can have the database print labels and or letters, personally addressed to each person by first or last name. Instead of "Dear Concert Presenter" or "Dear Sir" I can have it read "Dear David" or "Dear Mr. Smithson." I can also vary the content of the letter for different concert series. For example, I might use one letter for concert series with a budget of over $100,000 and another letter for smaller series with budgets of less than $10,000.

I keep a database of all my CD and other merchandise sales. It keeps track of all my customers, what they purchased, how much they paid, what method of payment they used (credit card, check, money order, PayPal, cash), when the purchase was made, credit card transaction numbers, and all their contact information including phone number and email address. I can print out invoices for each sale. The program specifies if an order has not been shipped, is in the process, or has been shipped. It keeps a running tab of the sales of every item I sell through my website, through Amazon.com, from concerts, and through other sources.

If I am going to give a concert in Little Rock, I can have the database find all the people in Arkansas who have purchased my merchandise and send a personalized email to each of them, giving the details of my upcoming concert.

I keep track of all my business expenses in various categories (recently I have moved business expense tracking into Quicken, the financial software program). At any time, I can add up all my purchases in different categories within any specified time period. For instance, at year end when I have to do my taxes, with a few keystrokes I can pull up all my purchases for the year: software purchases, CDs, books, equipment, or any other category I specify. If I need to find out when or where I bought that Neumann mic, I can do a quick search to find the information.

One of the most useful and powerful applications of FileMaker is to use it to help edit recordings. One day I was puttering about the FileMaker site. They had stories of how people in various industries use FileMaker. I clicked on the entertainment industry and read about several major film companies that use FileMaker. They keep track of everything (budgets, personnel, deadlines, equipment, you name it) with databases. They also use it for film editing. The number of camera shots taken in shooting a major motion picture is staggering. They use FileMaker to keep track of camera shots and special effects. As they edit, they search their FileMaker database for the clips they want which are each notated with information on camera angle, lighting, and other variables.

It occurred to me I could use it in a similar way to edit my recordings. Before FileMaker, I used pencil and paper to make lists of which takes I thought were good or bad, where they started and ended, and which ones I wanted to use. I had notes with crossouts, arrows, and highlighted numbers all over the place. Sticky notes were plastered everywhere. What a mess. Although it worked, it was confusing, draining, and laborious.

With FileMaker, I can set up a database for each song. I listen to the takes. For each take, I enter into the database the track number, the take's location (hours/minutes/seconds) on the recording timeline, name of the section of the song the take covers, measure numbers the take covers, whether the take is good or bad, notes about the performance, plus basic information about the track such as day and time it was recorded, mic technique used, and equipment used.

To edit a song, say I need to put together a section of music from measures 9–17. I can search my database for all the good takes that cover that section. Then, I can A/B them to find which is the best. As I "assemble" the recording, I note which takes I am using and where the "splices" are on the timeline down to the hundredth of a second. Because every detail is thoroughly, precisely, and clearly documented, any changes I need to make a few minutes or a few months later can easily be made without breaking a sweat. Keep in mind that I am only a solo guitarist. Imagine the power of this software application if you are editing a band or chamber music group. Phenomenal.

Just to give one other example of the flexibility and possible applications of FileMaker, here is an in-depth description from the FileMaker website on how the Dave Matthews Band uses FileMaker in their work:

> There's nothing quite like a live concert by a top band. There's an energy that flows directly from the stage and into the audience. You can listen to CDs, you can watch all the videos you want—but nothing beats a live performance— especially by a top concert act like the Dave Matthews Band. With their unique fusion of jazz and rock, and their accessible, grassroots style, Dave Matthews and his band mates make magic every time they take the stage.
>
> But creating that magic isn't easy. It requires tight organization and careful planning. And that's why whenever the DMB performs, they're accompanied by FileMaker Pro

and FileMaker Pro Server, the award-winning database software applications by FileMaker Inc.

A great stage band is more than musicians, more than songwriters. Live performance also requires a crack team of technicians—lighting experts, audio specialists, equipment managers. And then there are administrative personnel, the people who take care of all the details involved in putting on a show: working with each local venue, coordinating promotion, handling merchandise sales, making backstage arrangements. It's hard work, but for the Dave Matthews Band, FileMaker Pro makes it easier.

Ian Kuhn is the DMB's Monitor Engineer, and he's also responsible for introducing the band to FileMaker. As a long-time enthusiast of the Macintosh operating system, Ian's been using FileMaker since its earliest versions, and it didn't take him long to realize that FileMaker was a perfect fit for all the myriad tasks involved in putting together a show. Now, all these functions are tied together using FileMaker Pro Server—which Ian has running on a network that actually travels wherever the band goes. It's a cross-platform system he designed himself, with help from freelance consultant Rudy Arias, and everyone from the band can log in no matter what laptop they use, get email, surf the web and share files and printers—all over the network.

Routing the song list for each performance?

FileMaker Pro handles it—smoothly and efficiently. The set list has been entered into the FileMaker Pro Server on stage, and all the band and crew are plugged in through their own PowerBooks and laptops. Everyone knows instantly when each selection is coming up—and how often each song has been performed. There's even an instant messaging system so that changes in the routine and choices of encore songs are immediately available to everyone.

Need to work out a special lighting or audio effect?

FileMaker Pro handles that, too. The technical staff is also logged on to the FileMaker network during each performance, and adjustments can be made instantly. Everything from the lighting cues to minor technical details is instantly available via the FMP Server. In fact, up to 60 people can use the system at once, so no one is ever out of the loop.

Need to know the logistics for moving the band and its entourage from this venue to the next venue?

Well, FileMaker Pro handles that as well. The administrative team knows where the band is heading and what it'll find when it gets there, with all the advance work under control.

And once the show is over, FileMaker's job still isn't done. The Dave Matthews Band is well known for its live concert recordings, and once a performance is over, the master recording needs to be logged and filed. FileMaker Pro helps keep careful track of these valuable materials.

FileMaker's ease of operation is a vital part of its success, says Ian. "I've seen databases made with other software," he notes, "and they take forever! With FileMaker Pro we can build massive databases that just make people gasp at what they can do! The first few weeks we were using File-

Maker it was sort of an experiment—now it's an integral part of the band!"

Wherever the Dave Matthews Band travels, FileMaker Pro is there. And not just along for the ride. It's right there in the heart of every show.

As an entrepreneurial guitarist, you will be working on a great number of projects involving the management of much information and many expenses. A database will make it easier to keep your information organized, use it to your best advantage, track your expenses, and maximize your profits.

TIME TO BE RELIGIOUS— ABOUT BACKING UP YOUR DATA

They say death and taxes are the only sure things in life. They forgot one: your computer will crash. I don't care if you have an expensive computer or a cheap one. I don't care if you have a PC or Mac. It will crash. If it doesn't crash, I know you will do something stupid and lose data. YOU MUST BACK UP YOUR DATA externally. It doesn't matter what you are doing on the computer or how often you use it. YOU MUST BACK IT UP CONSTANTLY.

This goes for complex stuff like your FileMaker databases, your actual recording sessions, as well as the simplest most basic information you have on your computer. YOU MUST BACK UP YOUR DATA externally. Even *as* you are recording or working on a database or other important project, YOU MUST BACK UP YOUR DATA. Don't wait until the end of a recording session to back up your tracks. Take time during the session for backups. YOU MUST BACK UP YOUR DATA. Get it?

What do I mean by "externally"? Use an online backup service or external hard drive. I strongly recommend you do both. Or, back up to *two* external hard drives (even external hard drives fail—redundancy is the solution). Keep one at home and one at another location in case of fire, theft, etc. External hard drives (depending on how much information they store) can be purchased inexpensively—usually $100–$200 for a fairly capacious one. Online backup services such as Mozy and Carbonite back up your computer automatically. Your information is stored on their systems with redundancy. These services are very convenient. Use them.

But, if you are a performer and using a computer to record your music, you have a different situation. Ideally, you should be using a computer dedicated solely to recording music. This computer should be used *only* for music recording and should *not* be connected to the Internet—you don't want to risk getting spyware or viruses. Plus, firewalls, anti-virus, anti-spyware, and other security programs put extra demands on your computer. This can cause problems for your recording program, especially if you are using several tracks or plug-ins. If you are a Mac user, despite what friends say, Macs are also vulnerable to viruses and spyware—no computer is immune. Therefore, even a Mac used for recording should not be connected to the Internet. Since your music-recording computer won't be connected to the Internet, an online backup service is not a viable option. Use two external hard drives instead. The online services would definitely be an option for your everyday computer hooked up to the Internet. But some people have even lost data with the online services. So, they use the online backup service *and* an external hard drive.

Another option is an online storage service such as Box.net. An online storage provider is not an *automatic* backup service. You must back up your files manually. They provide 5 GB of storage space for less than $100/year or 15 GB for $200/year. Ultimately, that is more expensive than backing up to an external hard drive, but it has other advantages. Your files can be accessed from anywhere. You can share files with anyone else you specify (very useful if you are working with another band member or editor or mastering house in another area of town or different city). Files can be easily moved between computers. You could also use the site to provide downloads to your website customers who want to download individual songs from your CDs (just like iTunes). The difference is that you can give your customers more flexibility with how they want to use the songs and provide better-quality files (higher bit-rates).

So, you have the options of online or external-hard-drive backup for your regular computer. For your music recording computer you must use external-hard-drive backup only (two drives stored in separate locations). YOU MUST BACK UP YOUR DATA. Constantly!

PART FIVE:
You Are Running
a Business

YOUR PYRAMID

Yes, you are an artist. You spend your days working on songs, practicing, and writing new material. But, as an entrepreneurial guitarist, you must face the fact that you are also a business. You now own a business, a company. You must run this company. *You are a businessman.* Even Beethoven professed, "An artist must also be a businessman." That was in 1801.

Think of your company as a pyramid with five levels:

1. The foundation—cash flow
2. Sales and marketing
3. Quality control
4. Legal
5. The top—YOU

Ironically, the top level (you, the product) is the least important. You may protest, "But my music *is* me. My guitar playing is the important thing." Yes, artistically your music is the most important. But from a business standpoint, cash flow is number one. To get your company out of the starting gates, to develop it and keep it going so your artistic career can flourish, you will need continual cash flow. Otherwise, the company will begin to starve for oxygen, so to speak. If your company doesn't grow and develop, ten years from now you will find yourself still practicing the guitar in your room every day, and probably becoming quite a good guitarist, but without an audience to enjoy your talent. You will have to work a real job to support yourself.

LEVEL 1: THE FOUNDATION OF THE PYRAMID—CASH FLOW

That bottom level, cash flow, is the foundation upon which everything else rests. It feeds all the company operations that grow the business. Although you currently may be a poor, starving musician, you will soon see cash flowing into your bank account. You must put it to its best use to keep your career moving forward. One important principle to follow is not to spend money on something until you know where the money is coming from to pay for it (and when). Don't spend money on something unless you are very sure it will pay for itself in the near future. Be sure your purchase will be an *income-producing asset*. It needs to *produce* money for you, not eat it up. Keep your costs and spending as low as possible.

Use Your Own Money

You will need income in the early stages of your development not only to live on, but to fuel your career. Many companies rely on investors when starting out. In the music field, your most obvious and best investor is *you*. You can save as you go, and step by step build and ascend your career ladder.

If you are in a group, whether a pop group or a classical chamber music group, things are a little easier because investments can be divided among all the group members. In a group situation, be careful with loans. Most groups don't stay together long enough to pay off a loan. What a pain to still be paying off a loan two years after the group disbanded while you're trying to get a new group off the ground.

Shooting for the stars is a good idea. But, why set your sights low? *Shoot for a host of them.* In other words, don't put all your eggs in one basket, especially early in your career. Don't count on one project becoming a mega-success. Don't count on one person or contact making everything happen for you.

Instead of one stream of income, adapt a multiple stream of income approach. Until you have a Hedgehog Concept, the foundation of your business pyramid should be built on several "jobs" that all produce income. You may have some higher-risk projects that, if successful, will handsomely reward you. But they could also fail. Always have low-risk projects and strategies you can rely on for income. It could be teaching, playing gigs in small clubs, working in a music store, or a low-paying job in a recording studio or other music industry company.

Once you have your Hedgehog Concept, you can choose which income streams to eliminate and which to keep and develop to feed your economic engine. In the meantime, stay in the music arena as much as possible, both for the wellbeing of your spirit and to keep your thoughts and mind focused on things musical instead of the work schedule at Wal-Mart or QuikTrip.

Use Money From "Investors"

If you have difficulty finding money at some stage of your career, you could possibly raise money from friends and family, banks (admittedly, a long shot for a musician), organizations that support entrepreneurs, customers, suppliers (instrument manufacturers, guitar string manufacturers, publishers), and investors. Be a master of *using other people's money*. An entire book has been written on the subject, *OPM: Other People's Money*, by Michael Lechter.

If you are seeking to find people who will invest money in your career or latest project, a few things must be kept in mind. Ask yourself *why* they would want to invest in you. Number one is a no-brainer. Your investor wants to make money. Number two is that they may simply care about you. They may be family or a close associate. Number three is that many people who invest in the music business are looking for a little excitement. Call it what you want—glamour, adventure, action, publicity. They want to vicariously share the limelight, the "glitz" of the music world. After all, they might make money more reliably by investing in stocks, bonds, or real estate.

Put together an honest proposal that will appeal to them directly. If they want "glitz," invite them to V.I.P. parties or offer them special V.I.P. seating at concerts. Invite them to sit in on a recording session. Give them a title such as "Executive Producer" on a CD. Be as creative in this area as you are in your art. But be careful. Don't ever make promises to an investor that you can't keep. Nothing is a sure thing, especially in the music business. Be honest, and if anything, underestimate the return on investment. That way, the investor won't get nasty surprises. And if things do work out, you will really look good.

Most potential investors will be family, friends, or possibly a devoted fan. Regardless of who the investors are, approach them in a professional manner. Your financial figures must be honest and accurate, and it must be a money-making *plan*. The plan is called The Financial Prospectus. James Riordan, in *Making It In The New Music Business*, gives an excellent description of how to put together this document. Here are the key points:

1. Explain your goal.
2. Explain how you will accomplish your goal.
3. Explain how the investor's money will help accomplish the goal and make money for both of you.
4. Map everything out in timeline fashion.

I have additional relevant information in Chapter 41, "This Is the Part You Will Want to Skip Over." *Read it even if you aren't planning on having outside investors.*

If you are dealing with family or friends, you have an instant advantage: they trust you. When an investor trusts you, you are way ahead of the game. Friends and family are more likely to believe in you and are probably already familiar with your career, your devotion to it, and your potential. They have seen the hard work you have already put into your career and will want to help you go further. They are also more likely to have patience with setbacks and will keep rooting for you over the long haul.

If family or friends are reluctant to risk money on an investment in the music biz, you could simply ask for a straight loan that is not tied to your success. You agree to pay back the loan at a rate of X% and that's that. But again, you must plan. Work out the figures. For example, if you are wanting a loan to make a CD, figure out how many copies you can sell (be brutally honest here—ask some guitarist friends how many CDs they have sold) over a specific period of time. Don't ask for more money than your income from CD sales can produce. Make sure the timeline of paying back the loan matches the timeline of CD sales. In other words, don't ask for a ten-year loan if the majority of the CD sales will occur in the first 1–2 years.

You can also look farther afield for investors. Approach friends of friends, friends of your parents, fans, teachers, or anyone who has shown sincere interest in what you are doing.

Internet music investor websites such as SellaBand.com, SliceThe-Pie.com, and ArtistShare.com have surfaced in the past couple of years.

ArtistShare, founded in 2000, utilizes a "fan-funding" model to allow the general public to directly finance, watch the creative process of the recording, and in most cases gain access to extra material from an artist.

SellaBand supports upcoming bands by encouraging them to sell shares in their group to investors. Bands that successfully sell 5,000 "parts" are then rewarded with their own producer, studio time, and support from industry experts to help them record an album.

Similarly, SliceThePie.com allows bands to raise money directly from music fans and gives the fans the chance to be involved in the music production process. Fans who invest in the band or artist can earn money reviewing tracks as well as enjoy perks such as free album copies, their name on album sleeves, and a share in the financial returns from record sales. SliceThePie.com has also essentially created a stock exchange of its own, allowing investors to trade shares of their music between other holders within the market domain.

Other similar sites are available for various genres of music. If this sounds like something that may fit into your Hedgehog Concept, thoroughly research it before proceeding.

Remember that nearly everything in life (especially the entertainment business) is negotiable if you simply ask. If you wanted to book recording studio time, you could ask for a reduced rate in return for a cut of sales. You could arrange a similar deal when hiring an engineer or producer. Again, we must try to be as creative in our business dealings as we are in our music.

"I Don't Know Anyone Who Has Any Money"

Maybe you don't know anyone with money right now, but you will. You may think, "I just play the guitar. I have no connections with people who have money." Or, "I'm shy. I couldn't possibly ask someone for money." But if you read and research and follow every possible opportunity, you will be surprised at the new opportunities that continually unfold in front of you.

I once played at a luncheon (for no fee, paying my dues) for supporters of the Conservatory of Music and Dance, University of Missouri—Kansas City where I teach. One of the attendees was a prominent businessman, very much the entrepreneur. He was very taken with my playing. He invited me to lunch at his country club and to his palatial home for discussions. He was prepared to invest serious amounts of money in my career.

Unfortunately for me, he realized that even though I played the guitar well, I didn't sing, which therefore limited my potential in the commercial market. He felt that a classical guitarist would not give him a good enough return on his investment. He was thinking on the level of Madonna or Michael Jackson.

Even though that didn't work out, my point is that a major investor came forward to help me as a result of my playing a simple lunch gig. Other opportunities that did pan out came about from similar innocuous events:

> In my teens, when school was in session, I was practicing six hours a day. During the summer I would practice all day, literally from six in the morning till nine or ten at night. I used Aranjuez Strings. I went through hundreds of strings.
>
> During my junior year of college, I went to New York to study general music subjects at The Juilliard School. Back then they didn't even have a guitar program.
>
> The strings I used, Aranjuez Strings, were developed by Juan Orozco. He had a shop on West 56th Street. One day, my friend Vito and I decided to go down to Orozco's shop to see what it was like. Orozco was there, and we introduced ourselves. Orozco recognized my name and even remembered the fact that I was in Kansas City because I had ordered so many strings.
>
> I had my guitar with me and he asked me to play. It so happened he was starting up a guitar concert series at Carnegie Recital Hall. In his heavy Spanish accent he asked, "Would you like to play on my series? I will pay all the costs and promote it." I was nineteen or twenty years old. I couldn't believe what I was hearing. I just came to his shop on a lark to see where my strings were made.

I was being offered my New York debut at Carnegie Recital Hall, all expenses paid. (Today, playing a concert at the hall, now renamed Weill Hall at Carnegie Hall, costs $4,100 just for the hall rental. With promotional expenses, the cost easily hits $10,000.

It was as simple and serendipitous as that. Yes, I was a good guitarist and had practiced really hard to get to that level. But the actual opportunity came about in an unforeseen, almost random fashion. Opportunity does knock. Potential investors are all around you.

LEVEL 2: SALES AND MARKETING

The next level up from the foundation of cash flow is sales and marketing. For an artist, this one is *huge*. This is crucial. If no one knows you exist, you will be unable to sell anything.

For example, making the CD is the easy and fun part. Selling it is something else entirely. Once the CD is completed, the real work begins of promoting it and trying to sell it. You can have the best CD on the planet, but if no one knows about it, you will have 2,000 or more CDs sitting in your basement or garage for a very long time.

This level consists of everything you do to promote your product or your artistic creations. Regardless of the product, being able to sell it is a basic skill of all entrepreneurs. If you cannot sell, you cannot earn money to feed your cash flow, your foundation.

Who do you sell to? Your audience. Having an audience is the only guarantee of success. *There will never be a situation where you will not need an audience or fan base (customers) to sell to.* Whether your audience is a handful of people or hundreds of thousands, you must have customers to buy your product.

Sales and marketing are crucial to any business. It is essential to your success that you have a solid understanding of this subject. Thousands of books and tons of information on it are available. Start reading! You will discover hundreds of specific ideas you can use to sell your own products. In particular, check out Bob Baker at Bob-Baker. com. He is the author of the *Guerrilla Music Marketing Handbook* and many other books. He has hundreds of marketing ideas and articles on his website.

LEVEL 3: QUALITY CONTROL

Quality control applies to the quality of anything you release into the marketplace. That would include items such as CDs, performances (concerts, gigs, radio/TV appearances, Internet events), DVDs, publications, T-shirts, endorsements, software, and anything else you can think of. It includes order fulfillment and customer service and relations.

You can execute your sales and marketing plan well and sell a sizable amount of product. But the quality must be good. If the quality is subpar, you will have problems. For instance, let's say your product is a CD. Just on a basic level, aside from artistic considerations, if the printing is bad, the sound quality not equal or superior to other commercial releases, or the packaging defective, those thousands of CDs you successfully sold will be returned to you. Or, if the artistic quality doesn't live up to your marketing and sales pitches, sales will come to a grinding halt once word gets out that the CD is not really very good and that the marketing was just a bunch of hype. You can effectively put an end to your career right there.

LEVEL 4: LEGAL

Continuing up the pyramid, if you have the cash flow foundation, do your sales and marketing, and the quality is good, guess what? If your products aren't well protected legally, or if you don't have the proper accounting systems in place, the money from sales may not come to you. You have wasted valuable time and effort. Everybody else gets your money, not you.

As an entrepreneurial guitarist, your assets will largely be intellectual property. That property might be your songs, CDs, DVDs, videos, books, compositions or arrangements, etc. Remember what your mother told you! Bad people and pirates are everywhere. They will steal your stuff! If your guitar is stolen, yes, that is quite a heartrending loss. But it can be replaced. If someone steals the rights to your CD or song, however, the income from those can be lost forever. You must ensure that all benefits from your intellectual property accrue to you. These benefits may be royalties from the use and/or sale of your creations, mechanical license income, and of course the basic gross sales of your products.

Read, read, and read! Learn everything you can about copyright law, mechanical rights and royalties, licenses, etc. If you cannot figure it out, have an attorney explain it to you. Many states have associations of attorneys who provide legal advice to performing artists for free or greatly reduced fees. Do a Google search for "Lawyers for the Arts" and you will find a plethora of information.

Many other legal issues may crop up in the course of your career. Even the most basic service of giving music lessons in your home may require an occupational license. Or, you may at some point be accused of stealing someone else's riff or lyric. The alligators are out there waiting to take a bite out of you. Sometimes they will try to eat you alive. Protect yourself with knowledge and expert advice.

LEVEL 5: YOU

You are at the top of your pyramid. Ultimately, your product is *you*—your music and your artistic, creative ability.

Tend to Your Pyramid

As long as the four levels underneath you are solid, you are secure. Your company will thrive and you will thrive as an entrepreneurial guitarist. But if any one of those levels beneath you is rickety or rotten, watch out. Your pyramid will collapse and you will topple to the ground with grievous injuries. Take as much care of your company as you do your artistic development as a guitarist. Spend as much time attending to business as you do to practicing. Do not ignore the business side of your life as an entrepreneurial guitarist.

If any one level of your pyramid is weak, your career may fail or stagnate. It will certainly struggle financially. If you start to see problems, examine your pyramid, identify the problem, and tend to it. You are on top of the structure—keep an eye on what is under you.

How will you build and strengthen your pyramid? *Educate yourself.* Read and study up on each level. Take an introductory course or read a few books about accounting. Talk to a friend who is experienced with business to learn about managing your cash flow. I already mentioned the thousands of books about sales and marketing. You can buy some or borrow them from the library. As an artist, you already have a good feel for quality. But look around you and notice who is putting out quality work and who isn't. Study the differences. Learn everything you can about the legal issues of the music business. Look in my Recommended Reading List on my website, MillionDollarGuitarist.com. Order the books. Find them at the library. Read them.

chapter 40

YOU WILL NEED HELP

Inevitably, even with thorough research and reading about each level of your pyramid, you will realize your knowledge is deficient in one or more areas. Some of these levels are very foreign to performing artist types. Find people who can help you with your weak areas. *Seek qualified outside help.* You cannot be an expert on each level of your pyramid. You may have to occasionally hire someone to advise you or do some of the work. If you do not have the money right now, perhaps you could convince them to take their payment later, once the sales of your product or project begin to roll in.

For example, if you are about to embark on a costly project such as a CD or concert tour, hire an accountant to help you with a budget and cash flow analysis. He can give you a clear estimate of the cost of the project, how many CDs or concerts you will need to sell, and how much marketing you can afford. Large projects always cost more and take longer than originally planned. A good accountant will point out expenses you may have missed. Many artistic types such as guitarists lack knowledge of accounting practices and are very lax about record keeping. Those who lack math and number skills can get into trouble financially. Yes, an accountant will cost money. But the guitarist's lack of knowledge of accounting procedures and financial planning could result in financial chaos and ruin down the road.

Be sure your advisers are not financially needy. If an adviser is short on cash and you can't pay them on time, you might put them in a financial bind. After all, it's possible your sales won't begin to roll in when you thought they would. Be sure your advisers are specialists. Don't hire a generic attorney to advise you on a recording contract.

Make them a part of your team. That doesn't mean you have to employ them full-time. It means you should trust them. Be open about your plans. They must know everything that is going on. They should want to know everything that is going on. The more they know, the more they may be able to help you. They might even have insights into other areas of your career. If they are intimately familiar with who you are and what you are trying to achieve, they might come up with valuable advice even in areas outside their particular specialty.

And please: listen to your advisers! A common mistake is to ignore advice you don't like. But why pay for a good adviser and then ignore their advice? Patrick and Barbara Kavanaugh, in *Devotions from the World of Music*, relate this story about singer Johnny Cash, who took some hard-to-listen-to advice to heart:

> *Country great Johnny Cash's first big break was an opportunity to audition for Sam Phillips of Sun Records. Phillips helped launch the careers of Elvis Presley, Jerry Lee Lewis, Roy Orbison, B.B. King, and Ike Turner, among many others. Cash had high hopes because he knew Phillips could ignite his career. But Phillips was unimpressed. He turned*

Cash down, telling him to sharpen his talents or give it up. It hurt deeply, but Cash took Phillips' advice and put in countless hours of practicing, writing, and rehearsing. Cash set up another audition with Phillips. Phillips was very impressed that Cash had followed his advice and had worked so hard to improve. He knew he was working with someone who knew the value of hard work and would follow his advice. He signed Cash to Sun. Soon, Cash's career was on its way.

But you must be careful. "Experts" are not always correct. Listen to your inner voice as well. Again, from Patrick and Barbara Kavanaugh:

When Tchaikovsky played his now famous Piano Concerto in B-flat Major *(it was a dismal failure at its Russian premiere) for Nikolai Rubinstein, the finest pianist in Moscow, Rubinstein savaged it. It was unplayable, he said, broken passages, disconnected structure, unfixable. It was trivial and common. Rubinstein even accused him of having stolen passages from other people. Only one or two pages were worth keeping—the rest should be destroyed, he said. Of course Tchaikovsky was crushed. But his inner voice told him his piece was good. Better than good, it was a most excellent work. Realizing how distraught Tchaikovsky was at his comments, Rubinstein offered to perform it in concert if Tchaikovsky would alter it to his requirements. Tchaikovsky replied, "I shall not alter a single note." Today we are grateful Tchaikovsky did not follow the advice of the "expert."*

Let's make a distinction. You do not always have to follow the advice of the expert. But don't ignore it. Listen to it, and let it be a factor in your decisions. Your adviser's job is to be certain you make an informed decision. If you are contemplating taking a gamble, your adviser's job is to make sure you understand the risk you are taking. Your job is to make the decision.

Some of you may come from a Christian perspective. There will be times when you believe God wants you to do something, even when others around you are telling you not to. In that kind of situation pray, study the Bible for guidance, and ask advice from trusted people. Ultimately of course, the decision is yours to make, and you must be ready to deal with the consequences. It can be difficult to step out in faith, especially if the decision makes life difficult for you or negatively affects someone close to you. But there comes a time when you must take a stand for the Lord and do what you believe He is calling you to do. In those tough times, remind yourself that the Lord has promised to never leave you or forsake you.

Do not be a one-man show. You may be a really smart person. You may have street smarts or you may have excelled in school. You may be a PhD. But, sorry if I am the first one to tell you this: you do not know everything. Use mentors and advisers. Bring together a team whose members have street smarts and school smarts. The shared education and experience of your team will be priceless to you on your career path. They will help you avoid missteps, potholes, or even bottomless ravines.

chapter 41

THIS IS THE PART YOU WILL WANT TO SKIP OVER

Don't do it! Take a deep breath, focus, and keep reading.

You will have many great ideas for projects and products. If done well, they will generate good income. But a crisis or failure can occur if you do not properly plan for the long delay between the time when you have to start paying for production expenses and the time when money finally starts rolling in from sales. Let's take the example of making a CD.

If you decide to record it yourself, you have to purchase the recording equipment. This could cost several thousand dollars and will require at least a month to actually get the equipment and learn how to use it. If you go to a commercial recording studio, it could cost several thousand dollars. You may have to pay that cost up front. You may have to put down a deposit to reserve recording dates months ahead of time. You could put it on a credit card or borrow the money from someone.

Once the tracks are recorded and mixed (which will take a minimum of two months), the artwork will need to be done. That will take one or two months. Your graphic artist will want to be paid. So far, you have incurred several thousand dollars in recording costs and several hundred dollars for the graphic artist. At this point no money has started rolling in yet from sales of your new CD.

Then you send it off to a manufacturer to make one thousand or more CDs. That will cost over a thousand dollars, maybe two or three thousand dollars depending on the complexity of the CD, its artwork, and how many you order. Sure, put it on the credit card. Borrow the money from Dad. But realize that if you started in January, now it is probably at least May. That is a best-case scenario. Usually it will take longer than you think. It could be August. A sizable amount of money is on that credit card. You owe Dad a large chunk of money. And still no money is rolling in from CD sales. What about your website? Setting it up for selling your CD will drain even more time and money.

Finally, by early fall, the UPS truck stops in front of your house and your twenty or more boxes of CDs are stacked at your front door. If you have been thinking ahead, you have already done a significant amount of pre-promotion and your fans know the CD is coming. You put it up on your website, your shopping cart is turned on, you send some to CD Baby (who will set you up on iTunes and other download sites), maybe some to Amazon. The sales from your website will immediately roll in and the money deposited directly to your checking account. But the money from CD Baby and Amazon will not start to roll in for another month or so.

Get the picture? There can be a large gap between the time you begin work on a new project and the time it takes for the money to begin rolling in to pay the costs of its production, let alone make a profit. Unless you have income from other sources to pay these expenses, you can put yourself in a financial bind. Credit cards are fine if you do not mind the interest charges building up and as long as the project pays off not too far down the road. You do not want to be paying off that credit card for years if things don't work out. If you are planning to borrow the money from a family member or friend, be certain they understand they will not be repaid for many months, maybe a year or more.

You must plan your cash cycle. The following lists may seem overwhelming but you must be able to answer these questions if you intend to ask an investor or family friend to loan you money for your project. You also may be able to allay the fears and misgivings of your spouse if you have answers to these questions. You want your spouse on your side cheering you on and offering help and support. But, even if it's only your own money that's involved, you can keep yourself financially healthy if you have this information.

Some investors will want to thoroughly examine your answers to these questions. They will want to see how you have planned for the cash needs of your project and how it fits into your business/project plan. Hiring an accountant at this point would be worthwhile to help create the plan for your cash requirements and build the confidence of your investor. You might even be able to pry away a few *extra* dollars from the investor if they feel confident you have done your homework!

Okay, take a deep breath. Or take a break. Then go through these lists item by item. Think how each and every one of them might relate to your particular project/product.

WHERE IS YOUR CASH GOING TO COME FROM?

1. How much money will you need?
2. How much money from an outside investor (could be family or a friend) will you need?
3. Will you borrow money on a credit card or from a commercial lender?
4. Can you find a partner willing to put money into the project if they get a share of the profit?
5. Will you receive your payment from customers at the moment of sale? Will there be a delay? How long?
6. If you must extend credit to your customers, how long will it take to collect your money?
7. Is there a possibility of customers not paying you?
8. What level of bad debts might you have?
9. Will there be multiple production cycles for your project? If so, how many cycles will it take to see a profit?

HOW WILL YOU USE YOUR CASH?

1. Do you have a specific project or product in mind?
2. Have you taken steps to protect your project or product before you begin development?
3. Will you pay advisers (accountant, attorney, agent, recording engineer, graphic artist, PR person, producer, manager)?
4. Will you make demos or prototypes?
5. Do you have a source for supplies for your project (recording equipment, CD manufacturer, software, etc.)?
6. What payment arrangements can you negotiate with your

suppliers to avoid cash crunches?

7. Where will you store your products, once completed (at home, warehouse, storage unit)?

8. What office supplies will you need?

9. What office equipment will you need (computers, copiers, printers)?

10. How much money will you need to live on during the development of your project/product? Where will that money come from?

11. How much money will you need, and when will you need it, to produce the product/project? Make a timeline.

12. How will the product/project be packaged? What will that cost?

13. Will you need a website?

14. Will you set up credit card processing (shopping cart) on your website? How much are the bank fees? How much is the monthly fee? What is the cost per order processed?

15. How much will marketing materials cost?

16. How long will it take to replenish your inventory? If you sell all two thousand of your initial run of CDs, how long will it take to get more? When should you reorder? Will the money be there to reorder?

17. How will you take orders? Website/Internet only? Stores? Toll-free phone lines?

18. What is the cost of shipping each order? How will that affect your net profit?

19. Do you need insurance of some sort? Insurance on your inventory?

20. Is there a possibility of significant customer returns (dissatisfied customers, defective products) of your product? How will you deal with this? What will that cost?
21. Will you provide customer service of some sort?
22. If you are paying interest on loans or credit cards, how much interest will you owe by the time money from sales starts to roll in?

These are probably all questions you'd rather not think about. You would rather go practice. But look. Any potential investor, whether an outsider or a family member (or even your spouse!), will want to know the answers to these questions. Hearing the answers will help replace misgivings or doubts with confidence and support.

Answering these questions will also keep *you* focused on the proper execution of your project. Planning this out in advance will minimize the chances of your project and related finances going down in flames.

If the answers seem beyond you, this is the time to hire a professional accountant. This small investment now will save money later, and probably generate even more money for you in the long run.

Speaking of timelines, a scary thing to consider, especially in the field of popular music, is that the industry, and especially public taste, can change substantially from the time you begin your project until its completion. A project you considered "hot" when you began could cool off considerably by the time it is finished. For example, if you had planned to produce a disco CD toward the end of the disco craze, by the time the project had been completed, your market would have evaporated!

You also don't want to be distracted by having to focus on basic survival. The last things you want to have to think about, or hear, are things like:

- The CD manufacturer called to tell me my CDs are ready, but they won't ship them until I can pay the balance. But I have no money in the bank.
- I should be able to pay you soon. People owe me money, but temporarily I have nothing in my checking account.
- My spouse called and said, "We need groceries, but the checking account has no money."

These are red flags and will take your focus away from your career objectives. So again, be able to answer the questions in the lists above.

Be careful how you spend your time. In the beginning you will spend almost all your time on the future, creating and producing projects and ways to promote and market them. That is what energizes you and gets your career jump-started.

Unfortunately, as time passes, you may lose momentum. Or, if you are successful, you may get distracted by the day-to-day problems of managing what you have started. You will have to deal with taking orders, shipping, customer service, phone calls, emails, cash flow, record keeping, etc.

To keep your career rolling, keep your focus on the future. Don't rest on what you have already done. For example, you may have produced a great debut CD that sold well and got good reviews. But people forget very quickly. Unless you come up with something new to follow it, you will be forgotten and you won't be able to ride the momentum you created with your first release. Creating one great CD does not mean you have it made for the rest of your life. In the music industry, no one cares much about your past or early accomplishments. They want to know, "What are you doing *now*?"

PART SIX:
Once More,
With Feeling

chapter 42

THINGS I *MUST* DO

1. I will decide what I want out of life.
2. I will define my mission (beyond making a million dollars playing the guitar). I will pursue it with ferocious resolve. I will be obsessed by it.
3. I will develop my Hedgehog Concept.
4. I will make things happen instead of letting things happen to me. I will be decisive. I make my own luck, I make my own opportunities. I will create the circumstances I want. I will pursue every opportunity that might help me, no matter how small or inconsequential it may seem.
5. I will have an insatiable thirst for knowledge.
6. I will create definite plans and goals to achieve my mission. My plan will be executed with continuous action—no slacking off.
7. I will persevere. I will never give up. I might have failures, but I will learn from them and move on. I will not be discouraged by criticism.
8. I will maintain faith, but will not lose sight of reality. I will face the brutal facts of reality, but I will never lose faith.
9. I will work harder than I've ever worked before to achieve my mission. Nothing will stop me. I am fully willing to

pay a staggering price for this. I will do so gladly.

10. I will live BELOW my means.

THINGS I WILL *NEVER* DO

1. Make excuses
2. Blame others
3. Quit
4. Accept failure
5. Lose faith
6. Have a negative attitude
7. Hope or wish for an outcome
8. Wait for something to happen or someone to help me
9. Listen to others tell me I'm crazy, I'll never succeed, I'm being unrealistic, I'm not good enough

Bill O'Reilly offered this pragmatic advice that echoes several of the points above:

> *If you educate yourself, work hard, develop a skill, and are honest, you WILL succeed in the USA. And that is if you don't make bad personal choices such as drugs or alcohol or hanging out with the wrong people. If you don't follow this advice, you will be at the mercy of others. You will eventually be stranded—it isn't a matter of if, but when. Do not depend on anyone else—even your own family. Depend on YOURSELF.*

chapter 43

CODA AND FADE

This book is a summation of things I have learned and observed in my own life and career. By studying the lives of other successful, happy people, I learned some very effective principles of living. These principles enable people to accomplish their goals, lead happy, fulfilled lives, and make significant amounts of money by following their passion in life. Money can't buy happiness—we know that. But let's face it: we also know it can help make our lives more comfortable and possibly more productive and fulfilling.

Life provides no guarantees. Although I sincerely believe this book will help you in your career, keep in mind that sometimes the best students are the ones who never quite believe their professors! The perspicacious student applies a dose of healthy skepticism to what they hear and are told.

On the other hand, don't reject things you haven't tried. Don't give up on things a friend or family member says will never work or that they say *you* can't do. Don't ignore or sweep under the rug things that have implications you aren't too wild about. Be careful not to be a know-it-all and end up making bad choices.

The information I have presented is here for your consideration, not blind acceptance. Some things will require your very thoughtful and deep contemplation.

In your music, *you decide* how you want it to go and how you want it to sound. Likewise, you must be the final judge in all your "life decisions."

I often kid my son, "Go ahead, ignore my advice. Fall into a life of poverty, desperation, and despair." But, I know my son is his own man, thoughtful and intelligent. He may see that my perspective and recommendations are not quite right for him. He will choose a different path.

That is what your journey is all about. Don't follow someone else's path. Make your own. That is where your reward lies.

For updates, recommended reading, and resources; go to:

www.MillionDollarGuitarist.com

Where guitarists go for answers

Also, visit me at: **www.DouglasNiedt.com**

Hear and watch me play!

Listen to sound clips, watch videos, read guitar technique tips,

and much more.

SOURCES

Albom, Mitch. *Tuesdays With Morrie.* New York: Broadway Books, 1997.

Allen, Robert G. *Multiple Streams of Internet Income.* Hoboken, NJ: John Wiley & Sons, 2001.

Baker, Bob. *Guerrilla Music Marketing, Encore Edition.* St. Louis: Spotlight Publications, 2006.

Baker, Bob. *Guerrilla Music Marketing Handbook.* St. Louis: Spotlight Publications, 2007.

Baker, Bob. *Unleash the Artist Within.* St. Louis: Spotlight Publications, 2005.

Beeching, Angela Myles. *Beyond Talent.* New York: Oxford University Press, 2005.

Boggs, Bill. *Got What It Takes?* New York: HarperCollins, 2007.

Bordowitz, Hank. *Dirty Little Secrets of the Record Business.* Chicago: Chicago Review Press, 2007.

Brabec, Jeffrey and Todd. *Music, Money, and Success.* New York: Schirmer Trade Books, 2002.

Braun, Nick. *The Best Tax Busting Business Structures.* Kirkcaldy, UK: Taxcafe Ltd., 2008.

Britten, Anna. *Working in the Music Industry.* Oxford, UK: How To Books, 2004.

Brothers, Joyce. *How to Get Whatever You Want Out of Life.* New York: Simon and Schuster, 1978.

Burlingham, Bo. *Small Giants: Companies that Choose to Be Great Instead of Big.* New York: Penguin Group, 2005.

Cann, Simon. *Building a Successful 21st Century Music Career.* Boston: Thomson Course Technology, 2007.

Carnegie, Dale. *How to Win Friends & Influence People.* New York: Pocket Books, 1982.

Collins, James C. and Jerry I. Porras. *Built to Last.* New York: Harper-Business, 1997.

Collins, Jim (James). *Good to Great.* New York: HarperBusiness, 2001.

Eisenberg, Bryan and Jeffrey. *Call to Action: Secret Formulas to Improve Online Results.* Austin, TX: Wizard Academy Press, 2005.

Eisenberg, Bryan and Jeffrey. *Waiting for Your Cat to Bark?* Nashville: Thomas Nelson, 2006.

Ericsson, K. Anders. *The Making of an Expert.* Boston: Harvard Business Review, 2007.

Field, Shelly. *Career Opportunities in the Music Industry.* New York: Checkmark Books, 2004.

Gerardi, Robert. *Opportunities in Music Careers.* New York: VGM Career Books (McGraw-Hill), 2002.

Gladwell, Malcolm. *Outliers: The Story of Success.* New York: Little, Brown and Company, 2008.

Goldstein, Jeri. *How to Be Your Own Booking Agent.* Charlottesville, VA: The New Music Times, 2002.

Hatschek, Keith. *How to Get a Job in the Music and Recording Industry.* Boston: Berklee Press, 2001.

Hill, Napoleon. *Think and Grow Rich.* Greenwich, CT: Fawcett Publications, 1960.

Horn, Sam. *Pop! Stand Out in Any Crowd.* New York: Penguin Group, 2006.

Jennings, Jason. *Think Big, Act Small.* New York: Penguin Group, 2005.

Kavanaugh, Patrick. *Spiritual Lives of the Great Composers.* Grand

Rapids, MI: Zondervan Publishing House, 1996.

Kavanaugh, Patrick. *Spiritual Moments With the Great Composers.* Grand Rapids, MI: Zondervan Publishing House, 1995.

Kavanaugh, Patrick and Barbara. *Devotions from the World of Music.* Colorado Springs, CO: Cook Communications, 2000.

Kiyosaki, Robert T. and Sharon L. Lechter. *Before You Quit Your Job.* New York: Warner Business Books, 2005.

Kiyosaki, Robert T. and Sharon L. Lechter. *Rich Dad Poor Dad.* New York: Warner Books, 2000.

Levine, Michael. *Guerrilla P.R.* New York: HarperBusiness, 1993.

Levinson, Jay Conrad. *Guerrilla Marketing.* New York: Houghton Mifflin, 1993.

Levinson, Jay Conrad. *Guerrilla Marketing Excellence.* New York: Houghton Mifflin, 1993.

Mahler, Jonathan. *The Lexus Story.* New York: Melcher Media, 2004.

Nevue, David. *How to Promote Your Music Successfully on the Internet.* Eugene, OR: Midnight Rain Productions, 2007.

Passman, Donald. *All You Need to Know About the Music Business.* New York: Free Press, 2006.

Pinskey, Raleigh. *101 Ways to Promote Yourself.* New York: Avon, 1997.

Porras, Jerry and Stewart Emery and Mark Thompson. *Success Built to Last.* Upper Saddle River, NJ: Wharton School Publishing, 2007.

Pressfield, Steven. *The War of Art.* New York: Warner Books, 2002.

Rapaport, Diane Sward. *How to Make and Sell Your Own Record.* New York: Quick Fox, 1979.

Reed, John T. *Succeeding.* Alamo, CA: John T. Reed, 2006.

Reuting, Jennifer. *Limited Liability Companies for Dummies.* Hoboken, NJ: Wiley Publishing, 2008.

Riordan, James. *Making It In The New Music Business*. Cincinnati: Writer's Digest Books, 1991.

Schwartz, Daylle Deanna. *I Don't Need a Record Deal!* New York: Billboard Books, 2005.

Schwartz, Daylle Deanna. *Start & Run Your Own Record Label*. New York: Billboard Books, 2003.

Shagan, Rena. *The Road Show*. New York: American Council for the Arts, 1985.

Spellman, Peter. *The Self-Promoting Musician*. Boston: Berklee Press, 2008.

Stanley, Thomas J. and William D. Danko. *The Millionaire Next Door*. New York: Pocket Books, 1996.

Sweeney, Tim and Mark Geller. *Guide to Releasing Independent Records*. Torrance, CA: TSA Books, 1996.

LaVergne, TN USA
06 December 2009
166109LV00001B/1/P